# THE DICTIONARY OF WORDPLAY

# The
# Dictionary
## *of*
# Wordplay

*by*
## Dave Morice

Teachers & Writers Collaborative

New York

**The Dictionary of Wordplay**

**Library of Congress Cataloging-in-Publication Data**

Morice, Dave, 1946–
    The dictionary of wordplay / by Dave Morice
        p. cm
    Includes bibliographic references and index
    ISBN 0-915924-99-4 (alk. paper)-- ISBN 0-915924-97-8 (pbk. : alk. paper)
    1. Word games--Dictionaries. I. Title.

GV1507.W8 M593 2001
793.734'03--dc21

                                                    00-067621


Teachers & Writers Collaborative
5 Union Square West
New York, NY 10003-3306


Cover and page design: Christopher Edgar

Printed by Philmark Lithographics, New York, N.Y.
First printing

## Acknowledgments

A superultramegalosesquipedelian thanks to my editor Chris Edgar, who once said, "This book will be easier to do than most of our books," for his great patience, his many insights, and his sudden realization that his optimistic statement needed to be edited by replacing "easier" with "harder."

Thanks to the T & W staff, to Jordan Davis for his editing and close readings, and to Drew Gardner, Amy Gelber, Daniel Kane, and Linda P. O'Brien for their careful work on the manuscript.

A very special thanks to Ross Eckler for inviting me to be the editor of the "Kickshaws" column of *Word Ways* magazine.

Thanks to the many wordplay writers I've come to know in person and through correspondence, whose work provided much inspiration for the dictionary: Jay Ames, Jan Anderson, David Armstrong, Leonard Ashley, Ralph Beaman, Ralston Bedge, Howard Bergerson, Maxey Brooke, Eric Chaikin, Stephen Chism, Ted Clarke, Philip Cohen, Chris Cole, Edmund Conti, Fred Crane, Oren Dalton, Faith Eckler, Win Emmons, Willard Espy, Darryl Francis, Martin Gardner, Rex Gooch, Leonard Gordon, Jeff Grant, Paul Hellweg, Michael Helsem, John Henrick, John Holgate, Joyce Holland, Nyr Indictor, Michael Keith, Rich Lederer, Chris McManus, Charles Linnett, Daniel McGrath, Jed Martinez, Max Maven, John Meyer, O. V. Michaelsen, Sir Jeremy Morse, Mike Morton, Peter Newby, Harry Partridge, Murray Pearce, James Puder, Tom Pulliam, Bruce Pyne, Mike Reiss, Howard Richler, Lee Sallows, Mark Saltveit, Eric Seale, Anthony Sebastian, Will Shortz, Susan Thorpe, Dan Tilque, Ed Walpow, William Webster, David Woodside, and Monte Zerger.

Thanks to Mark Isham, Paul Ingram, Richard Carlin, Jack McMahon, Bill Gerhard, Milagros and Del Stevens, Jeanne Long, Jeannie Morice, and Tiny Advent.

And last but not least, thank God the book is done!

The work of Teachers & Writers Collaborative is made possible in part by grants from the New York City Department of Cultural Affairs and the National Endowment for the Arts, and with public funds from the New York State Council on the Arts, a State Agency. Teachers & Writers Collaborative is also grateful for support from the following foundations and corporations: Axe-Houghton Foundation, Bronx Borough President and City Council, The Bydale Foundation, The Cerimon Fund, Chase Manhattan Bank, The Saul Z. and Amy S. Cohen Family Foundation, Con Edison, E.H.A. Foundation, Thomas Phillip Johnson and Jane Moore Johnson Foundation, The Janet Stone Jones Foundation, Low Wood Fund, Inc., M & O Foundation, NBC, New York Community Trust (Van Lier Fund), New York Times Company Foundation, Henry Nias Foundation, North Star Fund, The Open Society Institute, Queens Borough President and City Council, Joshua Ringel Memorial Fund, Maurice R. Robinson Fund, Rush Philanthropic Arts Foundation, The Scherman Foundation, the Wallace-Reader's Digest Funds, and the Wendling Foundation.

```
                               CK
                             MOC
                           CKMO      M
                          OCKM      KM
                        KMOCKM    OCKM
           CKM           CKMOCKMOCKMOCK          CKM
          OCKMOCK        CKM  KMOCKMO          MOCKMOC
        KMOCKMOCKMO     KMOCKMOCKMO          CKMOCKMOCKM
      OCKMOCKMOCKMOCK    MOCKMOCK          MOCKMOCKMOCKMO
    KMOCKMOCKMOCKMOCKMO    CKMOC       OCKMOCKMOCKMOCKMOC
   CKMOCKMOCKMO KMOCKMOCKMOCKMOCKMOCKMOCKMOCKMO KMOCKMOCK
  OCKMOCKMOCK     OCKMOCKMOCKMOCKMOCKMOCKMOCK    MOCKMOCKM
 MOCKMOCKMO        CKMOCKMOCKMOCKMOCKMOCKM        CKMOCKMO
KMOCKMOCK            MOCKMOCKMOCKMOCK              KMOCKMO
KMOCKMO              MOCKMOCKMOCKMOCK               MOCKM
KMOCK                MOCKMOCKMOCKMOCK               MOC
 MOC                 MOCKMOCKMOCKMOC                MO
  O                 KMOCKMOCKMOCKMOC               K
                   CKMOCKMOCKMOCKMO
                  OCKMOCKMOCKMOCKM
                KMOCKMOCKMOCKMOCK
              OCKMOCKMOCKMOCKMOC
             MOCKMOCK   KM     OC
           CKMOCKMO    CK     MO
          OCKMOCK       K       C
        KMOCKM           M       M
      OCKM              KMOC      OCKM
    KM                 C M C       C M C
```

# Table of Contents

**Foreword**
by Ross Eckler
x

**Introduction**
by Dave Morice
xi

**Wordplay Entries, A–Z**
1

**After Word**
by Richard Lederer
255

**Appendix A:**
**Alphasets**
by Dave Morice
258

**Appendix B:**
**"Interesting" Number Names**
by Dave Morice
259

**Appendix C:**
**Inventors, Authors, and Sources for the Entries**
261

**Appendix D:**
**Bibliography**
285

# Foreword

*I used to be agnostic*
*Of the meaning of "acrostic"*
*I thought lipograms were messages one sent by word of mouth*
*The unique univocalic*
*Sounded far too encephalic*
*And a pal-in-drome? It had to be a friend in France's south*

As Roger Berry suggests in his poem, the vocabulary of wordplay has always been chaotic. Even for standard well-known terms there is often confusion of meaning. Take, for example, the term *anagram*. For most writers, an anagram is a rearrangement of letters of a word or phrase to form another word or phrase, but for members of the National Puzzlers' League, the term is reserved for transposals in which the rearranged word relates to the first in some meaningful way—an exact synonym, as *enraged* for *angered*, or a humorous allusion, such as *dirty room* for *dormitory,* or *woman Hitler* for *mother-in-law.* Similarly, some writers use *pangram* to refer to a word-list or sentence containing the 26 letters of the alphabet once each, whereas others use it to describe a sentence that uses each letter at least once, as in "pack my box with five dozen liquor jugs."

But matters are far worse. Because wordplay is an evolving field, new ways of manipulating letters or phonemes are constantly being devised. Often these are difficult to describe succinctly. Each writer invents his own name for a new wordplay idea, with the result that there are often many different names for the same concept (for example, word ladders, word golf, and doublets can all refer to the same thing).

Is this dictionary the last word with respect to the language of wordplay? Of course not—but it *is* the first word; such a dictionary has never before been compiled. As such it automatically becomes the standard against which later, more complete dictionaries will be judged. Samuel Johnson defined a lexicographer as "a writer of dictionaries; a harmless drudge." Webster, in turn, reminds us that a drudge is "one who does menial work" or "one whose work is routine and boring." Not so for *The Dictionary of Wordplay*! Dave Morice's work may have been lengthy or laborious, but I am sure it was never routine or boring. Mining disparate books of wordplay for relevant terms and melding these into a pleasing and consistent whole demands creativity and imagination of the highest order. One needs the vision of a poet as well as the patience of a bookkeeper!

—*Ross Eckler*

# Introduction

*by Dave Morice*

This book contains words that may surprise you. In it can be found the pun, the anagram, the palindrome, the lettershift, and the univocalic. It has words that can be made in special ways, with telephone dials, typewriter keys, Scrabble tiles, and Morse Code. It presents language most marvelous—words and sentences, lines of poetry, and other elements—behaving in a most unlanguagelike way. It is the first dictionary of wordplay.

Writers, students, teachers, word puzzlers, and anyone who has looked "beyond language" will discover many kinds of wordplay, familiar and not so familiar, within its pages. In fact, some of the wordplay has been around for thousands of years, and some of it slipped into the book just as it was going to press. This dictionary defines hundreds of terms, ideas, and facts of wordplay in English; and in doing so it shows the vast number of untapped resources available for experiencing the pleasure of language and discovering the play of words.

Wordplay is always just a word or two away from the words we speak, hear, read, and write. It is present in the home, the school, the office, the store, the streets. It's on television all the time (especially on ABC). It's in the movies (ultimately in the film titled *Z*). Sometimes it is intentional, and other times it is accidental.

New York City's highly acclaimed campaign to polish the image of the Big Apple was based on a rebus: I ♥ NY. Newspaper headline writers make mistakes (or are they mistakes?) founded on puns: MILK DRINKERS ARE TURNING INTO POWDER. On the other side of the word coin, poets use wordplay as a matter of course. In *Romeo and Juliet*, Mercutio, having just lost a swordfight in the worst way, has no recourse but to say pointedly, ". . . Ask for me tomorrow, and you shall find me a grave man." Perhaps poetry *is* the highest form of wordplay.

Wordplay has appeared most openly in books of puzzles, language games, and wordplay forms. In the nineteenth century, C. C. Bombaugh assembled hundreds of pages of wordplay in his book *Gleanings for the Curious from the Harvest Fields of Literature*. It is a classic collection ranging from acrostics to zeugmas, but it was not intended to organize them in any particular way.

## The Golden Age of Wordplay

During the past few decades, something amazing has happened to the English language. In his book *Language on Vacation* (Scribners, 1965), Dmitri Borgmann presented wordplay, which he renamed "logology," in an entirely new light: while wordplay is often considered a pastime, he pointed out that it is also a body of knowledge with its own concepts, principles, and terms. His book earned him the title "father of logology," and it ushered in a Golden Age of Wordplay that continues to this day.

In 1968, Borgmann founded *Word Ways,* the first magazine to give writers a forum for articles, stories, poems, puzzles, and challenges involving any and all wordplay forms. The following year, Howard Bergerson took over its editorship. Bergerson later wrote and published a groundbreaking book on palindromes and anagrams, appropriately titled *Palindromes and Anagrams* (Dover, 1973). In 1970, Ross Eckler became the editor, publisher, and distributor of *Word Ways*. He has brought out the magazine on a quarterly basis ever since then. Within its pages (over 9,000), a cornucopia of new forms has evolved, giving English the richest body of published wordplay in the history of the world.

Since the 1960s, wordplay has flourished. For the first time, small-press magazines—*Word Ways, Verbatim, Maledicta, The Palindromist, WordsWorth,* and others—have provided an accessible forum for wordplay writers, much as the "mimeograph revolution" of the 1950s gave poets a place to develop their voices and display their works. In fact, some of the new wordplay books, including specialized dictionaries and lexicons, were also published in alternative press format. The first palindromic novel, *Dr. Awkward in Oslo,* exists only in mimeograph form.

The massive amount of material generated in the past few decades has been collected in numerous books of wordplay. This proliferation suggested that chaos was once again in need of order. In 1998, Eckler published *Making the Alphabet Dance,* in which he defined "letterplay" as wordplay in which letters are manipulated like the pieces of a game or a puzzle. His book organized this complex field into a coherent whole made of many intricate parts. Eckler's and Borgmann's books serve as bookends on the shelf of modern wordplay.

Other developments expanded the audience for the other side of language. In 1988, Richard Lederer's book *Anguished English* came out from a small publisher, Wyrick and Company. The book presented real-life language bloopers in a rapid-fire, entertaining way. So entertaining was it that Jay Leno read from it for eight minutes on "The Tonight Show." After that, sales of the already-popular book shot through the roof. It was republished by Bantam Doubleday

Dell in a mass-market paperback edition that helped launch the Intrepid Linguist language series. It became the first wordplay book to make the *New York Times* bestseller list and launched Lederer's role as the great popularizer of wordplay. His subsequent wordplay books, including *Get Thee to a Punnery, Crazy English,* and *The Word Circus,* have sold well and have continued to bring wordplay to a wider audience than ever before.

In recent years, more wordplay books of all kinds—by Willard Espy, Will Shortz, Martin Gardner, Peter Newby, and others—have been published than ever before. Some focus on a specific, well-known form, such as the palindrome, the anagram, or the pun. Others attempt to cover the entire field by dividing it into major categories and presenting each category in a separate chapter. Still others present wordplay in puzzle books, cartoon books, joke books, almanacs, and other formats.

## Poetry, Prose, and Play

Wordplay has been a natural part of "mainstream literature" all along. Rhyme and regular rhythm are elemental forms that some people believe to be essential to poetry, but many other forms are also a natural part of it—assonance, alliteration, onomatopoeia, and others. In fact, all poetic forms are based on wordplay forms. What else could they be based on? Some forms are less constrictive than others. A free-verse poem is one of the least constrictive, but it, too, involves manipulating the sounds, meanings, and placements of words.

In the twentieth century, wordplay of different types became a significant, even major, part of works by writers such as James Joyce, Gertrude Stein, and E. E. Cummings. In *Ulysses,* Joyce layered the narrative with multilingual puns in order to tell a complex story in a way that was appropriately complex. In *Three Lives,* Stein gave words new meaning by altering the grammatical environment in which they existed. In poetry, Cummings broke single words apart to yield new meanings through typography. One wonders to what extent form determined content in these writers'—and other early Modernists'—work.

In the 1940s, Concrete Poetry began to show up around the world. More than ever before, poets let words do things that amounted to "art for wordplay's sake." Their writings, linked by the movement's catchy name, used different concepts to guide them. Some created works based on sound, some on shape, some on other linguistic elements. Works ranged from random letter poems such as those invented by the Lettrists to complex architectural/alphabetical structures such as John Furnival's "The Fall of the Tower of Babel." In the late 1960s, Something Else Press published *The Anthology of Concrete Poetry,* which became highly successful and influential in spreading the word about this avant-garde literary movement.

## Wordplay Writing

While free-verse poets and concrete poets have their own approaches, there is a special kind of writing endemic to wordplay: the writer chooses a specific wordplay form to use throughout a text. The choice of form almost always limits the choice of words. Word choice may focus on letters (palindromes, lipograms), sound (puns, rhymes), or meaning (slang terms, real names, made-up words).

In 1960, François Le Lionnais and Raymond Queneau founded Oulipo (an acronym of *Ouvroir de Littérature Potentielle*), a group of writers who devise literary structures based on wordplay. Many writers have consciously used wordplay, but few have used it so thoroughly and with such originality as Queneau, who wrote *100,000,000,000,000 Poems,* a sonnet sequence. It works like the children's books whose pages are cut into sections that combine to make different texts and pictures. In Queneau's sonnet sequence, ten pages with fourteen lines on each page are cut so that each line occupies a strip of paper. The strips can be turned like miniature pages to form different combinations of lines, and each combination makes a different sonnet. This, like many Oulipian strategies, extends the boundaries of convention. Oulipo writers have devised ways to use palindromes, anagrams, acrostics, puns, lipograms, and other wordplay forms listed in this dictionary.

Wordplay writers have engaged in similar techniques for centuries, calling it "constrained verse." In constrained verse, the writer attempts to achieve a goal, such as making a poem in which each line is a palindrome. Can it be done grammatically, syntactically, and semantically? For the Oulipo writer, the question is: What forms can be used to create poetry or fiction in a new way?

In every language at every time in history, poetry and wordplay have co-existed and interacted. Poets use wordplay to enhance their poetry; wordplay writers use poetry to enhance their wordplay. The English language, whose words come from more than 100 other languages, from Latin to Pig Latin, invites such cross-pollination.

## The Purpose of this Dictionary

The purpose of this dictionary is to bring some of the myriad forms of wordplay together and organize them in the most basic of ways—alphabetic order. Although it may seem simple, it has been very tricky. For one thing, wordplay books assume that the reader has a basic knowledge of wordplay; otherwise, he or she wouldn't be reading them. Thus many concepts were previously undefined, and many were identified by more than one term. The problem grew immensely. It was sometimes difficult to determine who did what. In some cases, one person came up with the concept, another the term, and another the example.

To put the dictionary together in the best way that I could, I took the following approach. First, I made a list of sources that I believe must be included. Then using some of the most basic on the list, such as those discussed above, I began choosing terms, definitions, and examples. After building a foundation of essential forms, I went through numerous sources and found other forms to add to the list. Thus the dictionary would contain the basic forms and many more based on the basics. Soon the problem became limiting the entries. There are so many forms that, without limitations, the book might have grown to the size of the *Oxford Unabridged Dictionary*.

I used three principles to guide my writing of definitions: be clear, be concise, and use interesting material. Defining words can be tricky, especially since definitions are made up of words, too. I tried to avoid making the definitions too simple on the one hand, and too detailed on the other. However, it sometimes became necessary to violate the principles in order to include important entries. Over a six-year period, I rewrote much of the dictionary two, three, or more times. There were many entries that didn't make the final cut.

Most entries in this dictionary define wordplay forms ranging from general to specific, from well-known to unknown, from acrostic to reverse bialphabetic word. Some entries define forms that are topical as well as linguistic: e.g., presidential anagrams, which are like other anagrams except that they use the names of presidents. Some entries define forms that are hybrids of other forms: combining palindrome with pangram results in a palindromic pangram (also called a pangrammatic palindrome). Some entries define other things that have held a special place in the lore of wordplay—for instance, Yreka Bakery and the Zzyxjoanw Hoax.

In arranging the entries, I often had to list related items in widely separated places and then cross-reference them. Ordinarily a book of wordplay talks about a major form like the anagram in a single, large section. A wordplay dictionary, however, must be a dictionary first. There is an entry for anagram, but there are also entries for, anagram name, palindromic anagram, and other anagrammatic forms that might otherwise be placed together in a single section.

A few wordplay terms were especially problematic. Recently some writers have tried to upgrade some of the older, more traditional terminology. Some believe that *pyramid* should be replaced with *triangle*. Some feel that redivider should replace *charade*. The terms in the dictionary are usually those that have appeared most often in print. Any other terms may be listed as synonyms, or they may appear as separate entries with a brief notation that cross-references them to the older terms.

In order to maintain consistency, the exact wording and spelling of some terms was changed slightly: for instance, *transposal* and *transition* mean the same in almost every case. *Transposal* appears to be the older, more frequently used of the two terms. Consequently, I changed *transition* to *transposal* whenever it had the same meaning. Similarly, I used the word *alphabetic* instead of *alphabetical* in all cases. Such alternate word changes are discussed and cross-referenced in the entries.

Of course, there may be errors, and these will be changed in future editions. And, of course, there are many terms that could have been included, some of which will be added later on. The dictionary is not entirely about individual terms but about the set of terms as they relate to each other. This interlocking of definitions shows the vast panorama of language facts that have become known as letterplay, logology, recreational linguistics, and, of course, wordplay.

### The Structure of the Entries

Most of the entries are structured in three blocks of text: (1) term, definition, and discussion in the first block—usually a single paragraph; (2) examples of the entry—a poem, a story, a list, etc.; and (3) synonyms and cross-references. In the example below, the first block has the term "Tom Swiftie" followed by its definition and a brief discussion to further illuminate the term's meaning. Next come two examples. The third block lists synonymous terms ("adverbial pun") and cross-references, in small capitals, to other entries in this dictionary (CROAKER, DOUBLE CROAKER, HERMAN).

•

**Tom Swiftie**: a sentence that has a quote attributed to Tom Swift (or anyone) and that ends with an adverb punning on the quote. Tom Swift was a character appearing in a series of books by Edward Stratemeyer in the 1920s. Tom sometimes spoke sentences of this type:

> "I'll try to dig up a couple of friends," said Tom gravely.
> "I got the first three wrong," she said forthrightly.

Also called "adverbial pun." See CROAKER, DOUBLE CROAKER, HERMAN.

•

There are, of course, entries that don't follow this basic structure. In some cases, especially for basic forms like ANAGRAM and PALINDROME, discussion and examples are followed by more discussion and examples. In other cases, there may be no need for discussion, examples, synonyms, or cross-references. In a few cases, the format differs out of necessity.

## A Word about "Word"

In most of the entries, the word "word" is used in the definition, even though in some cases the examples include names or phrases. In a some definitions, "word, name, or phrase" is used, for emphasis.

## 15 Commonly Used Terms and Their Definitions

The following list gives brief definitions for some of the broadest concepts. These should provide a quick introduction to the main body of the dictionary.

**ALPHABETIC VALUE**: the number signifying a letter's position in the alphabet. Examples: A = 1, B = 2, . . . Z = 26.

**ANAGRAM**: a word or words formed by rearranging the letters of another word or words related in meaning. Example: OCEAN = CANOE.

**BIGRAM**: a pair of letters considered as a single unit. Examples: AP, GH, NN, TO.

**CHARADE**: a word or words formed by redividing but not rearranging the letters of another word or words. Example: DOGMA—DOG MA.

**CIRCULAR ALPHABET**: the alphabet arranged in a circle so that it has no beginning or end and so that Z continues on to A.

**LADDER**: a series of three or more words formed by making a specific change in each word to generate the next word, as in this case each word has one letter replaced with another to form the next word. Example: DAWN—DARN—DARK—MARK—MURK—MUSK—DUSK.

**LETTERSHIFT**: a word whose corresponding letters are the same number of steps down a CIRCULAR ALPHABET. Examples: ADDS—BEET (one step), SLEEP—BUNNY (nine steps).

**NUMBER NAME**: one of the words used to signify the counting numbers. Examples: ONE, TWO, NINE VIGINTILLION.

**PALINDROME**: a word or words that read the same in both directions. Example: LEVEL.

**PANGRAM**: a sentence or other text that contains all the letters of the alphabet one or more times. Example: THE QUICK BROWN FOX JUMPS OVER THE LAZY DOG.

**PUN**: a word or phrase that has two meanings, one of which makes the text humorous.

**REBUS**: the representation of words by means of letters, numbers, or other symbols that are interpreted by their sound, placement on the page, et cetera. Examples: XPDNC = EXPEDIENCY, 10S = TENNIS.

**REVERSAL**: a word formed by spelling another word in reverse. Example: SLEEP—PEELS.

**TRANSPOSAL**: the same as an ANAGRAM, but the words in a transposal don't have to relate in meaning.

**TRIGRAM**: a set of three letters considered as a single unit. Examples: ABC, HKX, TOM, VVV.

**WORD SQUARE**: an arrangement of letters in a square format to spell words across and down. Example:

```
I T S
T H E
S E A
```

*To:*

D A N NY
P A N
P E N
P E A
B E A FURNER
B A A
B A M
J A M
J I M DENIGAN
H I M
H I E
H U E
S U E DENIGAN

**abbreviated rhyme**: a rhyming poem that uses abbreviations for some of its words, including the rhymes. "A Mrs. Kr. Mr." is a poem using real and made-up abbreviations (kr. = kissed her), beginning with these lines:

> The Mrs. kr. Mr.
> Then how her Mr. kr.!
> He kr. kr. kr.
> Until he raised a blr.

**abstemious word**: a word lacking the five vowels, AEIOU. The word *abstemious* (meaning "temperate") was chosen because it contains the five vowels in alphabetic order.

> GYPSY     NYMPH     PYGMY     SLYLY     RHYTHM

**accidental acrostic**: a poem or part of a poem in which the initial letters of consecutive lines going down spell a word. The opening stanza, or rubai, of the *Rubáiyát of Omar Khayyám* as translated by Edward Fitzgerald is an accidental acrostic:

> **W**ake! For the Sun behind yon Eastern height
> **H**as chased the Session of the Stars from Night;
> **A**nd, to the field of Heav'n ascending, strikes
> **T**he Sultán's Turret with a Shaft of Light.

See ACROSTIC.

**acro-equation**: the representation of a set of related words, such as the days of the week, as an algebraic equation in which the words are replaced by their initials. The group appears on one side of the equal sign and the name of the group appears on the other.

$\cdot S + M + T + W + T + F + S = W$  (Sunday + Monday + . . . = a Week)

$ME + NH + VT + MA + RI + CT = NE$
(Maine + New Hampshire + . . . = New England)

$4J + 4Q + 4K = FC$ (4 Jacks + 4 Queens . . . = the Face Cards)

**acronym**: a word formed from the first (or first few) letters of several related items (e.g., RADAR, SONAR, ANZAC).

**acronymic palindrome**: an ACRONYM that is also a PALINDROME. RADAR, one of the best known, is a palindrome about a palindromic process: radio waves go out and bounce back (RADAR = RAdio Detecting And Ranging).

**acrostic**: a text in which the initial letters of certain words are determined in advance. The commonest type of acrostic is a poem in which the initials of the lines from start to finish spell the name of the individual to whom it is addressed. Lewis Carroll concluded his second Alice in Wonderland book, *Through the Looking-Glass*, with an acrostic that spells the name of the real Alice, Alice Pleasance Liddell. (In the book, Alice Liddell is also punningly referred to as "little Alice.") The initial letters of the lines in the first two stanzas spell ALICE P:

> A boat, beneath a sunny sky
> Lingering onward dreamily
> In an evening of July—
> Children three that nestle near,
> Eager eye and willing ear,
> Pleased a simple tale to hear—

Acrostics can be written in a variety of prose and poetry forms. In ALPHA-BETIC POEMS, for instance, the word choice is guided by ALPHABETIC ORDER. In AUTOMYNORGAGRAMS, the choice is based on the letters as they occur in the text itself. The letters of the acrostic can appear in places other than the beginnings of the words, too (SEE DOUBLE ACROSTIC, TELESTICH, TRIPLE ACROSTIC).

**acrostic dictionary**: a dictionary in which the words are arranged by first and last letter (A–A, A–B, A–C, . . . Z–Z), and then alphabetically by the letters within each first-last letter combination. Thus, if *dear* precedes *deed* in a regular dictionary, *deed* would precede *dear* in an acrostic dictionary, since D–D words come before D–R words.

**acrostic equation**: a numerically correct equation made of NUMBER NAMES whose initials on one side of the equal sign spell the answer on the other side.

> One hundred – Ninety-one – Eight = ONE      $100 - 91 - 8 = 1$
> Twenty + Eighty – Ninety = TEN      $20 + 80 - 90 = 10$

**acrostic poem**: an ACROSTIC. (Usually the word "poem" is unnecessary—most acrostics are poems.)

**acrostic puzzle**: a poem composed of riddling lines whose solutions form an acrostic that spells out the answer to the puzzle. One 10-line poem written in praise of a lady posed five riddles with solutions whose first letters spelled out the lady's last name (Green):

> G R A V E
> R I N G
> E V E N I N G
> E A S E
> N O

**add-a-line couplet**: a two-line poem formed by taking a well-known line from a classic and adding a rhyming line that turns the original into a humorous parody of itself.

> I think that I shall never see—
> My contact lens fell in my tea.
>
> Tyger, Tyger, burning bright,
> How you save electric light!

**adjacent-letter switch**: a transposal in which two letters next to each other in a word change places to form another word. This is a special case of METALLEGE.

> SALVE = SLAVE      NUTHATCH = UNTHATCH

**adjacent pronoun speller**: a word with strings of consecutive letters that spell a large number of different pronouns. The letters in USHERS can spell five:

```
USHERS
US
  SHE
  HE
  HER
  HERS
```

**adjacent word speller**: a word with strings of consecutive letters that spell a large number of words. The letters in THEREIN can spell ten.

| ERE | HER  | HEREIN | RE   | THE   |
|-----|------|--------|------|-------|
| HE  | HERE | IN     | REIN | THERE |

**AEGINRST transposal problem**: the challenge of finding as many words as possible that are TRANSPOSALS of the letters AEGINRST, one of the ULTIMATE TRANSPOSAL SETS. The words can come from any published source. So far, some 150 transposals of AEGINRST have been found. In the examples below, the first line has five tranposals that are common words. The next five lines have transposals that are uncommon words, each followed by its definition and source.

ANGRIEST   GRANITES   INERT GAS   INGRATES   RANGIEST
EAST'RING: poetic shortening of *eastering* (see *west'ring* in *Oxford English Dictionary*)
NEGRITAS: plural of *negrita*, serranoid fish of the West Indies (*Funk & Wagnalls New Standard Dictionary of the English Language*)
REASTING: dialect term meaning becoming rancid, as bacon (*English Dialect Dictionary*)
STAINGER: surname of John Stainger (1991 Calgary Telephone Directory)
TRANGIES: towns such as Trangie in New South Wales (*Times Atlas of the World*)

**AEIOU abbreviation**: an abbreviation using all five vowels. AEIOU (without periods) was the abbreviation for the bilingual motto of Emperor Frederick III of Austria (1440–1493). The vowels are the initials of two five-word sentences, one in Latin and one in German, which have roughly the same meaning in both languages. Their meaning can be translated into an English sentence with the very same initials.

Austriae Est Imperare Orbi Universo (Latin: "It is for Austria to rule the world.")

Alles Erdreich Ist Oesterreich Untertan (German: "The whole world is subjected to Austria.")

4

**AEIOU word**: a word in which the five major vowels appear once each in any order.

DIALOGUE        EQUATION        SEQUOIA

**AEIOUY word**: a word in which all six vowels appear once each in any order.

AUREOMYCIN        BUOYANCIES        EURYOMIA

**Agamemnon word**: a word containing three or more consecutive tri-grams, each of which is a three-letter palindrome, as in AGA-MEM-NON. An Agamemnon word may have extra letters. In these examples, the left column has nine-letter words, while the right column has longer words with extra letters.

| | |
|---|---|
| ILICACEAE | proBABILISTS |
| SUSUHUNAN | noNENTITIZIng |
| MIMICISMS | chOROCOCCACEAE |

**aibohphobia**: fear of PALINDROMES.

**ailihphilia**: love of PALINDROMES.

**A-invariant**: a UNIVOCALIC with A as the only vowel.

ARCHCHARLATANS        CATCH-AS-CATCH-CAN

**Alberti disc**: a code wheel in which the letters of the alphabet are arranged around the inner circumference of a circle as well as the outer circumference. Each turn of the circle can line up the letters to form one of 26 SUBSTITU-TION CODES.

**all-consonant word**: a word that consists of consonants only; that is, a word that excludes all six vowels, AEIOUY:

GRR        NTH        TSK

For longer all-consonant words, it is necessary to go beyond unabridged dictionaries. The following words fall into the categories noted in parentheses:

CRWTHS, CWMTWRCH (words of Welsh origin using W as a vowel)
STLP, TRSTJ (words of Eastern European origin using L and R as vowels)
Joe BTLFSPK by Al Capp, PTHWNDXRCLZP by James Joyce (coined words)
PHFFFT, BZZBZZ (slang interjections)

Also called "no-vowel word."

**alliterative acrostic**: an ACROSTIC in which all the words in each line begin with the same letter and and in which those letters going down the poem spell the subject's name. The following is about the poet William Butler Yeats:

> You yawn, you yearn, yet yon you yield
> Each eye. Each enigmatic ear
> Awakens, and an army adds
> The truth to touch the timeless tear!
> So seek some swordsman's shield.

**alliterative eulogy**: a statement of high praise using words in succession that begin with the same consonant sounds.

> If boundless benevolence be the basis of beatitude, and harmless humanity a harbinger of hallowed heart, these Christian concomitants composed her characteristics, and conciliated the esteem of her contemporary acquaintances, who mean to model their manners in the mould of their meritorious monitor.

**all-vowel pun pair**: a pair of words that sound alike and contain all five vowels between them.

AURICLE + ORACLE    ADIEU + ADO    GORILLA + GUERRILLA

**all-vowel word**: a word consisting of one or more of the six vowels and no consonants. The vowels may appear one or more times in any order. I, AY, AYE, and EYE are four all-vowel HOMOPHONES (first meaning).

AIAIAI    EUOUAE    OO-OOO-OO    O-O-O-O-O-O-O-O-O-O

**alphabet-crashing word**: a word whose initial letter and one or more other letters are the same distance apart in the word as they are in the alphabet. They CRASH where the corresponding letters are the same.

ABIDE                INKLI NG
ABcDE                I j KLmNo

See INVARIANT LETTER, LOCALLY INVARIANT LETTERS.

**Alphabet Cube**: an imaginary machine composed of little lights arranged in a 3-D cube of twenty-six rows, twenty-six columns, and twenty-six planes. Each light has on it one of the 17,576 possible TRIGRAMS, going from AAA to ZZZ. By pressing a specific button on the console, the operator lights up certain trigrams. For instance, the PALINDROME button lights up all the palindromic trigrams. Other buttons light up other trigrams displaying different kinds of wordplay, such as anagrams, letter shifts, etc. Its purpose is to show the patterns of wordplay in three dimensions. Its limitation is that it only works with three-letter words or strings. Words of any length can be represented by WORD WORMS.

**alphabetic** (*adj.*): using the letters of the alphabet in a specific way; arranged in the conventional order; relying on or related to the alphabet.

**alphabetic advertisement**: an advertisement that uses words beginning with each letter of the alphabet. The following appeared in the London *Times* in 1842:

> TO WIDOWERS AND SINGLE GENTLEMEN.—WANTED by a lady, a SITUATION to superintend the household and preside at table. She is Agreeable, Becoming, Careful, Desirable, English, Facetious, Generous, Honest, Industrious, Judicious, Keen, Lively, Merry, Natty, Obedient, Philosophic, Quiet, Regular, Sociable, Tasteful, Useful, Vivacious, Womanish, Xantippish, Youthful, Zealous, &c. Address X.Y.Z., Simond's Library, Edgeware-road.

**alphabetical** (*adj.*): see ALPHABETIC. As these two adjectives have the same meaning, *alphabetic* will be used throughout this dictionary for the sake of consistency.

**alphabetically** (*adv.*): in a manner that uses the letters of the alphabet or that causes letters or words to be arranged in alphabetic order.

**alphabetically-ordered AEIOU word**: a word in which the five major vowels appear once each in alphabetic order.

| CAESIOUS | FACETIOUS | LAWN TENNIS COURT |

**alphabetically-ordered AEIOUY word**: a word that uses all six vowels once each in alphabetic order.

ABSTEMIOUSLY          FACETIOUSLY

**alphabetically-ordered consonant word**: a word in which the consonants appear in alphabetic order.

COMMEMORATIVE          ADIADOKOKINESIAS
C  MM  M  R T V          D  D  K  KN S  S

**alphabetic equality names**: names whose letters have alphabetic values that add up to the same amount. In these examples, the alphabetic values are based on different arrangements of the alphabet. For the normal alphabet, A = 1, B = 2, . . . Z = 26, but for the reverse alphabet, Z = 1, Y = 2, . . . A = 26. The sum and the specific alphabet are listed in parentheses:

Saddam Hussein = Richard Nixon (137, normal alphabet)
Lyndon Johnson = John Kennedy (172, REVERSE ALPHABET)
Gorbachev = Harry Houdini (127, TYPEWRITER KEYBOARD ALPHABET)
Joe McCarthy = Adolph Hitler (124, ALTERNATING ALPHABET)
Norman Schwarzkopf = Theodore Roosevelt (182, HALF-SWITCH ALPHABET)

**alphabetic neighbor**: a letter that comes before or after another letter in the alphabet. C and D are alphabetic neighbors, but C and E are not. In the CIRCULAR ALPHABET, Z and A are alphabetic neighbors, too.

**alphabetic order**: the traditional arrangement of the letters from A to Z.

**alphabetic pattern**: the arrangement of letters in the alphabet in relation to the arrangement of letters in a word.

**alphabetic poem**: a poem whose lines are organized around the alphabet. In one type, the words in each line begin with the same letter, starting with A's in the first line and ending with Z's in the last line. Here are the first three and the last four lines of "The Siege of Belgrade":

An Austrian army awfully array'd
Boldy by batter besieg'd Belgrade;
Cossack commanders cannonading come,
. . .
Xerxes, Ximenes, Xanthus, Xavier?
Yield, yield, ye youths, ye yeomen yield your yell;

Zeno's, Zorpater's, Zoroaster's, zeal
Attracting all, arms against acts appeal.

**alphabetic recital**: a story, poem, or other text in which the words sound similar to the alphabet recited from A to Z. The words are HOMOPHONES (first meaning) or near-homophones of the spoken letters. Here are two examples:

Hay, be seedy! He-effigy, hate-shy jakey yellow man, oh peek, you are rusty, you've edible, you ex-wise he!

Abby sized Dee's effigy, hijackcd Elle's minnow, piqued curest tease. "You've double-uscd," ex-wiscd Zee.

Also called "alphabet story."

**alphabetic sentence**: a 26-word prose text in which each word begins with a different letter and in which all 26 words occur in alphabetic order. An alphabetic sentence can be more than one sentence long.

Able bodied conscientious dustmen emptying filthy garbage handle indescribable junk. Kitchen leftovers make noxious odours producing quite revolting stenches. This unwholesome vegetation won't exactly yield zeal.

**alphabetic sequence**: **1.** two or more letters that are next to each other in the alphabet, such as FG or LMNOPQR. Using the CIRCULAR ALPHABET, an alphabetic sequence can make the jump from Z to A, too, as in WXYZAB. Thus there are 26 sequences of 25 different lengths. Each letter is an ALPHA-BETIC NEIGHBOR of the other. An alphabetic sequence can appear in a word in several ways, including:

Adjacent in order: UNDERSTUDY, SIZABLE
Not necessarily adjacent but in order: AMBUSCADE, PRIZEFIGHTING
Not necessarily adjacent, not necessarily in order: FEEDBACK,
    QUADRUPLICATIONS

Also called "alphabetic letter sequence."

**2.** a group of letters occurring in alphabetic order in a word. In this definition, the letters do not have to be adjacent in the alphabet. A single letter can also be considered an alphabetic sequence. Most words can be divided into two or more alphabetic sequences each composed of a different set of letters. Shown below are two of several ways that the word POETRY can be divided into three alphabetic sequences.

```
POETRY        POETRY
P - - T - Y    P - - T - -
_ O _ _ R _    - O - - - Y
_ _ E _ _ _    - - E - R -
```

**alphabetic step**: the distance from one letter to the next in the alphabet. A is one alphabetic step from B, two alphabetic steps from C, and 25 alphabetic steps from Z. This concept is used in various wordplay forms, especially the LETTERSHIFT.

**alphabetic substitute-letter transposal chain**: a SUBSTITUTE-LETTER TRANSPOSAL chain in which a different letter of the alphabet is substituted at each step up to a possible 26 steps forming a 27-word chain. This was the basis of a contest in *Games* magazine. The winning entry was a 23-step chain of 13-letter words, which started with the four words below. The underlined letter in each word was dropped and replaced by the underlined letter in the next word, and the new set of letters was transposed to form the new word. Entries were scored by multiplying the number of words in the chain by the number of letters in the words.

C̲APITALNESSES—SK̲EPTICALNESS—TY̲PICALNESSES— PLICATE̲NESSES— . . .

**alphabetic tetragram**: a TETRAGRAM consisting of four consecutive letters. Words with alphabetic tetragrams are hard to find.

ABCDarian          oMNOPon          supeRSTUd

**alphabetic transaddition**: a series of words formed by adding in turn the letters from A to Z to the same starting word, and then rearranging them if necessary. In this example, AT is the starting word, and each added letter is capitalized:

| | | | | | | |
|---|---|---|---|---|---|---|
| tAa | Eat | aIt | Mat | Qat | taU | taY |
| Bat | Fat | taJ | taN | aRt | Vat | Zat |
| Cat | taG | Kat | Oat | Sat | taW | |
| taD | Hat | aLt | aPt | Tat | taX | |

**alphabetic trigram**: a TRIGRAM consisting of three consecutive letters. The following words have alphabetic trigrams in them:

| | | |
|---|---|---|
| crABCatcher | HIJinks | liverwuRST |
| graDEFinder | pOPQuiz | zUVWlla |

**alphabetic value**: the number representing a given letter's position in the alphabet: A = 1, B = 2, . . . Z = 26. The concept of alphabetic value provides the major (non-algebraic) key to manipulate letters as numbers in wordplay.

| | | | | | | |
|---|---|---|---|---|---|---|
| A = 1 | E = 5 | I = 9 | M = 13 | Q = 17 | U = 21 | Y = 25 |
| B = 2 | F = 6 | J = 10 | N = 14 | R = 18 | V = 22 | Z = 26 |
| C = 3 | G = 7 | K = 11 | O = 15 | S = 19 | W = 23 | |
| D = 4 | H = 8 | L = 12 | P = 16 | T = 20 | X = 24 | |

**alphabetic value of (a letter in any SCRAMBLED ALPHABET)**: the number representing a letter's position in any rearrangement of the alphabet. The alphabetic values of the letters in the REVERSE ALPHABET are Z = 1, Y = 2,... A = 26.

**alphabetic word**: a word whose letters occur in alphabetic order. An example is AN, but not THE.

| | | |
|---|---|---|
| BILLOWY | ADELOPS | AEGILOPS |

**alphabetic word challenge**: the challenge of rearranging the alphabet so that the sum of the letters spelling the longest word forward and the longest word in reverse is maximized. In the following arrangement, the two words have a total of 25 letters:

```
          JKMQVWXZSUNCOPYRIGHTABLFED
Forward:            UNCOPYRIGHTABL E
Reverse:            S  N  O    I   TA LFED
                   (DEFLATIONS)
```

See ALPHABETIC WORD, CIRCULAR ALPHABET, SCRAMBLED ALPHABET.

**alphabetic wordplay**: wordplay based on alphabetic order in some way. Some alphabetic wordplay involves finding and using the first or the last entry in a dictionary or a phone directory. Other alphabetic wordplay involves looking for words containing letters that occupy specific positions in the alphabet, forming groups of words in this way, rearranging the alphabet, or assigning numerical values to the letters.

**alphabetized integers**: NUMBER NAMES placed in alphabetic order.

**alphabet of silent hosts**: the alphabet as a set of letters that are pronounced in words but that don't appear in them. All 26 letters can be found in silent hosts. Here are six examples:

|   |   |
|---|---|
| A: eight | X: decks |
| B: W-shaped | Y: wine |
| C: sea | Z: xylophone |

**alphabet of silent letters**: the alphabet as a set of letters that appear in words but that aren't pronounced in them. All 26 letters can be silent. Here are six examples:

|   |   |
|---|---|
| A: bread | X: Sioux |
| B: subtle | Y: crayon |
| C: yacht | Z: rendezvous |

**alphabet rearrangement**: see SCRAMBLED ALPHABET.

**alphabet ring**: a circle with all 26 letters written in any order around the circumference. If the letters appear in alphabetic order, the ring is the CIRCULAR ALPHABET.

**alphabet shift**: an alignment of a portion of the alphabet that results in a set of one or more letters occupying the same relative positions in the alphabet. These are called LOCALLY INVARIANT LETTERS. A word can have more than one alphabet shift formed by different alignments of letters. WRETCH, for example, has four shifts.

```
WRETCH      WRETCH      WRETCH      WRETCH
|           | |          | |        |
WXYZAB      QRSTUV      CDEFGH      YZABCD
```

**alphamagic square**: a magic square (a square of numbers that add up to the same amount horizontally, vertically, and diagonally) in which the sums of the letters in the number words also form a magic square. In this example, the numbers add up to 45 in each direction, and the letter amounts add up to 27.

| Numbers | | | Number Names | | | Letter Amounts | | |
|---|---|---|---|---|---|---|---|---|
| 5 | 22 | 18 | five | twenty-two | eighteen | 4 | 9 | 8 |
| 28 | 15 | 2 | twenty-eight | fifteen | two | 11 | 7 | 3 |
| 12 | 8 | 25 | twelve | eight | twenty-five | 6 | 5 | 10 |

**alphametic**: an arithmetic problem in which each digit is replaced by a letter. The digits are chosen so that the letters can be decoded to spell words, one letter per digit. Alphametics can use addition, subtraction, multiplication, and division. This one adds up to an urgent message:

```
    5  4  7  8            S  E  N  D
    1  6  2  4            M  O  R  E
 +  9  6  3  8        +   G  O  L  D
 ─────────────        ──────────────
 1  6  7  4  0        M  O  N  E  Y
```

**alphanumeric value**: see ALPHABETIC VALUE.

**alphapositional value**: see ALPHABETIC VALUE.

**alphatoon**: an animated cartoon showing one letter changing to another letter. See SHAPE-SHIFT (*v.*).

**alphome**: a set of alphabetically ordered letters of which at least one arrangement is a word. For example, the alphome ABINR can form at least one word, BRAIN. There are four types of alphomes based on the letters they contain. Here is one word of each type:

CARPET = A + C + E + P + R + T (alphabetically-isolated letters; a VICINAL)
MOCKED = CDE + K + M + O (alphabetically-isolated letters and alpha-
  betically consecutive letter groups)
MOUTHING = GHI + MNO + TU (no isolated letters; a NON-VICINAL)
BACED = ABCDE (single group of alphabetically-consecutive letters)

**alphomic word**: see ALPHABETIC WORD.

**alternade**: a word that can be broken up into its odd-numbered and even-numbered letters (i.e., two sequences of every second letter) to form shorter words. See QUATERNADE, QUINADE, TRINADE.

```
    CALLIOPES           TRIENNIALLY
    C  L  I  P  S       T  I  N  I  L  Y
    A  L  O  E          R  E  N  A  L
```

Also called "drop-letter reversal."

**alternating alphabet**: BADCFEHGJILKNMPORQTSVUXWZY, the alphabet with the letters in each pair switching positions. In other words, all odd letters appear in even positions, and vice versa.

**alternating monotony**: a word with the same letter in every other position for three or more occurrences. MONOTONY, for instance, has the letter O in the second, fourth, and sixth positions. There are three kinds of alternating monotonies, distinguished by whether they are composed of vowels, consonants, or both. See CONSONANTAL ALTERNATING MONOTONY, DOUBLY-INTERTWINED ALTERNATING MONOTONY, VOCALIC ALTERNATING MONOTONY.

**alternating vowel-consonant number name**: a NUMBER NAME in which vowels (AEIOUY) and consonants alternate in spelling the word.

ONE  TEN   ELEVEN  NINETY-SEVEN

**amalgam**: an anagram of the names of two real or fictitious people in a phrase or a sentence that relates them in some way.

 DIANA + CHARLES = I hear scandal.
 CLEOPATRA + VALENTINO = O, can love pair talent?
 SAINT + DEVIL = invalid set

**ambigram**: an ANAGRAM ambiguously apposite or opposite in meaning from the starting text.

 THE NUCLEAR REGULATORY COMMISSION = Your rules clone atomic nightmares.

**anagram**: a word, phrase, or sentence formed by rearranging the letters of another word, phrase, or sentence. An anagram usually relates in meaning to the original text, but not always (see TRANSPOSAL). Many other wordplay forms involve anagrams.

 The Greek poet Lycophon is credited with inventing the form about 260 B.C. It works by the simplest strategy, moving letters around like the pieces of a puzzle, and yet a well-crafted anagram is a miniature work of art.

In fact, the word ANAGRAMS transposes to ARS MAGNA, the Latin for "great art." Like tiny haiku, some anagrams create delicate and beautiful images, such as MOONLIGHT = THIN GLOOM. To invoke the muse, AN INSPIRED POET might say, "SPIRIT, PEN AN ODE!"

At least 10,000 anagrams have been published in English. Here are some masterpieces of the form (and MASTERPIECES itself can be anagrammed to ART SEEMS EPIC):

PITTANCE = a cent tip
DESPERATION = A rope ends it.
GOLD AND SILVER = grand old evils
THE NUDIST COLONY = no untidy clothes
THE MARRIED MAN = I'm her darn mate
IS PITY LOVE? = Positively!

The following three words are especially noteworthy for being the longest anagrammatic trio related in meaning.

PARENTAL = PATERNAL = PRENATAL

In the next example, the singular and the plural of the same word generate opposite meanings:

DORMITORY = dirty room          DORMITORIES = tidier rooms

The most well-known long word forms a normal-sounding sentence that could have been spoken by the artist Picasso:

ANTIDISESTABLISHMENTARIANISM = I am an artist, and I bless this in me.

Schoolchildren (third and fourth graders in this case) like to make anagrams of their own names.

MAXIM = I'm Max.                    ZACHARY = Ah, crazy!
DANIEL = nailed                     AMELIA = am a lie
MARK T. = K-Mart                    JAMES STONE = same jet, son
SEAN = sane
KARA CHAPMAN = Hark, a Pacman!

The old riddle, "Why did the chicken cross the road?" is given a new answer by anagramming one sentence into the other:

THE CHICKEN CROSSES THE ROAD = She checks corn at other side!

Also called "apt anagram," "apposite anagram."

**anagram classification system**: a method of categorizing anagrams based on the change in letter order from one word to the other. The first word's letters are numbered by position, and the second word's letters are represented by rearranging the positional numbers of the first word. For example, PAST (1234) anagrams to TAPS (4213). Since the first word's letters are always numbered consecutively, it is enough to know the numeric arrangement of the second word to figure out the first word: if TAPS = 4213, then 1=P, 2=A, 3=S, 4=T, which spells PAST.

**anagram equation**: a numerically correct equation whose NUMBER NAMES on each side are rearrangements of the same letters. There is only one anagram equation in English. In Spanish, however, there are two, each with the sum of 15.

> ELEVEN + TWO = TWELVE + ONE
>
> UNO + CATORCE = CUATRO + ONCE (1 + 14 = 4 + 11)
> DOS + TRECE = TRES + DOCE  (2 + 13 = 3 + 12)

Also called "apposite numerical transposition."

**anagrammar chain**: a sequence of words in which each adjacent pair forms a longer word that is not related in meaning.

> CAD-AVERS-ION (CADAVERS, AVERSION)
> EPIC-ENTER-TAIN (EPICENTER, ENTERTAIN)

**anagrammatic cross-reference**: an anagram in the form of a library cross-reference. The ANAGRAM uses directional words such as SEE, FIND, etc.

> SEPARATE = See "apart"
> INFIDEL = Find "lie"
> TELEVISION SET = See "It's not live"
> DISEASE = See "AIDS"

**anagrammatic definition**: a dictionary definition that is an ANAGRAM of the word it defines.

> GIFOLA: [New Latin, anagram of *Filago*] synonym of *Filago* (in *Webster's 3rd*)
> GRANATE: a garnet (in *Webster's 2nd*)

**anagrammatic pangrams**: two or more PANGRAMS that are ANAGRAMS of each other. In the two lines below, each line is a pangram using the six vowels (AEIOUY) twice and the twenty consonants once. Thus, the lines are anagrams of each other as well.

> Why jog exquisite bulk, fond crazy vamp,
> Daft buxom jonquil, zephyr's gawky vice?

**anagrammatic sonnet**: a six-line poem with four feet per line, in which each foot is an ANAGRAM of another word or words. The poem is not a traditional sonnet, but it *is* anagrammatic. There are a total of 24 feet. The challenge is to figure out the 24 anagrams. Here is a first line, followed by two anagram versions:

> As to the war, try elm. I tried.

> Oats. wreath. myrtle. tidier.

> So at the raw myrtle it ride.

**anagrammatic translation**: a word in one language that turns into its equivalent in another language when the letter at one end is moved to the opposite end. Each word is an anagrammatic translation of the other.

> AND = DAN (Indonesian)
> THE = HET (Dutch)
> TUNA = ATUN (Spanish)

**anagrammatic verse**: poetry based on ANAGRAMS in one way or another. In the poem "Dorothy Was Once in the Emerald City of Oz," each line is an anagram of the title. Here is the first stanza:

> Dorothy was once in the Emerald City of Oz.
> She tried the way to Oz, forced in many cool
> Woods nicely on the road for the city maze.
> The icy dew froze Tinman. "Choose a dry tool," . . .

Also called "anagrammic poetry."

**anagrammed story**: a story in which the letters of each word can be transposed to form the correct word in the original story. "Eth Stinted" ("The Dentist") begins with these sentences:

"Sinned Hurts, Stinted," dear het malls gins tedious eth moor. "Logans:
On nipa, on agin. Mug seaside, pastel, unrested."
Shote sword ewer ton grenadine. Eros dare gams, ton oot knee whit
binge ether.
Het idea acme, sliming. "Eth cod si dreary."

Translation:

"Dennis Hurst, Dentist" read the small sign outside the room. "Slogan:
No pain, no gain. Gum disease, plates, dentures."
Those words were not endearing. Rose read mags, not too keen with being there.
The aide came, smiling. "The doc is ready."

**anagram name**: see TRANSPOSAL NAME.

**anagram puzzle verse**: a poem with blank spaces that have to be filled in
with words that are ANAGRAMS of each other. In the following example, the
missing anagrams are MELONS, SOLEMN, and LEMONS.

> "The _ _ _ _ _ _ are terribly small,"
> Say I to my wife in the hall.
> Her big _ _ _ _ _ _ eyes
> Open wide: she replies:
> "It was _ _ _ _ _ _ I ordered: that's all!"

**anagram word square**: **1.** a WORD SQUARE in which all the words are
ANAGRAMS of each other. As shown below, an anagram square is actually four
squares in one. Each square can be rotated 90 degrees clockwise to form the
square on its right or, in the case of the last square, to form the first square.
Rotation also changes a square in another way: The first is a single square, the
second a double square, the third a single, and the fourth a double.

```
A R E    E R A    R A E    E A R
R E A    A E R    A E R    R E A
E A R    R A E    E R A    A R E
```

**2.** a word square that contains the same letters and mirrors the pattern of at
least one other square. Each square below is an anagram word square of each
of the other two.

```
T A N    T A N    R A N
A R E    E R A    A T E
N E T    N E T    N E T
```

**3.** a word square made of the letters in a single nine-letter word. Each of the two squares below is a three-square made of GALENGALE, and each is also an ANAGRAM WORD SQUARE (meaning 2) of the other.

```
N A G        L E G
A L E        E N A
G E L        G A L
```

**ananym**: a pseudonym that an author forms by reversing the letters of his or her last name. The term is derived from *anonym*, a synonym of *pseudonym*. See REVERSAL PSEUDONYM.

John COLLARD (English writer) = DRALLOC

**anatonym**: a part of the body that has shifted in usage from noun to verb.

TOE the line.     FOOT the bill     FACE the music.

**anchored palindrome**: a word, phrase, or name that is PALINDROMIC except for one or more letters (the "anchor") at its beginning or end.

SENSUOUSNESS     DANNY LLEWELLYN

**anchored reversal**: a pair of words that are REVERSALS of each other except for their first or last letters. When the appropriate anchor (first or last letter) is dropped, the remaining letters are reversals. GRIT - G = RIT, and STIR - S = TIR.

NAIROBI—CIBORIA          TESSERACT—CARESSETH

**anchored transposals**: two or more words in which only the interior letters are transposed. The first letter and the last letters stay the same.

FIELD = FLIED = FELID
CAVERN = CRAVEN = CARVEN

**anchored word**: a word considered in terms of its first letter and its last letter only. Every word of two or more letters can be considered an anchored word. One challenge is to create a TYPE-COLLECTION of anchored words from A–A to Z–Z. Here is the section representing A–A to A–Z. At this time, two combinations have not been found.

AreA, AraB, AcademiC, AnD, ArE, AlooF, AmonG, AlthougH, AlkalI, A–J, AsK, AiL, AM, AN, AlsO, AsleeP, A–Q, AfteR, AS, AT, AdieU, AlloW, AX, AnY, AdZ.

## animal anagram: an ANAGRAM of an animal name.

EWE—WEE                    OSTRICH—RICH SOT
LEOPARD—PAROLED            PLATYPUS—SALTY PUP

## animal beheadment: the BEHEADMENT of a word that results in an animal name.

CRAM—RAM                   SCAT—CAT
REGRET—EGRET               THEN—HEN

## animal curtailment: the CURTAILMENT of a word that results in an animal name.

APEX—APE                   BOARD—BOAR
BEARD—BEAR                 BOAST—BOAS

## animal charade: a CHARADE of an animal name.

DONKEY—DON KEY             PARROT—PAR ROT
FLAMINGO—FLAMING O         ROBIN—ROB IN
HERRING—HER RING           STALLION—STALL ION

## animal kangaroo: a KANGAROO WORD that has an animal name within it.

BOTANY—BOA                 RECTANGLE—EAGLE
HYPHENATE—HYENA            TRIGGER—TIGER

## animal letter substitution: an animal name that becomes another animal name with the change of a single letter—initial, middle, or terminal.

DONKEY—MONKEY    BEAR—BOAR    COD—COW
HARE—MARE        FOAL—FOWL    COON—COOT

## animal looper: a looping anagram (or CYCLIC TRANSPOSAL) that has an animal name as one of its words.

DRAKE—RAKED                EMANATE—MANATEE
EMUS—MUSE                  LOW—OWL

**animal palindrome**: a PALINDROME that includes the name of an animal.

> Elk cackle.
> He goddam mad dog, eh?
> Lay a wallaby baby ball away, Al.
> Was it a car or a cat I saw?

**animal-within-animal beheadment**: the BEHEADMENT of an animal name that results in another animal name.

BASS—ASS
BEAGLE—EAGLE

FOWL—OWL
WASP—ASP

**animal-within-animal charade**: a CHARADE of an animal name that results in a shorter animal name (and one or more other words).

ANTELOPE—ANT ELOPE
PIGEON—PIG EON

MEADOWLARK—MEAD OW LARK
MEADOWLARK—MEAD OWL ARK

**animal-within-animal kangaroo**: a KANGAROO WORD that is an animal name with a shorter animal name within it. The most meaningful of all is CH<u>ICK</u>EN—HEN.

<u>CR</u>O<u>CO</u>D<u>I</u>LE—COD
<u>M</u>ON<u>GOO</u>SE—MOOSE

<u>O</u>R<u>A</u>NGU<u>TA</u>N—RAT
<u>W</u>E<u>A</u>S<u>EL</u>—EEL

**animultitude**: a NOUN OF MULTITUDE associated with a specific animate object. All of the following are real:

SKULK OF FOXES
PLAGUE OF LOCUSTS
COWARDICE OF CURS

PARLIAMENT OF OWLS
OSTENTATION OF PEACOCKS
PITYING OF DOVES

**antibeheadment**: a BEHEADMENT that produces a word with a meaning that contrasts with the starting word.

BONUS—ONUS
LAWFUL—AWFUL

PREVIEW—REVIEW
SHE—HE

**anticharade**: a CHARADE that means the opposite of the original text.

NOWHERE (not present) = NOW HERE (present)
UN-HUNH (yes) = UNH-UNH (no)

SEARING SUN LIT ISLAND = SEA RINGS UNLIT ISLAND

Also called "charade-antigram."

**antidisestablishmentarianism**: the most famous long word of all (28 letters), listed in *Funk & Wagnalls New Standard Dictionary of the English Language*. In the nineteenth century it meant "opposition to the separation of church and state." A literal interpretation of its parts gives it the meaning "a doctrine against the dissolution of the establishment." It may have been coined as early as 1869. British Prime Minister William Gladstone (1809–1898) is reputed to have used it once, possibly in the adverbial form ending with "-ICALLY."

**antigram**: an ANAGRAM that means the opposite of the original text or that sharply contrasts with it. (Originally this term meant "reversal.")

A DIET = I'd eat.                    GIANT = I, gnat
FORGET-ME-NOT = forgotten me    LEMONADE = demon ale

Also called "antonymogram," "antonymous anagram," "opposite anagram."

**antikangaroo**: a KANGAROO WORD that conceals its own opposite.

COMMUNICATIVE—MUTE          PEST—PET
EXIST—EXIT                          WONDERFUL—WOEFUL
FRIEND—FIEND

**anti-lettershift pair**: a pair of words in which no letters in corresponding positions are shifted the same number of steps along the alphabet. WORD PAIR is one anti-LETTERSHIFT pair: W shifts 19 steps to P, O shifts 12 steps to A, R shifts 17 steps to I, and D shifts 14 steps to R. Here is a longer anti-lettershift pair with its shift values subtracted on the right.

| S | T | A | T | E | S | M | A | N | | 19 | 20 | 1 | 20 | 5 | 19 | 13 | 1 | 14 |
|---|---|---|---|---|---|---|---|---|---|----|----|----|----|----|----|----|----|----|
| I | N | T | E | R | P | R | E | T | - | 9 | 14 | 20 | 5 | 18 | 16 | 18 | 5 | 20 |
| | | | | | | | | | | 10 | 6 | 7 | 15 | 13 | 3 | 21 | 22 | 20 |

**anti-lettershift sentence**: a set of anti-lettershift words arranged to form a sentence in which neighboring words make an anti-lettershift pair.

Statesmen interpret community.

**antiphonetabet**: the alphabet of sounds represented by different letters than "normal" to make the sounds. The "a" sound in "cat" has the same sound as "au" in "laugh." The "au" sound is in the antiphonetabet.

"ay" (as in "day") = "et" (as in "fillet")   "p" = "gh" (as in "hiccough")
"d" = "t" (as in "Taoism")                "r" = "l" (as in "colonel")
"j" = "dg" (as in "hedge")            "v" = "f" (as in "of")
"m" = "mn" (as in "autumn")       "z" = "x" (as in "xylophone")

**antiphonetic spelling**: a variant spelling of a word in which the letters are replaced with other letters having the same sounds occurring in certain other words. To demonstrate the difficulty of English orthography, the playwright George Bernard Shaw, a champion of spelling reform, used an antiphonetic spelling of FISH as GHOTI ("gh" as in "enough," "o" as in "women," and "ti" as in "nation." Here are two more antiphonetic spellings:

TET = DAY ("d" as in "missed," "ay" as in "fillet")
OUGNAMP = ONION ("ou" as in "rough," "gna" as in "lasagna," "mp" as in "comptroller")

**antirebus**: a SYLLABIC REBUS that goes in the other direction—i.e., words form letters. In regular syllabic rebuses, RUN would signify ARE YOU IN. Conversely, in an antirebus, ARE YOU IN would signify RUN. The individual words of an antirebus sound like letters.

Oh, any. (ONE)
Hello, Angie. I see. Why are—oh, hey, Dee! Yes? (LONG, ICY ROADS)
Age? Oh, tee 'em! A tee? See age. (HOT MATCH)

**antonymic reversal**: a REVERSAL of another word or longer text with opposite or contrasting meaning.

TUNA = A NUT              ALLEN = NELLA
EMBARGO = O, GRAB ME!    NATASHA = AH, SATAN!

**antonymic substitution**: the replacement of every word in a text with the word opposite in meaning.

Now is the winter of our discontent
Never isn't a summer to your happiness

**antonymic transdeletion**: deleting one letter in a word and transposing the remaining letters to create a new word opposite or contrasting in meaning to the original.

GIANT – I = GNAT.
RELIGIOUS ACTS – T = SACRILEGIOUS

**apostrophe word**: a word with an apostrophe in it that spells another word if the apostrophe is removed. The two words have different meanings and (usually) different pronuncations.

I'LL—ILL        CAN'T—CANT        SHE'LL—SHELL

**apostrophic poem**: a poem using APOSTROPHE WORDS and their una-postrophized equivalents as off-rhymes. "Apostrophe to Love" begins with these two stanzas:

When she said we'd
Be shortly wed,
Her dad said, "He'll
Be damned to hell."

She asked if I'd
Obeyed my id.
I asked if she'll
Remove her shell.

**apostrophic sentence**: a sentence with a large number of apostrophes replacing a larger number of letters. In this example, most of the abbreviated forms can be found in the poems of Robert Burns. The 45 apostrophes replace 56 letters.

'Tis o'er ev'ry fo'c's'le th' bo's'n's look'd wi' min' pu'd 'til fu' o' fa', e'en t' nor', tho' mis'ry's awfu', 'n' ca's'll've sigh'd thro' ha's e'er sin' a' kiss'd, car'd, wish'd, an' clasp'd, ne'er ev'n i' lo'e.

**aptagram**: an ANAGRAM strongly related in meaning to the original word or words.

ARISE = RAISE            IMPREGNATE = PERMEATING
DETOUR = ROUTED          NOTE = TONE
EVIL = VILE              STATEMENT = TESTAMENT

Also called "aptanagram," "synanagram."

**aptly named author**: an author whose name is especially appropriate for the topic of the book.

*The Art of Editing* by Jack Scissors and Floyd Baskette
*Diseases of the Nervous System* by Baron Brain
*Motorcycling for Beginners* by Geoff Carless

**aptronym**: a person's name that is particularly suited to its owner's profession.

Larry SPEAKES (White House spokesperson)
Sally RIDE (astronaut)
DAN DRUFF (barber)
James BUGG (exterminator)

**artagram**: an ANAGRAM made by rearranging the letters that spell the term used to identify a specific art movement or any member of it. The resulting artagram makes a statement about art. One way is to change -IST to IT'S, as in MINIMALIST = IT'S MINIMAL. Another way is to begin with ART and rearrange the other letters, as follows:

SURREALIST = Art is rules.
REALIST = Art lies.
ABSTRACT ARTIST = Art acts art's bit.
OP ARTIST = I spot art.
POP ARTIST = Art pops it!
HARD EDGE ARTIST = Sh! Great art died.

**art movement name**: the name of an art movement, especially an art movement of the twentieth century. Some art movement names are as imaginative as the art they name.

| | | |
|---|---|---|
| AIR ART | FUNK ART | FOOD ART |
| ANTI-ART | NO ART | KITCHEN SINK ART |
| OP ART | COP ART | POP ART |

**asymmetrical letters**: F, G, J, L, N, P, Q, R, S, and Z, the letters of the alphabet that lack both horizontal and vertical symmetry. See HORIZONTAL MIRROR LETTERS and VERTICAL MIRROR LETTERS.

**A-to-Z word list**: a series of words having all 26 letters of the alphabet appearing in order. Here is the shortest list using words from the *Pocket Mer-*

*riam-Webster* (allowing A and I but no other single-letter words, and no abbreviations such as ABC or TV):

nAB CoDE FiG HIJacK LiMN OP QuRSh TurVes WaXY Zip

**augmented number name**: a NUMBER NAME whose letters appear in correct spelling order at the beginning and the ending of a longer word. Here are ONE to FOUR, each augmented with an internal pentagram to form a longer word. See CONCEALED CARDINAL, EMBEDDED NUMBER NAME.

OvertoNE      TWelvemO      THREnodizE      FOUndatoR

**autological** (*adj*.): self-descriptive (said of a word). E.g., PRINTED is printed, FINISHED is finished, and VISIBLE is visible. See GRELLING'S PARADOX.

**automobile noise**: one of the seven classifications of sound that General Motors engineers assigned to the noises that an automobile can make.

| | | | |
|---|---|---|---|
| SQUEAK | THUMP | KNOCK | HISS |
| RATTLE | GRIND | SCRAPE | |

**automynorcagram**: a text in which the initial letter of each word is determined by every single letter in order of appearance. For instance, in T̲HE H̲ORSE E̲ATS H̲AY O̲R R̲IPE S̲TRAW E̲VERYDAY, the first letters (underlined) spell THE HORSE. If this were continued, the next four words would begin with the letters in EATS HAY . . . (e.g., E̲VEN A̲S T̲HE S̲UN H̲EATS A̲LL Y̲ELLOW . . .). "The Automynorcagrammatical Raven," a version of "The Raven" by Edgar Allen Poe. begins with words that spell MIDNIGHT, the first word:

Midnight intombed December's naked icebound gulf.
Haggard, tired, . . .

**autoshiftgram**: a word that is a SHIFTGRAM of itself—that is, the letters of one word shift to a string of letters that transpose to the same word. All known examples shift 13 steps.

TANGER + 13 = GNATRE = TANGER
EMBLAZONRY + 13 = RZOYNMBAEL = EMBLAZONRY

Also called "identity shiftgram."

**avenumenclature**: the naming of streets. This little-explored area of word-play offers many possibilities. Here are some unusual street names:

LA RUE DE LA VAL DE LA MARE (New Jersey)
WHIP-MA-WHOP-MA-GATE (New York)
EVERY STREET (Leicester, England)
GIPSY LANE / GYPSY LANE (dually named, Chesterfield, England)

**average letter weight**: the sum of the ALPHABETIC VALUES of the letters in a word divided by the number of letters in it. The sum of the alphabetic values of the five letters in SEVEN is 19 + 5 + 22 + 5 + 14 = 65, and 65 divided by 5 = 13. In this case, 7, the lucky number, has an average letter weight of 13, the unlucky number.

**average numerical value of the alphabet**: the sum of the ALPHABETIC VALUES of all the letters (1 + 2 + 3 + . . . 26 = 351) divided by the number of letters (26), which is 13.5. By coincidence, 351 and 13.5 are numerical ANAGRAMS. The value, 13.5, marks the midpoint of the alphabet, located between M and N.

**backswitch**: the transformation of a word or phrase into a second word or phrase by changing (or switching) the last letter and reversing the remaining letters.

AUTUM<u>N</u>—MUTUA<u>L</u>

**backward alphabet**: see REVERSE ALPHABET.

**backward multiple charades**: short words formed by reversing the letters of a single long word and redividing them.

> ADENOFIBROMATA
> reverses to
> ATAMORBIFONEDA = AT + AM + ORB + IF + ON + ED + A

See CHARADE.

**backward spiraling alphabet**: the alphabet written in a clockwise spiral over and over starting with Z and continuing with the REVERSE ALPHABET. As with the SPIRALING ALPHABET, one purpose of the backward spiraling alphabet is to find words spelled in a line. Two words are highlighted, but others appear in the spiral, which can be extended indefinitely.

```
J  I  H  G  F  E  D
K  F  E  D  C  B  A
L  G  T  S  R  Q  Z
M  H  U  Z  Y  P  Y
N  I  V  W  X  O  X
O  J  K  L  M  N  W
P  Q  R  S  T  U  V
```

**backward substitution code**: a code in which the letters of the alphabet are replaced by the letters of the REVERSE ALPHABET. Thus A would become Z, B would become Y, and so on, as shown below. The word CAB would now read XZY.

```
A B C D E F G H I J K L M N O P Q R S  T U V W X Y Z
Z Y X W V U T S R Q P O N M L K J I H  G F E D C B A
```

**bad mixer**: a word of three or more letters that cannot be transposed in full or part to form another word. None of the transposals (or partial transposals) of TRY spells a word in the *Shorter Oxford English Dictionary*:

> TRY:   RYT  YTR  YRT  TYR  RTY
>        TR  TY  RT  YT  RY  YR

**balanced word**: a word with an AVERAGE LETTER WEIGHT of 13.5. The shortest balanced word must have two letters, as in the word, LO. The sum of LO's ALPHABETIC VALUES divided by the amount of letters in it equals 13.5 (L=12, O=15; 12+15=27; and 27 divided by 2 = 13.5).

> LOGOLOGY = 108 / 8 = 13.5

INTERCRYSTALLIZATION = 270 / 20 = 13.5

Also called "alphabetically balanced combination," "alphabetically balanced collocation."

**Baltimore deletion**: a form of DELETION in which each letter in turn is removed to form a new word.

PEAT—EAT—PAT—PET—PEA

**Baltimore transdeletion**: a type of TRANSDELETION in which a word or entry phrase is turned into a series of others by removing each letter in turn and rearranging the rest.

**bananagram**: a rhymed couplet containing a pair of ANAGRAMS to be solved. One of the rhyming words is one of the anagrams. (The answers to the example below are BEARD and BREAD.)

We don't hire hippies. So Personnel said.
I shaved off my ——. I needed the ——.

**base 27 number system**: a word considered as a number in a base 27 number system that uses the letters from A to Z for the numbers 1 to 26 and a blank space for zero. A = 1, B = 2, . . . Z = 26, Z( blank) = 27, ZA = 28, etc. All words and all strings of letters in general represent numbers. In some instances, base 27 words can perform numerical operations that give a word for an answer:

ANTI + BULK = DIET          ANTICS + REVEAL = STONES
AT x KING = STOVE          AN x AN + I x I = AM x AM

**base 26 number system**: in letterplay, a number system that uses the letters from A to Z for the numbers 0 through 25. This was the first system to use all 26 letters as numeric constants. The one flaw was that, because A = 0, certain words such as WAKE and AWAKE represent the same number. The solution was to change to a BASE 27 NUMBER SYSTEM.

**base 26 word**: a word considered as a number in a base 26 number system that uses the letters from A to Z for the numbers 0 to 25. This was the first system to use all 26 letters as numeric constants. The one flaw was that when A= 0, then certain words, such as WAKE and AWAKE, would rep-

29

resent the same number. To assure that all words would have unique numeric equivalents, it was necessary to devise a BASE 27 NUMBER SYSTEM.

**baseword**: starting word; the word on which a wordplay operation is performed. For ANAGRAMS, the baseword is the word whose letters are rearranged to form the ANAGRAM. In the anagram pair NOTE-TONE, NOTE is the baseword that anagrams to TONE. The operation works the other way, too: TONE is the baseword that anagrams to NOTE. Some operations aren't reversible. In the BEHEADMENT pair, SNOW-NOW, SNOW is the baseword that beheads to NOW; NOW can't behead to SNOW.

**beastly English**: an animal name that has become a verb to express human behavior.

> CROW: to brag about an accomplishment
> BIRD-DOG: to try to win over another's date
> SPONGE: to live off others
> GOOSE: to poke with the finger

**beau présent (beautiful in-law)**: a poem addressed to a person or subject, using only the letters of that person or subject's name. Oulipian. See ACROSTIC.

**beautiful English word**: an English word that an individual considers beautiful. More than 50 years ago, American writers were polled for their choices of English words they considered to be the most beautiful in the language. Some responses and their respondents include:

> LAUGHTER—Louis Untermeyer          LOVELY—George Balch Nevin
> GOSSAMER—Dr. Wilfred Funk          PAVEMENT—Arnold Bennet
> HOME—Lowell Thomas                 NEVERMORE—Elias Lieberman

**beauty parlor/barber shop nomenclature**: a beauty parlor or barbershop name that uses one or more forms of wordplay—rhyme, alliteration, assonance, HOMOPHONE, literary allusion, etc.—to achieve a hair-raising effect.

> CROP MOP SHOP          FOX & HAIR
> BRUSH STOP             BLOW-N-GO
> JACK THE KLIPPER       HAIRTAKERS
> FOLLICLE FOLLIES       SPIRAL HAIRCASE

| | |
|---|---|
| MANE STREET | COFFEE 'N' COIFFURE |
| CURL UP AND DYE | E-CLIPS |
| AMERICAN HAIRLINES | SCISSORS OF OZ |
| CLIPTOMANIA | |

**beheadment**: the removal of the first letter of a word to create a new word.

| | |
|---|---|
| CLIMB  LIMB | CACHE  ACHE |
| THERE  HERE | SPECULATION  PECULATION |
| ALONE  LONE  ONE | |

Also called "apheresis," "decapitation," and "decollation."

**beheadment homophone**: a word that becomes its own HOMOPHONE when its first letter is removed.

| | | |
|---|---|---|
| AISLE—ISLE | SCENT—CENT | WRAP—RAP |
| KNIGHT—NIGHT | WHOLE—HOLE | WRITE— RITE |

**beheadment poem**: a poem that uses BEHEADMENTS to make its rhymes. This is the third stanza of "Paradise" by George Herbert.

Enclose me still for fear I start.
Be to me rather sharp and tart,
Than let me want thy hand and art.

**beheadment sentence**: a sentence made of words resulting from BEHEADMENTS of the corresponding words in another sentence.

Show this bold Prussian that praises slaughter, slaughter brings rout. Teach this slaughter-lover his fall nears.

How his old Russian hat raises laughter—laughter rings out! Each, his laughter over, is all ears.

**belle absente (beautiful outlaw)**: a poem addressed to a person or subject, excluding the letters of that person or subject's name. Oulipian.

**Bermuda Triangle of definitions**: three definitions, each of which refers to the other two.

ANT (*n*.): n. emmet or pismire
EMMET (*n*.): ant or pismire
PISMIRE (*n*.): ant or emmet

**bialphabetic order**: an arrangement of letters that consist of two interwoven ALPHABETIC SEQUENCES (second meaning). For example, the letter string AXBYCZ can be separated into ABC and XYZ or into ABCZ and XY. Also called "dialphabetic order."

**bialphabetic word**: a word whose letters are in BIALPHABETIC ORDER— that is, whose letters can be divided into two interwoven sequences, each of which is in its own alphabetic order. This example shows two of several ways that FEMININITY can be divided:

| FEMININITY | FEMININITY |
|---|---|
| F   I  I  ITY | F M NN  Y |
| EM N N | E  I  I  IT |

**biconsonantal word**: a word that contains two different consonants, each appearing one or more times, with no restriction on vowels.

| BUGABOO | INSANENESSES |
|---|---|
| VOODOOED | TATTOOAGE |
| HALLELUIAH | ZOWIE |

**bicycle**: a WORD CYCLE of two words. Read in either order, the two form a familiar compound word or two-word expression.

BOAT  HOUSE = HOUSEBOAT

**bidigital word**: a word whose letters have ALPHABETIC VALUES using two digits throughout.

| Letters: | V | A | L | V | U | L | A |
|---|---|---|---|---|---|---|---|
| Alphabetic values: | 22 | 1 | 12 | 22 | 21 | 12 | 1 |

**bigram**: a pair of letters considered as a single unit. There are 676 bigrams (AA, AB, AC, . . . ZX, ZY, ZZ).

**bigram beheadment**: the removal of the first two letters of a word or phrase to create a new word. See BEHEADMENT.

**bigram curtailment**: the removal of the last two letters of a word or phrase to create a new word or phrase. See CURTAILMENT.

SATIETY—SATIE

**bigram deletion**: the removal of two consecutive interior letters from a word to create a new word. See DELETION.

      CATENARY—CANARY

**bigram-frag square**: a WORD SQUARE made of words divided into BIGRAMS. The first square below uses eight-letter words, and the second uses ten-letter words. Each row and each column is a single word formed by the bigrams in it. See REAL WORD SQUARE.

| | | | | | | | | | |
|---|---|---|---|---|---|---|---|---|---|
| DA | TA | BA | SE | | RE | ME | DI | AB | LE |
| TA | BU | LA | RE | | ME | LA | ST | OM | AD |
| BA | LA | DI | NE | | DI | ST | RA | IN | ER |
| SE | RE | NE | LY | | AB | OM | IN | AB | LE |
| | | | | | LE | AD | ER | LE | SS |

**bilingual palindrome**: a line in one language that reverses to a line in another language. The meaning is approximately the same in both directions. This bilingual PALINDROME is English in one direction and Latin in the other:

Anger? 'Tis safe never. Bar it! Use love.
Evoles ut ira breve nefas sit; regna!
(Rise up, in order that your anger may be but a brief madness; control it!)

**binary cipher**: a substitution CIPHER in which each letter is represented by a binary number. In one of the simplest forms, the letters are replaced by the binary numbers from 0 to 11010, so that A = 0, B = 1, C = 10... Z = 11010.

**birthday terminology**: a word designating a special variation on "birthday."

UNBIRTHDAY: a day that isn't your birthday. In most years, you have 364 unbirthdays.
EXBIRTHDAY: the belated birthday that a friend wishes you a few days too late. Exbirthday cakes are stale, and exbirthday presents come from secondhand stores.
ALTERBIRTHDAY: the substitute birthday that the unlucky person born on leap day celebrates during non-leap years.

**bisogram**: a pair of two words in which no letter is repeated, such as BLACKSMITH, GUNPOWDER. See ISOGRAM.

**blank sonnet**: a list of 14 rhymed words written in a column to be made into a sonnet. An early-nineteenth-century poet named Dulot wrote page after page of such lists of rhymes, which he had intended to fill in with sonnet lines later on. However, he was robbed of his papers, and he told his friends that he had lost most of his three hundred sonnets. When they responded with surprise that he'd written so many, he replied, "They were blank sonnets." He explained BOUT-RIMÉS, and the idea caught on. Soon it became the fashion to make up rhymes to fill in with lines. See also INVISIBLE SONNET, NO-LETTER POEM.

**Boggle**: a game in which each player tosses 16 lettered dice onto a tray and makes words from the top faces by moving from one letter to any letter adjacent to it—up, down, right, left, or diagonally. Like Scrabble, it has been the inspiration for wordplay challenges. One basic challenge is to find the Boggle sequence that generates the most words. The best solution to date, found using a computer, generates 2,047 words:

```
G N I S
D T R P
S E A C
D B L S
```

**bookend word**: a word that contains two shorter words, one formed by consecutive letters within the starting word and the other formed by the remaining letters. For instance, DEBATER has BAT in the middle and DE . . . ER at the ends.

| | |
|---|---|
| BETRAYER = BEER + TRAY | LIGAMENT = LINT + GAME |
| DEMEANED = MEAN + DEED | RESIDENT = SIDE + RENT |

**Book of Truth, the**: an imaginary book of 100 numbered pages. The first page says, "The sentence on page 2 is true." The second page says, "The sentence on page 3 is true." It continues this way to page 100, which says, "The sentence on page 1 is false." When the reader turns back to page 1, the book has magically changed the sentence to make it true. Now it says, "The sentence on page 2 is false." Each succesive reading changes the text until it cycles back to its original state.

**boustrophedon word**: a word that can be divided into two sequences of letters, one in ALPHABETIC ORDER and one in REVERSE ALPHABET:

ABSCONDENCE
AB  C    DE    E   (in alphabetic order)
    S  ON   NC   (in reverse alphabetic order)

**bout-rimés**: a list of rhymed words. *Bouts-rimés* means, literally, "rhymed endings." The rhymed words are chosen in advance for the challenge of writing a poem ending with them. The form was inadvertently invented by a poet named Dulot in the early eighteenth century (see BLANK SONNET). The basic concept has appeared in different types of poetry, including Dada, Surrealism, and Concrete Poetry, in the twentieth century. Some poems use only rhyme:

> Boy,
> Gun;
> Joy,
> Fun.
> Gun,
> Bust.
> Boy,
> Dust

**bow-wow theory**: the theory that human speech originated as an imitation of sounds produced by animals, birds, water, and other natural phenomenon. This term is used by detractors of the theory, who point out that the same animal's sound is represented by different words in different languages. For instance, here are few for a rooster's sound:

COCK-A-DOODLE-DOO (English)    CHICCIRICHI (Italian)
COQUELICO (Spanish)    KOKKO-KOKKO (Japanese)
COCOROCO (French)

**braille alphabet**: the alphabet in which each letter is represented one or more raised dots in a specific pattern. The braille alphabet was invented to enable blind people to read by running their fingers over the dots.

**brand-name palindrome**: a commercial name that spells the same in both directions.

AZIZA (cosmetic line)    MUM (deodorant)
CIVIC (car by Honda)    PEP (cereal)

ELLE (magazine)                    PIZZAZZIP (pizza oven)

**brand-name reversal**: a commercial name that spells a different word in reverse. The two on the right are intentional reversals.

EVIAN (mineral water)              REGAL (beer)
TUMS (antacid)                     SERUTAN (vitamin tonic)

**British back slang**: a slang word formed by reversing the letters of the word it represents.

BOTTLE = ELTTOB          TOBACCO = OCCABOT
POLICE = ECILOP          WALNUTS = STUNLAW

**British broadcast blunder**: a blooper broadcast on British radio.

"He's got a fresh pair of legs up his sleeve." (BBC Radio, Scotland)
"The reason he is struggling to bowl straight is because his head is in the
   wrong place." (Radio 3)
"The chief dietician at Crew Hospital had only a skeleton staff." (Radio 4)
"They'd spent the weekend in a ditch waiting for a duck to fly over with a
   shotgun." (Radio 4)

**Brookline letter change**: the substitution of one letter for another at each position in a word that results in a new word each time.

RICE: NICE—RACE—RILE—RICH

**buildup reversal**: a pair of REVERSALS formed by adding one or two letters to the beginning or ending of a shorter pair of reversals.

TINKER = REKNIT          DRAWER = REWARD
STINKER = REKNITS        REDRAWER = REWARDER

Also called "build-on reversal, buildup."

**buried word**: a word whose letters appear in order within a longer word. There are two main types of buried words. In one type, the letters are embedded consecutively with no extraneous letters separating them. In the other type, the letters are scattered throughout like the letters of a JOEY found in a KANGAROO WORD.

MEAT:   ME, EAT, AT (contiguous letters)
MEAT:   MET, MAT (noncontiguous letters)

**burlesque**: a witty or derisive literary imitation.

**cadence**: a set of identical letters spaced at equal intervals in a word. All words except those that are ISOGRAMS have at least one cadence. The length of a cadence is the number of letters in it, and the spacing is the number of positions from one of its letters to the next within the word. See ALTERNATING MONOTONY.

EFFERVESCENCE (length 5, spacing 3)

NONCONTAMINATION (length 4, spacing 5)

**Caesar's alphabet**: a CIPHER in which each letter is shifted the same amount of steps along the CIRCULAR ALPHABET. Julius Caesar was one of the first to use such a code. In Caesar's alphabet, the letters were shifted three steps, so that A became D, B became E, and so on.

**calligraphic portrait**: a drawing of a famous person's face made of the letters in his or her name. This picture of William Shakespeare uses only the letters in SHAKESPEARE:

**Canada Dry**: a text that appears to involve wordplay but does not. (Associated with the soft drink's slogan: "the champagne of ginger ale.") Oulipian.

**capitonym**: a word whose pronunciation and meaning change when it is capitalized.

| | | |
|---|---|---|
| LAME | TANGIER | NICE |
| POLISH | AUGUST | REVEL |

**capitonym poem**: a poem that uses a CAPITONYM in both lowercase and uppercase form in each line, as in "Herb's Herbs":

> An herb store owner, name of Herb,
> Moved to rainier Mt. Rainier,
> It would have been so nice in Nice,
> And even tangier in Tangier.

**car-name anagram**: a word or phrase made by rearranging the letters of a car name.

> CAMRY = MY CAR
> COUPE DE VILLE = EVIL CLOUD PEE
> DIABLO = BAD OIL
> ELANTRA = A RENTAL
> MONTE CARLO = CLEAN MOTOR

**car-to-car anagram**: a car name that is the ANAGRAM of another car name.

> ELECTRA = A TERCEL
> PREVIA = A VIPER

**catch riddle**: a RIDDLE that catches the listener off guard with its simple answer. The first catch riddle below is probably the most famous:

> Why did the chicken cross the road?
>    To get to the other side.
>
> If you went over a cliff, what would you do?
>    Fall.

**caudation**: insertion of a letter at the end of a word. This is the reverse of CURTAILMENT.

**celebrity palindrome**: a PALINDROME that includes the first name, last name, nickname, or any name that refers to a famous person or creature, real or fictional, in any field. *Games* magazine spurred a lot of people to write celebrity palindromes when it held a contest titled "Palindromes with Personality." Thousands of celebrity palindromes were entered in the contest. Here are eight of the results. The first on the list won first prize. The others were runners up or honorable mentions.

> Lisa Bonet ate no Basil.
> To Idi Amin: I'm a idiot.
> Oh no! Don Ho.
> Plan no damn Madonna LP!
> Man, Oprah's sharp on AM.
> Vanna, wanna V?
> O, Geronimo, no minor ego!

**centered lettershift pyramid**: a series of LETTERSHIFT words whose letters form a pyramid aligned on the center column.

```
      .  .  .  I  .  .  .
      .  .  T  A  P  .  .
      .  V  I  P  E  R  .
      I  R  E  L  A  N  D
```

**cento**: a poem made of lines taken from the work of one or more other poets. The earliest centos appear in ancient Greece in some of the plays of Aristophanes, who uses lines by Homer and Aeschylus. The first known cento in English is *Collection of Poems by Several Hands* (1775) by Robert Dodsley, who connected lines from Shakespeare's plays to celebrate the bard's birthday. In the following quatrain, part of a longer poem, each line is by a different poet:

> I only know she came and went,    (Powell)
> Like troutlets in a pool;    (Hood)
> She was phantom of delight,    (Wordsworth)
> And I was like a fool.    (Eastman)

Also called "mosaic" and "patchwork verse."

**central number**: the number whose NUMBER NAME appears at the middle position when an odd number of number names is alphabetized. For the numbers 1–9, the central number is ONE; for 1–19, it is also ONE; for 1–99, it is still ONE. But for 1–999, it is ONE HUNDRED NINETY–TWO, which is also the central number for 1–9999.

**C-graph**: a type of WORD GRAPH formed by a three-dimensional PAVEMENT made of tetrahedrons.

**chain-link sentence**: a sentence in which the last two letters of each word become the first two letters of the next. Will Shortz asked listeners of the National Public Radio program "Weekend Edition" to make chain-link sentences. Here are a few responses:

> Can an anteater erase several almost stonelike Kenyan anthills?
> Frankenstein intimidated Edith through ghoulish shenanigans.
> Madonna—naked!—edifies Estonia's asexual aldermen.
> Martha has aspirin in industrial allotments.
> The helium umbrella lacked edging.

**chain verse**: **1.** poetry in which the last word of one line is repeated as the first word of the next.

**2.** poetry in which the last line of one stanza is repeated as the first line of the next.

Also called "concatenation verse" in boths meanings.

**challenge**: a word problem of one of three types: (1) To find the most extreme example of a word or set of words—e.g., to find the longest word in a published source; (2) to locate examples of words to fill a TYPE-COLLECTION—e.g., to compile a list of 26 words, each beginning with a different doubled letter; (3) to construct a group of words with a specific relationship—e.g., to construct a WORD SQUARE.

**Chandlerism**: a description of a person modeled on this line written by Raymond Chandler, hard-boiled detective story writer: "She was the kind of blonde that could make a bishop kick a hole through a stained-glass window."

> She was the kind of gal who could make a dogcatcher get the rabies.
> She was the kind of lady who could make a linguist speak in tongues.

**changeover**: the transformation of one word or phrase into a second word or phrase when one letter changes to another and moves to a new location.

HOLSTER—OLDSTER

**"characteristic initials" method**: a method of generating a phrase describing someone by using the initials of his or her name as the initials of the phrase.

GEORGE WASHINGTON = GREAT WARRIOR
FRANKLIN PIERCE = FOURTEENTH PRESIDENT
ABRAHAM LINCOLN = ASSASSINATED LEADER

**charactonym**: a literary character's name that especially fits his or her personality. Charles Dickens was a master of the charactonym. Here are some of his creations:

SCROOGE—tightfisted miser
MR. GRADGRIND—tyrannical schoolmaster
JAGGERS—rough-edged lawyer
MISS HAVESHAM ("have a sham")—jilted spinster living an illusion

**charade** (*n*.): a set of words formed by respacing but not rearranging the letters of another word, phrase, or sentence.

BEDEVIL = BED + EVIL          CRUMBLED = CRUMB + LED
CHICAGO = CHIC + AGO          PLEASURE = PLEA + SURE
SOAP OPERA = SO A POP ERA
BOATHOUSE = BOA + THOU + USE

**charade** (*v*.): to respace a text to form another text. Also called REDIVIDE.

**charade-anagram**: a CHARADE that aptly describes the original word.

An ISLAND . . . IS LAND.
A DAREDEVIL is one who has DARED EVIL.

**charade poetry**: verse in which the CHARADE forms the basis for word choice in some or all of the lines. There are various forms of charade poetry.

**charades**: a game in which two teams alternate taking turns trying to figure out a target word or phrase, the title of a book, a movie, a TV program, etc. One member of the team acts out the syllables for his or her teammates to guess. In some versions the actors answer questions. The CHARADE most likely began as a written form, turned into a parlor game in nineteenth-century England, and died out in the twentieth century. In the 1950s, charades regained popularity as a suburban party game in America. Variations included

Adverbs, Proverbs, and The Game. (*Note:* In all entries but this one, *charades* is the plural of the wordplay term CHARADE. This is the only entry where it is the name of the acted-out game.)

**charade sentences**: sentences that are CHARADES of one another.

> Flamingo: pale, scenting a latent shark!
> Flaming, opalescent in gala tents—hark!

> O, had a man developed a way!
> Oh, Adam and Eve loped away.

**charade square**: a word square made by dividing a nine-letter word into three segments and arranging them in a column to spell three words across and three words down. LACERATED and PALAVERED can form charade squares:

```
L A C        P A L
E R A        A V E
T E D        R E D
```

**charadist**: a person who composes charades.

**charitable word**: a word that changes to another word when any one of its letters is deleted.

> PLEATS:   _LEATS   P_EATS   PL_ATS   PLE_TS   PLEA_S   PLEAT_

**cheater's** (*possessive n.*): indicates that the form following it has been altered to allow made-up words to be spelled in any way necessary. This enables the writer to be more creative in certain forms of wordplay, such as the ANAGAM and the PALINDROME, which are traditionally more resrictive in word choice.

**cheater's amalgam**: an ANAGRAM of the names of two people that allows made-up words to be used.

> NOAH WEBSTER + MARY PICKFORD FAIRBANKS = "FRFRPABOHBARKS"

**cheater's anagram**: an ANAGRAM that uses made-up words.

> MISSPELLINGS = SIMPL, SINGELS

**cheater's palindrome**: a PALINDROME in which made-up words are used to balance the real words. Anything expressed in letters counts as a word, as this cheater's palindrome explains: "DROWASI" IS A WORD.

> Capable was I ere I saw Elbapac.
> We drink Nir dew.
> "De ret tume," he muttered.
> Oolginani's evil Eskimo, "Nomik Se," lives in an igloo.
> Samorael bats at times emit testable aromas.
> "Gniebne! Ilaeht! Demaercsiiiiii!" screamed the alien being.
> Madam, I'm not Onmimadam.
> Purcell, a base note detones a balle crup!
> "Emord nil apaflah," sed Ivor P., "provides half a palindrome."

**cheater's palindrome play**: a play in which the characters speak in CHEATER'S PALINDROMES. "It's a Nice Night in Nithginecinasti" is about two tipsy celebrants meeting at a party. It begins:

> SHE: My name's Emanym.
> HE: How are you? I'm Miuoy E. Rawoh.
> SHE: May I call you Uoy Llaciyam?
> HE: Uoy Llaciyam? Tah! What may I call you?
> SHE: Me? Em.
> HE: It's a nice night in Nithginecinasti.
> SHE: Drink, nird.

**checkerboard word square**: a WORD SQUARE in which the letters are placed in checkerboard fashion to spell four-letter words across and down and an eight-letter word along one diagonal. "Skeezik" invented the form in 1877.

```
   M   A       S   T
S  C       A   R
   A   L   A       R
H  O   V       E
   S   E   R       E
O  R       E   S
   S   E   N       T
E  A   S   T
```

**chemical element symbol**: a letter or set of letters assigned to represent a chemical element. The symbols for the first 103 elements are listed alphabetically below. They appear in ELEMENTAL WORDS and other wordplay-forms. The names of the elements along with their respective symbols can be found in most collegiate and unabridged dictionaries.

```
Ac  Be  Cm  Fe  Ho  Md  No  Pr  Sb  Te  Yb
Ag  Bi  Co  Fm  I   Mg  Np  Pt  Sc  Th  Zn
Al  Bk  Cr  Fr  In  Mn  O   Pu  Se  Ti  Zr
Am  Br  Cs  Ga  Ir  Mo  Os  Ra  Si  Tl
Ar  C   Cu  Gd  K   N   P   Rb  Sm  Tm
As  Ca  Dy  Ge  Kr  Na  Pa  Re  Sn  U
At  Cd  Er  H   La  Nb  Pb  Rh  Sr  V
Au  Ce  Es  He  Li  Nd  Pd  Rn  Ta  W
B   Cf  Eu  Hf  Lr  Ne  Pm  Ru  Tb  Xe
Ba  Cl  F   Hg  Lu  Ni  Po  S   Tc  Y
```

**chemical element word-weight**: the sum of the ALPHABETIC VALUES of the letters in a chemical element. The first two elements below are the only whose WORD-WEIGHTS match their atomic numbers, and the third element comes closest of all to matching word-weight with atomic weight.

ERBIUM = 68     HAFNIUM = 72     IRON = 56
(atomic weight = 55.857)

**chemical element word-weight group**: a group of two or more elements that have the same WORD-WEIGHT. The largest group has five elements, each with a word-weight of 85:

CURIUM   FERMIUM   FRANCIUM   SILVER   VANADIUM

**chemical symbol equivalent**: the representation of a word or name that has chemical element names in it by replacing them with CHEMICAL ELEMENT SYMBOLS. The best-known example appeared in the 1964 presidential campaign. Candidate Barry Goldwater's last name was represented by transforming GOLDWATER to $AuH_2O$.

**chess notation symbols**: a letter currently used to signify a pawn or a piece in chess.

| | | |
|---|---|---|
| K = king | R = rook | N = knight |
| Q = queen | B = bishop | P = pawn |

**chess word**: a word containing two or more CHESS NOTATION SYMBOLS. Most chess words have other letters in them as well:

BB = two bishops              KP = a king and a pawn
Quasi-BaNKRuPt = all six chess pieces     KaKKaK = four kings
BaRBaRiaN = two bishops, two rooks, and a knight

Also called "chess piece word."

**children's alphabet**: a children's poem in which every line (or almost every line) starts with a different letter of the alphabet and goes from A to Z. One of the first published children's alphabets begins and ends as follows:

> A was an apple-pie;
> B bit it,
> C cut it,
> [. . .]
> W wanted it,
> X, Y, Z, and ampersand
> All wished for a piece in hand.

**chronogram**: an inscription that contains Roman numerals adding up to the date of an event. Chronograms are written most often in Latin, although the ancient Romans never wrote them. They appear on bells, church windows, medals, title pages, and tombstones. Here are two chronograms written in English:

> IaMes by the graCe of goD, Is a kIng, noVV neVer Vnhappy.
> (MDCVVVVIII = 1623, the 21st year of King Jame's reign.)
>
> praIse hIM o yee ChILDren
> (MDCLIII = 1653, the year the tower of St. Edmund's Church in Salisbury was rebuilt.)

**chronogrammatic epitaph**: an epitaph in which the lines give the full date of the deceased's death. The epitaph of a sschoolmaster who died in 1651 concludes with two lines, each a CHRONOGRAM representing that year:

> the Last nIght of DeCeMber      (MDCLI = 1651)
> he resteD froM aLL hIs Labors.      (MDLLLI = 1651)

**cipher**: a method of representing the alphabet using the letter as the basic unit to represent the message. A cipher is usually simpler than a CODE.

**cipher alphabet**: an alphabet that provides the match between the plaintext letters and the coded letters. For two examples, see BACKWARD SUBSTITUTION CODE and SINGLE-SHIFT CODE.

**circular alphabet**: the alphabet arranged in a circle with the letters going from A to Z, and then continuing at A, just as the numbers on a clock go from 1 to 12 and continue at 1. The circular alphabet plays an important part in LETTERSHIFT words, ALPHABET MATHEMATICS, and certain other types of LETTERPLAY. Also called "clock alphabet."

**circular palindrome**: a word that can be read clockwise or counterclockwise when its letters are written in a circle. In the first example, ASSESS can be read in either direction starting at A. In the second, PIPE can be read clockwise starting with the top P and counterclockwise starting with the bottom P.

**circular reversal**: a pair of words that are reversals of each other when their letters are written in a circle and read clockwise and then counterclockwise. In the first circular reversal below, SNOOP and SPOON start with S in both directions. In the second, REVERSE starts clockwise with the top R, and REVERES starts counterclockwise with the bottom R.

**clock alphabet**: see CIRCULAR ALPHABET.

**code**: a method of representing a message by using words, phrases, letters, or syllables to replace the text. A code is usually more complicated than a CIPHER. However, "code" is often used to mean the same as "cipher."

**collinear words**: words whose ALPHABETIC VALUES have differences that are proportional between successive pairs. They are like LETTERSHIFT words, except that the shift values vary from one letter position to the other. In this example, the shift values are (1, -4, -3). Thus, GYP (7, 25, 16) + (1, -4, -3) = (8, 21, 13) = HUM. The rest of the words and letter strings are generated the same way.

GYP—HUM—iqj—jmg—KID—LEA

**colorful rhyme**: a word that rhymes with PURPLE, ORANGE, and SILVER, the color names often cited as having no rhyming words. Some writers have found unusual, but perfectly valid, words that do rhyme. See TRIPARTITE COLOR RHYME.

PURPLE—CURPLE (hindquarters, esp. of a horse)
ORANGE—BLORENGE (a hill near Abergavenny, Wales)
SILVER—CHILVER (a ewe lamb)

**combination padlock**: a PADLOCK with the added feature that the overlap is a word, too.

SCAR + ARAB = SCAB (the lock)
SCAR + ARAB = SCARAB (the combination)

**comic alphabet**: an ALPHABETIC POEM or other text that plays on the sounds and meanings of words. Here are the first three and last three letters of a comic alphabet:

A for 'orses (hay for horses)
B for mutton (beef or mutton)
C for yourself
[. . .]
X for breakfast
Y for husband
Z for breezes (zephyr breezes)

**comic book onomatopoeia**: the use of made-up words to represent sounds in comic books. Comic book writers can be quite creative in their use of language. Here is a selection of words that are as expressive in their comic book onomatopoeia as the cartoon actions they represent:

FFFFFFFFFWOPP (head hit by pie)
SLOR-SLOR-SLOR-SLOR-SLORRREERRRRK-K-K (drinking last
   juice through straw)
HUPUNNNNNGGG (eyes bug out in surprise or terror)
WOO-OP W-P-P W-WOO WOO-OOP (man falls in outhouse pit)
YAKAKAKAKAKA (gargle)
THPT (anteater tongue shoots out, catches fly)
SLUUUCK (sucking cheese off lasagna)

**commonest letters**: see ETAOIN SHRDLU.

**common-gender pronoun**: a personal pronoun that refers to a person of unspecified sex. Many have been proposed since the 1850s, but none have achieved general usage. Here are 8 sets of pronouns from a list of 26 sets. The traditional set of masculine and feminine pronouns for the cases would be *he, his, him* and *she, her, her.*

| Proposer and Date | Nominative | Possessive | Objective |
| --- | --- | --- | --- |
| Unknown, 1850s | ne | nis | nim |
| C. C. Converse, 1884 | thon | thons | thon |
| Funk & Wagnalls, 1913 | heer | hiser | himer |
| Lincoln King, pre-1936 | ha | hez | hem |
| A. Cringle, 1971 | z | | |
| Don Rickter, 1973 | xe | xes | xem |
| Various, 1974 | | hisher | himmer |
| C. M. Elverson, 1975 | ey | eir | em |

**complementary transposal**: a pair of words related in meaning that are formed by rearranging the letters of another word.

LOITERING = LION, TIGER
MATRICES = RATS, MICE

**compound epithet**: a disparaging or abusive compound word made up to scorn someone.

**compound epithet epigram**: A poem that uses COMPOUND EPITHETS. The following satirizes the philosophers known as Sophists. Originally in Latin, here is an English translation:

Loftybrowflourishers,
Noseinbeardwallowers,
Brigandbeardnourishers,
Dishandallswallowers,
Oldcloakinvestitors,
Barefootlookfashioners,
Nightprivatefeasteaters,
Craftlucubrationers;
Youthcheaters, Wordcatchers, Vaingloryosophers,
Such are your seekersofvirtue philosophers.

**compound palindrome**: a word, phrase, or sentence that is made of two or more palindromic parts. Every two-part compound palindrome is also a CIRCULAR PALINDROME. Here are two words and a sentence, with their palindromic parts below them:

NONLEVEL          RARENESS
NON + LEVEL       RAR + ENE + SS

EGAD! AN ADAGE WAS A SAW!
EGAD AN ADAGE + WAS A SAW

**computer-error poetry**: poetry written using words from the "Error Listing from Algorithm" that appeared as the appendix to the 1966 U.S. Government report on computer spelling. The misspelling looks like Middle English or Scots dialect. The excerpt below is from a poem written in iambic pentameter, "The Sorserer's Lost Lover." Fifty percent of the words are spelled according to the error listing. The poem begins:

A, once apon a time, the prity dauter
Of an oald pirot dove intew the wauter.
Sow inosent was shee, air shee was taecen
By pation's kice, hoos  eco wood awaecen
The riem and rithm of a luver's pleser.
Shee left her father's suny otion treser
And swam ashore.

**computer spelling algorithm**: a four-step algorithm of 3,130 rules intended to "teach" a computer how to spell. In 1966, a U.S. Government research team programmed the computer with the algorithm and the rules, and they gave it a spelling test. The computer attempted 17,009 words and got 8,483 correct, 6,195 with one error, 1,941 with two, and 3,890 with three or more. Its score: 49.87 percent. The algorithm worked half the time, and the other half it systematically produced errors. It proved what everyone knew: that English has a very broad set of rules for spelling. The report's appendix, "Error Listing from Algorithm" is a treasure trove of misspelled words.

**concealed cardinal**: a NUMBER NAME embedded within a larger word. See AUGMENTED NUMBER NAME, EMBEDDED NUMBER NAME.

> mONEy      drifTWOod      hEIGHTen      laTENess

**concrete poetry**: see SHAPED POETRY.

**connected diamond**s: a form in which two DIAMONDS are placed in tandem so that the middle lines touch.

```
        S               S
    B   I   T       B   O   A
S   I   G   H   T   S   O   U   N   D
    T   H   E           A   N   D
    T                   D
```

**consecutive dotted letters**: the lowercase "i" and/or "j" appearing two or more times in a word. Few words have more than two in a row.

> hijinks      Beijing      Fiji      Lake Mijijie

**consecutive-identical-letter sentence**: a sentence constructed to include the same letter as many times in a row as possible.

> The farmer's wife shouted at her son, "Stop shooting, Robb; BB bullets can injure the chickens!" (5 B's)

> The children's answers were incorrect except for Bess's "SS's S's stand for Schustzstaffel." (9 S's)

**consecutive-identical-letter word**: a word in which the same letter appears two or more times in a row. Doubled letters are common, but tripled and quadrupled letters are scarce:

| | | | |
|---|---|---|---|
| 3 letters: | GODDESSSHIP | WALLLESS | BRRR |
| 4 letters: | EEEEVE | ESSSSE | BRRRR |

**consecutive letter-pairs**: doubled letters occurring two or more times in a row. The five-pair example below is a coined word meaning as "the individual who keeps house in a nook on the moon."

BOOKKEEPER                SUBBOOKKEEPER
SWEET-TOOTHED             MOONNOOKKEEPER

**consecutive paragraph acrostic**: a word spelled by taking the initial letters of any series of consecutive paragraphs as they occur. This concept originally appeared as a contest in *Games* magazine. The longest word, SYNONYMS, was found on page 10 of *Heart of the Eagle* by Elizabeth Graham.

**consecutive pronoun speller**: a word with strings of consecutive letters that spell a large number of different pronouns. The letters in USHERS can spell five:

USHERS
US
  SHE
   HE
   HER
   HERS

**consistent sesquipedalianism**: the property of being a long word beginning and ending with the same letter. Some letters begin and end much longer words than other letters do. These are among the longest for their respective letters:

ELECTROLUMINESCENCE          JURAJ
STEREOPHOTOMICROGRAPHIES     WHEELBARROW

**consonantal alternating monotony**: a word with the same consonant in every other position for three or more occurrences.

COCKCROW          OVOVIVIPAROUS

LILYLIKE          PUPIPARA

**consonym**: a word having the same consonants in the same order as another word. Each is a consonym of the other.

eTHNiC—THeNCe          SPoNGe—eSPioNaGe

**constant sum pair**: a pair of words whose corresponding letters have ALPHABETIC VALUES that add up to the same total in each case. The alphabetic values of BIG = 2, 9, 7 and LEG = 12, 5, 7. The sum of the values in each position is 14 (2 + 12, 9 + 5, 7 + 7). Each of these pairs is followed by its constant sum:

    FREER + MANN (19)          SHELF + GRUNT (26)

**contronym**: a word or phrase having two or more opposite or contrasting meanings. See JANUS-FACED WORD.

> ALOHA: hello or goodbye (Hawaiian)
> BOLT: to secure in place, or to dart away
> DUST:  to remove fine particles from, or to sprinkle fine particles on
> LEFT: departed from,  or remaining
> SCREEN: to view, or to conceal

Also called "antilogy," "contranym," "Janus-faced word."

**constrained verse**: poetry written under a specific, predetermined rule, or constraint, involving wordplay. Two basic types of constrained verse are ANAGRAMMATIC VERSE and PALINDROMIC POETRY.

**conundrum**: a riddle that depends on a pun.

> When is coffee like the soil? When it is ground.
> Why is a thought like the sea? Because it's a notion (an ocean).

Also called "punning riddle."

**crash** (*v.*): to have the same letter occupying the same position in two words. DEVIL and FETCH crash at the letter E. Words may crash at more than one position.

**croaker**: a sentence like a TOM SWIFTIE except that it ends with a verb, and not an adverb, punning on the quote.

> "My pet frog died," Tom croaked.
> "That's no beagle; that's a mongrel," Tom muttered.

**crossword**: a CROSSWORD PUZZLE.

**crossword pack**: a WORD PACK in the format of a CROSSWORD PUZZLE. The letters can form words in two directions, horizontal to the right and vertical going down. Letters occupying adjacent positions have to be part of the same word, and each word has to be connected to at least one other word. In this example, the names of the seven rainbow colors fit into an 8 x 8 grid:

```
        Y
        E
    V I O L E T
  G   N   L
  R E D   O       B
  E   I   W       L
  E   G           U
  N   O R A N G E
```

**crossword puzzle**: a puzzle composed of blank squares that are to be filled in with letters spelling words horizontally and vertically. Black squares or bars separate the words, which are clued in various ways. American crossword puzzles use simple definitions to clue the words. British crossword puzzles, however, use cryptic statements that incorporate ANAGRAMS, words hidden in a phrase or another word, CHARADES, REBUSES, REVERSALS, and other clues that are intentionally ambiguous. As a result, British puzzles are more difficult than American puzzles.

Arthur Wynne, a journalist who emigrated to New York from Liverpool, is credited as the inventor of the crossword puzzle. His first puzzle appeared in the *New York World* on December 21, 1913. He called it "word-cross." About a month later, the name was changed to "cross-word." It evolved from two ancient wordplay forms, the ACROSTIC and the WORD SQUARE. In 1924, Simon and Schuster published a book of 50 crossword puzzles under the imprint "The Plaza Publishing Company" in order to avoid the bad feedback they were anticipating. Instead, the book was so popular that crosswords became the biggest puzzle craze ever. Crossword puzzles' popularity continued full blast into the Great Depression. Today they are the most popular word game in the world.

**cryptarithm**: a puzzle in which letters replace digits in an arithmetic problem. When the solution results in meaningful words, the cryptarithm is an ALPHAMETIC.

**cryptographic sentence**: a sentence consisting entirely of ISOGRAMS of the same length. This sentence uses 16 seven-letter isograms:

Various younger aunties obviate fadeout, outlive unideal adipose obesity, acutely enamour toadies echoing buoyant elation.

**curtailment**: the removal of the last letter of a word to make a new word.

PINE = PIN      MACARONIC = MACARONI = MACARON

**curtailment homophone**: a word that becomes its own HOMOPHONE (first meaning) when its last letter is removed.

| | | |
|---|---|---|
| BEE—BE | DAMN—DAM | PLEASE—PLEAS |
| BUTT—BUT | INN—IN | WEE—WE |

**cyclic transposal**: a TRANSPOSAL in which the first letter of a word is moved to the last position to form a new word or phrase.

STOPPING—TOPPINGS          EMANATE—MANATEE
DEVALUATE—EVALUATED        GELATIN—ELATING

Some cyclic transposals result in two words having no element of pronunciation in common.

EACH—ACHE      ECHOIC—CHOICE          SHOE—HOES

In this example, the two parts relate in meaning:

CABARET—A BAR, ETC.

Also called "cyclic, head-to-tail transposal," "incomplete cyclic transposal."

**cyclic transposal sequence**: a series of words formed by moving the first letter of one word to the last position to form the next word and then repeating the process. If the last word in the sequence generates the first word, the sequence is complete, as in the first three examples below. Otherwise, it is incomplete, as in the last example:

EAT—ATE—TEA
LAME—AME—MELA—ELAM
ESTER—STERE—TERES—EREST—RESTE
STABLE—TABLES—ABLETS

Also called "cyclic transposal."

**cylinder**: a story or other text that can be read beginning at any point without substantially altering the meaning. Oulipian.

**daffynition**: a punning definition.

> ACOUSTIC: What you play pool with.
> HIJACK: A tool for changing airplane tires.
> INCONGRUOUS: Where bills are passed.
> MOON: What cows are always doin'.
> PROPAGANDA: A socially correct goose.
> STUCCO: What you get when you sit on gummo.

**definitional literature**: the substitution of dictionary definitions for the original words in a text. Oulipian.

**deletion**: a word formed by deleting a letter from the interior of another word.

> FRIEND = FIEND
> UNINFORMED = UNIFORMED = UNFORMED

Also called "elision" and "syncopation."

**deletion antonyms**: two opposites formed by deleting the same letter or letters from the two starting words.

> COMET-GOT = COME-GO  SILL-SWELL = ILL-WELL
> PEARLY-PLATE = EARLY-LATE  MARK-PARK = MA-PA
> SHOT-SCOLD = HOT-COLD  DON-DOFF = ON-OFF
> HEATH-SHEATH = HE-SHE  TOWN-FROWN = TO-FRO

**diagonal square**: a WORD SQUARE in which words are spelled from left to right in three directions: horizontally, diagonally from top to bottom, and diagonally from bottom to top. In this example, LAND, LEND, WARD go each respective direction:

```
L A N D
M E R E
T A N E
W O R D
```

**diamond:** a FORM (second meaning) in a diamond shape. As in a WORD SQUARE, the words are spelled across and down. The first diamond (1870), shown below, had five lines. Another FORMIST, "Nypho," built a double 15-line diamond and a single 17-line diamond. Since then, a 17-line diamond has been created, as well as a double 15-line diamond.

```
      A
    A N D
A N N I E
    D I D
      E
```

**difference pyramid**: a set of words formed by taking a starting word and making successive DIFFERENCE WORDS from it. This example shows a difference pyramid on the left and its ALPHABETIC VALUES on the right:

```
B O X T Y        2   15  24  20  25
  M I D E            13   9   4   5
    D E A             4   5   1
      A D             1   4
```

**difference word**: a word formed by subtracting the ALPHABETIC VALUES of adjacent letters. In each pair, the smaller alphabetic value is subtracted from the larger to obtain a difference. The difference is treated as an alphabetic value and converted to the letter it represents. The resulting set of letters spell the difference word. VASE forms the difference word URN in the following way:

| Word =            | V  | A  | S  | E |
|-------------------|----|----|----|---|
| Alphabetic values = | 22 | 1  | 19 | 5 |
| Differences =     | 21 | 18 | 14 |   |
| New word =        | U  | R  | N  |   |

**different end-letter rhymes**: two or more words with the same rhyming sound, but with different final letters.

| | | | |
|---|---|---|---|
| DAY | FLEA | LIE | SHOE |
| GOURMET | SKI | NIGH | TRUE |

**different end-letter rhyming poem**: a poem in which every line ends with the same rhyming sound but with a different letter. The four lines below begin a 15-line poem in which each line ends in the same sound (long O), but in a different letter (in order of appearance, HEMAFDPSLWTOUXG).

> O for a muse of fire, a sack of dough,
> Or both! O promissory notes of woe!
> One time in Santa Fe, N.M.,
> Ol' Winfield Townley Scott and I . . but whoa.

**digital anagram**: a word, phrase, or sentence whose letters have ALPHABETIC VALUES composed of digits that can be rearranged to form a different set of alphabetic values that convert to letters spelling a different word, phrase, or sentence. For instance, the alphabetic values of the letters in LED are 12, 5, 4. Their digits, 1254, can be rearranged to 1524, and then respaced as 15, 24, which are the alphabetic values of the letters spelling OX.

> SOUR (19, 15, 21, 18) = AERIAL (1, 5, 18, 9, 1, 12)
> WORDS (23, 15, 18, 4, 19) = HI! BAN ME. (8, 9, 2, 1, 14, 13, 5)
> CORN (3, 15, 18, 14) = DREAM (4, 18, 1, 5, 13) = ARCADE (1, 18, 3, 1, 4, 5)

Also called "numbergram."

**digital charade**: a word whose letters have ALPHABETIC VALUES with the same digits in the same order as another word. The words differ because the the digits are redivided to make different alphabetic values signifying different letters.

> LOVE (12, 15, 22, 5) = ABOVE (1, 2, 15, 22, 5)

Also called "numbergram charade."

**digital palindrome**: a word whose letters have ALPHABETIC VALUES composed of digits that read the same in both directions. For instance, IS = 9, 19. Three examples follow; the first uses all different letters, the second is both a digital palindrome and a LETTER-UNIT PALINDROME, and the third is the longest known digital palindrome:

DAEMON (4, 1, 5, 13, 15, 14)
DEIFIED (4, 5, 9, 6, 9, 5, 4)
INSULINS (9, 14, 19, 21, 12, 9, 14, 19)

Also called "numberdrome."

**digital reversal**: a word whose ALPHABETIC VALUES have digits that can be reversed and redivided to form a new set of alphabetic values representing letters that spell a new word.

ABASH (1, 2, 1, 19, 8) = HIKU (8, 9, 11, 21)

Also called "numbergram reversal."

**digital wordplay**: wordplay involving the digits in the ALPHABETIC VALUES of letters. In some cases, this means considering the pattern of the digits (as in DIGITAL PALINDROMES); and in other cases, it involves manipulating the digits to form new alphabetic values (as in DIGITAL REVERSALS). In digital wordplay, K is a digital palindrome because its alphabetic value is 11. Y is a DIGITAL CHARADE because its alphabetic value is 25—those digits separately are 2 and 5, the alphabetic values of the letters spelling BE.

**digram**: see BIGRAM.

**disassembled poem**: a poem that has been copied as an alphabetized list of words to be rearranged to form a new poem, the RECONSTRUCTED POEM. See VOCABULARYCLEPT POETRY.

**doctored name**: a name formed by taking a word beginning with DR, adding a period, and ending with the rest of the word's letters. The original word is supposed to represent the fictitious doctor's specialty.

DR. AIN (doctor for plumbers)
DR. EAMLAND (for fantasizers)
DR. IVES (for motorists)
DR. OPPER (for clumsy oafs)

**domunym**: a word that identifies people from a particular place.

PHILADELPHIANS    RHODE ISLANDERS    LIVERPUDLIANS

**double acrostic**: an ACROSTIC poem or puzzle in which the first letters of the lines spell out one text going down the page, and the last letters of the lines spell out another.

**double beheadment**: **1.** a WORD RING in which the last two letters of one word are the same as the first two of the next.

> MEAN
>   ANNA
>     NAME
>       (MEAN)

**2.** the removal of the first two letters of a starting word, one letter at a time, to produce two new words. In each of the following examples, all three words are related in meaning:

> ALONE      UPRAISE
>  LONE       PRAISE
>   ONE        RAISE

**double beheadment homophone**: a set of four HOMOPHONES (first meaning), two of which can be beheaded to form the other two.

> WRITE—RITE; WRIGHT—RIGHT

See BEHEADMENT.

**double croaker**: a sentence like a TOM SWIFTIE except that it ends with two words, such as a verb and an adverb, punning on the quote.

> "This meat is hard to chew," Tom beefed jerkily.
> "I have grape beverages," Tom whined with clarity.
> "I hate reading Victor Hugo," said Les miserably.

**double-cross**: the process of converting two words into two other words by dividing each word into two parts and switching the second parts.

> MAIDS RAPTURE—MATURE RAPIDS

**double-crostic**: a type of CROSSWORD in which the squares are numbered in the grid and the letters are numbered in the clues. When the letters of the correct answers are placed in the corresponding squares, they spell out a literary quotation.

**double half-square**: an INVERTED HALF-SQUARE in which the words going across are different from those going down.

**double homoliteral**: a text in which each word has two or more letters in common with the word preceding it. SHE READS AND NODS is a double homoliteral. The common letters appear in parentheses here: SHE (SE) READS (AD) AND (ND) NODS.

**doubled letter**: a letter occuring twice in a row. E.g., in LETTER, "T" is a doubled letter.

**double mirror letters**: H, I, O, and X, the letters that are symmetrical along both a vertical line and a horizontal line drawn through the center of each: The top half mirrors the bottom half, and the left half mirrors the right half. Each double mirror letter is also a HORIZONTAL MIRROR LETTER and a VERTICAL MIRROR LETTER.

**double mirror palindome**: a palindrome made of DOUBLE MIRROR LET-TERS. The line below appears the same rightside up and upside down both on paper and in a mirror. It reflects a censor's thoughts on the rating of a porno film.

OH HO—XXX—OH HO

**double mirror word**: a word spelled with DOUBLE MIRROR LETTERS. Held upside down in front of a mirror, they read the same. Printed in a verti-cal column and held right side up in front of a mirror, they also read the same. Very few common words work this way. The vast majority are:

I HI HO O OH OX XI

**double oxymoron**: a phrase composed of two consecutive OXYMORA.

FRESH FROZEN JUMBO SHRIMP

**double-play word**: a word spelled by using a KEY on a telephone keypad twice before moving on to another key for each pair of letters.

| CALLED | SPACED | DEBARRED |
|--------|--------|----------|
| 225533 | 772233 | 33227733 |

**double shiftword**: see CYCLIC TRANSPOSAL.

**double sound pun**: a PUN in which one sound generates two meanings. The first meaning is that of the word itself, and the second meaning is that of a different word having a similar sound. In the first line below, WADING suggests WAITING.

> Bathing beauty: a girl worth wading for. (Anon.)
> When shooting elephants in Africa, I found the tusks very difficult to remove, but in Alabama the Tuscaloosa. (Groucho Marx)

**double square**: a WORD SQUARE in which the words going across are different from the words going down: A double square has double the amount of different words as a SINGLE SQUARE. In 1871, the first double square appeared in print:

> T E R M
> A L O E
> P L A T
> S A M E

**doublet**: a WORD LADDER. "Doublet" is the term that Lewis Carroll invented and preferred for his popular pencil-and-paper game (his original term was "Word-links"). The "Doublet" is the pair of words to be connected in a word ladder (HEAD and TAIL in the example). A "Link" is each of the connecting words (HEAL, TEAL, TELL, TALL). The "Chain" is the complete series. Carroll called people who played the game "Doubleteers."

> HEAD
> HEAL
> TEAL
> TELL
> TALL
> TAIL

**double transposal square**: a TRANSPOSAL SQUARE in which the rows and the columns transpose to all different words. A square measuring 6 x 6 letters would transpose to six six-letter words across and six different six-letter words down.

**double vowelindrome**: a VOWELINDROME in which each of the five vowels appears as a DOUBLED LETTER between pairs of the same consonant.

**doubly-intertwined alternating monotony**: a word with the same vowel/consonant combination occurring consecutively three or more times.

> KUKUKUKU

**drop-letter reversal**: a word formed by dropping the first or the last letter of another word and then reversing the order of the remaining letters.

> <u>A</u>SSUAGED—DEGAUSS        ANIMATIV<u>E</u>—VITAMIN A
> <u>R</u>EUNITER—RETINUE        ROTATIVEL<u>Y</u>—LEVITATOR

**dropout** (*n.*): the process of joining two words, dropping out a third word from the middle, and forming a fourth word by joining the leftover letters.

> REAMER + ITCH = REAMERITCH = REACH + MERIT

**dual identity word**: a word in which adding one S to the end forms its plural and adding another S to the end forms a new singular. In some cases, the second S forms the feminine version of the original word; in other cases, it forms a new word:

> MILLIONAIRE = MILLIONAIRES = MILLIONAIRESS
> CARE = CARES = CARESS

**echo verse**: poetry in which the last word or last few syllables of each line is repeated as an "echo." The echo makes an ironic comment on the line itself. This form seems to have been familiar to the Romans. In English, echo verse became popular in the sixteenth century thanks to Sir Philip Sidney and others, but by the nineteenth century it had fallen out of favor. One of the best known examples of the form is George Herbert's "Heaven." Here are the beginning and ending lines:

> O who will sow me those delights on high?
> Echo:                              I.
> Thou, echo, thou art mortal, all men know.
> Echo:                              No.
> [. . .]
>
> But are there cares and business with the pleasure?
> Echo:                              Leisure.
> Light, joy, and leisure; but shall they persever?
> Echo:                              Ever.

**editorial kangaroo**: a KANGAROO WORD that contains one or more shorter words that can be used to express an editorial opinion, as in the following sentences:

> These days, POLITICIANS make us want to throw POTS and PANS at them.
> If IMPERIALISM is a PERIL, is DEMOCRACY in DECAY?
> Much AIR POLLUTION is caused by the AUTO.
> Is the INTERNAL REVENUE SERVICE fraught with INNER VICE?
> PUBLIC RELATIONS can hide a bunch of LIES.

**eight-square**: a WORD SQUARE measuring 8 x 8 letters. The first (shown below) was puiblished in 1884. Almost a month and a half later, two other people each published the same square, which they had constructed without knowing of the original.

```
G A D A W A R A
A N E L A C E S
D E T A S T E S
A L A N T I N E
W A S T I N G S
A C T I N I A S
R E E N G A G E
A S S E S S E D
```

**E-invariant**: a UNIVOCALIC with E as the only vowel.

STRENGTHLESSNESSES          SELF-CENTEREDNESSES

**elementally-spelled element**: an element from the periodic table whose name can be spelled using only elemental symbols. There are exactly a dozen, including these four:

    ArSeNiC        TiN

    XeNoN        PHOsPHORus˙

**elemental word**: a word having a chemical element symbol in it that can be replaced by the element's name to form a new word. For example, FEY contains FE, the symbol for IRON. When IRON replaces FE, then FEY becomes IRONY.

    AGED—SILVERED     SIC—SULFURIC     BASIS—BASILICONS

**embedded double letter removal**: deleting a DOUBLE LETTER pair within a word to form a new word by connecting the ends.

    CRIBBED—CRIED         MUZZLE—MULE

**embedded number name**: a NUMBER NAME whose letters appear in the correct order in another word. The letters may appear in a consecutive string (clONE, mONEy), or they may be broken apart by other letters (ThEN, sTrEamliNe).See AUGMENTED NUMBER NAME, HIDEAWAY NUMBER NAME.

**embedded palindromic sequence removal**: deleting a palindromic sequence within a word to form a new word, by connecting the ends. See PALINDROME.

    JUICILY—JULY         BANANALAND—BLAND

**embedded tautonymic sequence removal**: deleting a TAUTONYM within a word to form a new word by connecting the ends.

    LONENESS—LOSS        FIDDLEDEEDEE—FIDDLE

**emblematic poetry**: poetry written in a specific shape in order to express the theme chosen by the writer. In the seventeenth century, emblematic poetry reached its peak of popularity. Writers produced verse in a wide variety of unusual forms. Hearts, fans, and knots were used for love songs; wineglasses, bottles, and casks for drinking songs; altars, pulpits, and monuments for religious verses and epitaphs. In the twentieth century, concrete poets have written SHAPED POETRY, which is a kind of emblematic poetry.

**emoticon**: a combination of punctuation marks, letters, and other symbols to make a typographic image. This usage of linguistic symbols originated in computer e-mail. The most commonly used emoticon is the sideways "smiling face" made of a colon, hyphen, and close parenthesis. But many other, more complex, emoticons have been devised, including a sequence representing the moves of the short-lived Macarena dance. Inserted in a text, emoticons can add humor, sarcasm, etc., which may not be obvious in the words alone. In these examples, the first three are supposed to be viewed sidewise, and the last two are upright (seated):

| :-) | :-)) | ;-) | ⌒I⌒ | ⌒I__⌒ |
|:---:|:---:|:---:|:---:|:---:|
| smiling face | laughing face | winking face | regular ass | fat ass |

**ender**: a word that ends a NETWORK.

**English/foreign language blend**: a combination of the names of two languages, one being English, that refers to a mixture of the two:

FRANGLAIS: French with many English words and expressions
FRINGLISH: English with French words and expressions
HINGLISH: a blend of Hindi and English spoken in India
JAPLISH: a blend of Japanese and English spoken in Japan
SPANGLISH: a blend of Spanish and English spoken in parts of the western U.S. and Latin America
VIETLISH: presumably a blend of Vietnamese and English spoken in Vietnam

**enigma**: **1.** a RIDDLE in verse format. Sir Thomas Wyatt (1503?–1542) was perhaps the first to write such enigmas. The answer to this one by Wyatt could be a kiss:

> A lady gave me a gift she had not,
> And I received her gift I took not.
> She gave it me willingly and yet she would not,
> And I received it albeit I could not.
> If she give it me, I force not,
> And if she take it again she cares not,
> Consider what this is and tell not,
> For I am fast sworn I may not.

**2.** a word or phrase clued indirectly through wordplay.

**enigmatic rebus**: a LETTER REBUS that must be solved like a RIDDLE. In some cases, the REBUS hides the letter within the word or phrase. REVOLUTIONLESS EVOLUTION means R because REVOLUTION less EVOLUTION leaves R. In other cases, the rebus presents a description of the letter. RINGTAILED means Q, because Q has a ringtail.

> DAUNTLESS AUNT = DAUNT LESS AUNT = D
> A CIRCULAR LETTER = O

**eodermdrome**: a word whose WORD GRAPH has two connector lines that cross. Most words can be graphed without such a crossing, but some longer words require it, such as these two:

> METASOMATOSES          TRINITROPHENYLMETHYLNITRAMINE

**"equation" equation**: the equation showing the sum of the ALPHABETIC VALUES of the vowels in the word *equation* to be equal to the sum of the alphabetic values of its consonants.

> E + U + A + I + O           =     Q + T + N
> (5 + 21 + 1 + 9 + 15 = 51)         (17 + 20 + 14 = 51)

**equiliteral numbers**: a set of NUMBER NAMES, each member of which has the same quantity of letters. ONE and TWO are equiliteral numbers. Every number is equiliteral with at least two other numbers. The shortest equiliteral numbers—ONE, TWO, SIX, TEN—have three letters. The longest has 758 letters, and there are approximately one sextillion numbers of that length, enough to fill 15 quintillion books, each the size of a 100,000-word novel. The first three sets of equiliterals can be written on the back of a postage stamp:

> ONE TWO SIX TEN
> FOUR FIVE NINE
> THREE SEVEN EIGHT FORTY FIFTY SIXTY

Also called "equiliteral number words."

**equivalency**: a set of NUMBER NAMES that can be arranged in a specific pattern to show surprising equivalency between them. In this example, the numbers from ZERO to NINE go down and up the column. Each pair of numbers adds up to nine, and each line has nine symbols in it:

```
Z E R O + N I N E
O N E + E I G H T
T W O + S  E V E N
T H R E E + S  I X
F O U R +  F I V E
```

**equivoque**: a poem that can be read in two different ways because its lines are in two different orders. In some equivoques, the meaning changes if one reads the alternate lines only. In others, the meaning changes because two stanzas are placed next to each other in two columns: The lines can be read down, stanza by stanza, for one meaning; and they can be read across for another. Also called "equivocal verse" and " Jesuitical verse."

**Ernulphus curse**: an ACROSTIC POEM written to condemn the subject. Here are the first four lines of an Ernulphus curse on Benedict Arnold:

> B orn for a curse to virtue and mankind,
> E arth's broadest realm ne'er knew so black a mind.
> N ight's sable veil your crimes can never hide,
> E ach one so great, 'twould glut historic tide.

**ETAOIN SHRDLU**: the twelve letters most often appearing in printed text, arranged in order of decreasing frequency. E, the commonest, appears an average of once every five letters.

**ETAOIN SHRDLU poetry**: verse using only the twelve letters most often appearing in printed text (see ETAOIN SHRDLU). The title and each line of the poem below is an anagram of those letters:

### Old Train's Hue

The loud rains!
His outer land!
Old hue? Trains:
"I rule hot sand."
The rail sound!
Ah, line or dust.
Sail? The round
Lie had no rust.

**euonym**: a name with an especially favorable meaning.

| | |
|---|---|
| DAVID ("beloved") | Harry TRUMAN |
| JESUS ("savior") | Martin Luther KING |

**even letters**: B, D, F, G, J, L, N, P, R, T, V, X, and Z, the letters occupying even-numbered positions in the alphabet.

**even-letter word**: a word spelled with EVEN LETTERS. Since none of the vowels are even letters, there are few even-letter words.

    NTH         PHFFFT

**even-numbered letter**: a letter occupying an even-numbered position in a word or other LETTERSTRING. This should not be confused with EVEN LETTERS.

**everyday phrase professional terminology**: terminology to upgrade the phrases and sayings of everyday speech. The new terms mimic medical terminology:

    AMOROUS TERRICIRCUMFLEXION: love makes the world go round
    CHRONOCIDE: killing time
    FELINOLINGUAL SEIZURE: cat got your tongue
    HYPERCULINARY PUTREFACTION: too many cooks spoil the broth
    SIMIOLUMINOSITY: monkeyshines

**exclamation point name**: one of the many names used for the punctuation mark (!). All but the last two appear in dictionaries:

| | | |
|---|---|---|
| EXCLAMATION MARK | ASTONISHER | SHOUT |
| EXCLAMATION POINT | CHRISTER | SHRIEK |
| MARK OF EXCLAMATION | SCREAM | FLASH |
| MARK OF ADMIRATION | SCREAMER | SPARKLE |

**exonym**: a place name that foreigners use instead of the name that natives use. In these examples, the exonym is in uppercase letters:

| | |
|---|---|
| COLOGNE—Köln | MOROCCO—Maroc |
| FLORENCE—Firenze | MOSCOW—Moskva |

**exquisite corpse**: a poetry game for three or more players. Each player writes an article and an adjective on a sheet of paper and then folds the paper to cover the words. The players exchange papers, add a noun to the new paper, and fold the paper again. They repeat this procedure with a verb and then with another article and adjective, and they finish with another noun. The results are read aloud to general bafflement.

**extended metaphor riddle**: a RIDDLE in which the answer is concealed in a complex and elaborate metaphor. Lewis Carroll made up such a riddle, calling it "An Explication of an Enigma." It discusses the things found in a large box, such as two lids, two caps, two lofty trees, and other baffling items, which signify a chest, two eyelids, two kneecaps, two palms, etc., that are clues for the answer (man).

**extensive mutation pair**: the two sets of numbers that are anagrams of the words EXTENSION and EXTENSIVELY. Arranged in the order shown below, their digits form NUMERICAL REVERSALS (1106, 6011); added together, their sums also form DIGITAL REVERSALS (17, 71):

EXTENSION—ONE, TEN, SIX—1, 10, 6—1106
EXTENSIVELY—SIXTY, ELEVEN—60, 11—6011

EXTENSION—ONE + SIX + TEN—17
EXTENSIVELY—ELEVEN + SIXTY—71

**ex-word**: a dictionary word beginning with EX- (meaning "out of," "not," or "former") that has been given a new definition that relies on the third meaning ("former").

EXCITATION: residue of tearing up a traffic ticket
EXILE: Atlantis
EXPORTER: someone who used to work on the railroad
EXPUNGE: used to be that funny sea creature you could wash your car with
EXTERMINATOR: Arnold Schwarzenegger, if he stops making movies

**eye-rhyme**: the poetic device of rhyming words whose endings are spelled the same but are pronounced differently.

**false derivative**: a word formed by inappropriately applying some grammatical change to another word. In fact, the two words are not related in meaning.

> BUTTER—BUTTRESS (false feminine)
> SENT—PRESENT (false antecedent)
> LIMB—LIMBER (false comparative)
> SHILL—SHILLING (false gerund)
> PLUS—NONPLUS (false negative)
> TREAT—RETREAT (false reiterative)

**false number name**: a word composed of two or more NUMBER NAMES that signifies something other than a normal number. Most false number names still refer to numbers in a specific context, such as TWENTY-TWENTY (eyesight). However, *Webster's Second Abridged* defines TWENTY-EIGHT as "a West Australian yellow collared parakeet," not as a cardinal number.

> ONE-ONE (logic, math)  THREE-FOUR (music)
> ONE-TWO-THREE (fencing)  SIX-THREE-THREE (education)

**false past tense**: a compound word with a part that sounds like the past tense of the corresponding part in another word.

> SEAHORSE—SAWHORSE

**family of palindromes**: a series of PALINDROMES formed by changing only the first and last words of a starting palindrome. The palindrome "Able was I ere I saw Elba" can generate a large family. Each new palindrome is made by reversal pairs filling in the blanks in this formula: "____ was I ere I saw ___."

> Mad was I ere I saw dam.
> Drab was I ere I saw bard.
> Spot was I ere I saw tops.
> A nut was I ere I saw tuna.

**famous last anagram**: a well-known person's FAMOUS LAST WORDS derived by anagramming the letters of the person's name.

> WILLIAM BUTLER YEATS: "Art, beauty will smile."
> THOMAS STEARNS ELIOT: "So I'm there at last, son."
> ERNEST HEMINGWAY: "Where's my neat gin?"

**famous last words**: a well-known person's final utterance.

> Matthew Prior, English poet: "The end."
> Victor Hugo, French novelist: "I see black light."
> Dylan Thomas, Welsh poet: "I've had 18 straight whiskeys—I think that is the record."

**feminist surname**: a last name that is traditionally a woman's first name. The following are the first and last names of real people:

| | | |
|---|---|---|
| Margaret ANNE | John JAYNE | Glen PAM |
| David CHRISTINE | Andrea LARA | Derrick SHIRLEY |
| Philip DOROTHY | Bryan MAY | John WINNIE |

**Fibonacci letters**: A, B, C, E, H, M, and U, the letters with ALPHABETIC VALUES equal to Fibonacci numbers. In the Fibonacci series, each number is the sum of the previous two numbers: 0, 1, 1, 2, 3, 5, 8, 13, 21, etc.

**Fibonacci word**: a word spelled with FIBONACCI LETTERS. All seven letters appear once each in the phrases BE A CHUM and EACH BUM.

> BACCHAE          CACHUCHA

**film title oxymoron**: a movie title that is inherently contradictory.

> *Advance to the Rear*
> *Hide in Plain Sight*
> *True Lies*

**first-half letters**: A, B, C, D, E, F, G, H, I, J, K, L, and M, the first thirteen letters of the alphabet.

**first-half word**: a word spelled with FIRST-HALF LETTERS. Short first-half words, like LIKE and HALF, abound. Only a few have twelve or more letters.

FIDDLE-FADDLED    ILL-EFFACEABLE    HIGGLEHAGGLED

**first lady anagram**: an ANAGRAM of the name of an American president's wife.

ELEANOR ROOSEVELT   role: to serve alone
MAMIE DOWD EISENHOWER   We deem war mood; he is in.
JACQUELINE KENNEDY ONASSIS   is as queenly on deck in jeans.

**first-name lettershifts**: first names that are LETTERSHIFTS of each other.

| BEA | BOB | IDA | GUS |
|-----|-----|-----|-----|
| SAL | NAN | JEB | MAY |

**first-and-last-name lettershifts**: a person's first name and last name that are LETTERSHIFTS of each other. A search of a national computer telephone database turned up one name, but there are certainly others.

GAIL
KEMP   [4 listings]

**first-and-last name partial lettershifts**: a person's first and last name that are PARTIAL LETTERSHIFTS of each other. Here are three of several found on a national computer telephone database:

| ART . . . . | . TOM . . | JUDY . . |
|-------------|-----------|----------|
| JACKSON | KNIGHT | GRAVES |
| [349 listings] | [54 listings] | [17 listings] |

**five-square**: a WORD SQUARE measuring 5 x 5 letters. The first American five-square was published in 1868:

```
L I G H T
I D L E R
G L A R E
H E R O N
T R E N T
```

**five-vowel word**: a word that uses the five major vowels, once apiece in any order.

> EUNOIA     DIALOGUE     SULPHONPHTHALEINS

**flip-flop definition**: an imaginary definition in which a compound word or two-word entry is defined by switching its parts around. *Webster's Second* has an entry that defines LION ANT as ANT LION. In these made-up entries, switching the parts changes the meaning:

> COWBOY = BOY COW
> UPHOLD = HOLD-UP
> TABLE DRESSING = DRESSING TABLE
> CAST IRON = IRON CAST
> TRAVEL TIME = TIME TRAVEL
> HOUSE CAT = CATHOUSE
> NIGHTFALL = FALL NIGHT

**floccinaucinihilipilification**: the longest word (29 letters) in the *Oxford English Dictionary,* meaning "the categorizing of something as worthless or trivial." It dates back to 1741.

**foldable permutation**: a TRANSPOSAL in which one word changes to another when its letters are written on a piece of paper, folded the correct way (as on a road map), and read from the top down. Some are foldable one way, but not the other: VINE-VEIN works, but VEIN-VINE doesn't. Also called "roadmap anagram."

**forbidden letter**: a letter that must not appear in a text. The forbidden letter is determined in different ways. In a LIPOGRAM, the writer chooses in advance to exclude a certain commonly used letter from the text. In an ANAGRAM, the writer uses the letters in a given text as often as they occur and excludes any additional letters.

**form**: **1.** generally, any type of wordplay, from major forms such as PALINDROMES to minor forms such as DIGITAL CHARADES.

**2.** specifically, a set of letters arranged in a pattern so that they spell words in two or more directions. In this case, "form" refers to letters in a geometric shape. The best-known form is the WORD SQUARE.

Originally, forms were similar to CROSSWORD PUZZLES, but without the black spaces separating words. (In fact, the modern crossword puzzle evolved from this concept.) In the twentieth century, forms evolved into structures of free-standing letters. These are regarded as works of logological art, and the FORMISTS who create them as artists of LETTERPLAY.

**formist**: a person who constructs WORD SQUARES or other FORMS (second meaning).

**form puzzle**: see FORM.

**forward-and-backward multiple charades**: many short words formed by redividing the letters of a long word in both directions. Each word of the forward CHARADE is a reversal of the corresponding word in the backward charade (SUP-PUS, ER-RE, MAT-TAM, etc.).

SUPERMATHEMATICAL = SUP + ER + MAT + HE + MA + TIC + AL
    Reverses to
LACITAMEHTAMREPUS = LA + CIT + AM + EH + TAM + RE + PUS

**found poem**: a poem made from a prose text that already exists, such as a news story, a magazine article, etc. The poet organizes the words into lines and stanzas to emphasize the poetic aspect of the words.

**four-square**: a WORD SQUARE measuring 4 x 4 letters. One of the earliest four-squares was published in 1859:

J U S T
U G L Y
S L I P
T Y P E

**four-word pangram problem**: The problem of making a PANGRAM-MATIC sentence using words from any published sources. The following four words form a pangrammatic set, but they don't make a sentence:

FJORDHUNGKVISL (river in Iceland)
PECQ (town in Belgium)
WAMB (obsolete spelling of WOMB)
ZYXT (obsolete form of the verb, SEE)

**four-word word**: a specific type of CHARADE in which one word becomes four words.

AMENITIES = A MEN I TIES     PERTINACITY = PERT IN A CITY

**frag**: a part of a word used in certain types of NETWORKS.

**frame words**: two or more words of equal length whose corresponding letters go in alternating directions of the alphabet. In the examples below, the letters appear in alphabetic order from top to bottom in the odd-numbered columns and from bottom to top in the even-numbered columns.

```
F R A M E        A W A Y
W O R D S        G R E W
                 J O L T
                 L I O N
                 M E S H
                 R A T E
```

**frequency-alphabet**: the alphabet with the letters arranged in order of the relative frequency in which they appear in ordinary English text, going from most to least frequent. This frequency alphabet includes ligatures:

E T A O I N S H R D L U C M F W Y P G B V K J Q X FI FF FL Z FFI FFL

**frequency value**: a numeric value assigned to a letter based on the number of times it occurs in printed text.

**friendlier word**: a FRIENDLY WORD whose replaced letters also spell a word.

BANE = PANE BONE BARE BANK = PORK

**friendliest word**: a word in which every letter, every two letters, every three letters, etc., can be replaced by the letter(s) in the corresponding positions in a different word to make a new word in each case. BANE, for example, is friendliest with MITT, with which it trades letters to form 14 other words:

| BANE + 1 letter = | MANE | BINE | BATE | BANT | | |
|---|---|---|---|---|---|---|
| + 2 = | MINE | MATE | MANT | BITE | BINT | BATT |
| + 3 = | MITE | MINT | MATT | BITT | | |

Also called "garble group."

75

**friendliest word pair**: a pair of words, each of which is a FRIENDLIER WORD of the other. Each letter of one word can be switched with the corresponding letter of the other to form a set of new words, as in:

| | | | | |
|---|---|---|---|---|
| CAT = | H̲AT | CO̲T | CO̲D̲ | = HOD |
| HOD = | C̲OD | HA̲D | HO̲T̲ | = CAT |

**_____-friendly alphabet**: a CIRCULAR ALPHABET in which each set of adjacent letters of the same length can be found in a dictionary word. A trigram-friendly alphabet and a hexagram-friendly alphabet have been constructed for three-letter and five-letter sets.

**friendly word**: a word that can spell another word by changing any one of its letters to another letter. This begins a trio of wordplay forms—friendly word, friendlier word, friendliest word—that progress in complexity. Otherwise, it means the same as ONALOSI. The term "friendly word" originally appeared in the index to *Beyond Language*, but not in the text.

| | | | | |
|---|---|---|---|---|
| BANE = | LANE | BONE | BADE | BANK |

**function shift**: the change that a word can make from one part of speech to another. The commonest variety of function shift is the transfer of a noun into a verb, as in ANATONYM. See NOUN-ADJECTIVE-ADVERB-VERB MATRIX.

**Game of Conditionals, the**: a poetry game in which each player writes a sentence beginning with "If . . ." or "When . . ." and then folds the paper to cover the words. The players exchange papers, and each player then writes a sentence in the conditional or future tense. The results are then read aloud.

**Game of Definitions, the**: a poetry game in which each player writes a question on a piece of paper and folds the paper to cover the words. The players exchange papers, and each then writes an answer on the new paper. The results are read aloud to the mystification of all. Also called the "question-and-answer game."

**garble group**: See FRIENDLIEST WORD.

**gematria**: the study of words as classified by sums of ALPHABETIC VALUES. Historically, people have attached religious significance to the fact that related words have the same sums, such as JESUS and MESSIAH, whose alphabetic values add up to 74 in each case. Most wordplay experts regard such sums as interesting, but not mystical.

**gender-neutral term**: a word in which MAN has been replaced in order to make the word gender-neutral. In some cases the gender-neutral term is a tongue-in-cheek replacement, such as this sequence of changes to make HUMAN the ultimate in political correctness: HUMAN = HUPERSON = HUPERCHILD = HUPEROFFSPRING.

| | |
|---|---|
| MAILPERSON | PERSONHOLE |
| DOBERPERSON | PERSONPOWER |

**geographical link-o-gram**: a word that links both parts of a two-word place name. SANG is a link-o-gram connecting LOS ANGELES. Others appear in:

| | | |
|---|---|---|
| BETHEL PARK | EAST RIVER | ORE MOUNTAINS |
| COSTA RICA | NEW HAMPSHIRE | SARATOGA SPRINGS |

**geographic name speller**: a word or phrase whose letters can spell the names of geographic locations. In each name, no letter can be used more often than it appears in the place speller. The word PALINDROMES spells the names of 15 French and Italian cities. The phrase A CHANDELIER spells the name of at least 18 nations, including these eight:

| | | | |
|---|---|---|---|
| ADEN | CHILE | CHAD | ICELAND |
| ARCADIE | CHINA | CHALDEA | IRELAND |

**geographic name-to-word reversal**: a community whose name is a word spelled in reverse.

TESNUS (TX) = SUNSET          DELEVAN (NY) = NAVELED

**geographic partial lettershift**: a PARTIAL LETTERSHIFT of a country to one or more words or other text. In the first two examples, each country name partially shifts to its own abbreviation. In the third, the country name shifts to several words that make a sentence.

```
B R I T A I N        A M E R I C A        A . . . . .
U K . . . . .        . . . . . U S        . . D I M .
                                          . L O T . .
                                          . . I N . .
                                          N O R W A Y
```

**geographic reversal**: a community whose name is another community's name spelled in reverse. The communities below are located in the U.S.; the last two are in the same state.

> COLVIN (AL)—NIVLOC (NV)
> CALVERT (TX)—TREVLAC (IN)
> FOSTER (RI)—RETSOF (NY)
> DOTSERO (CO)—ORESTOD (CO)

**geographic spelling variants**: different spellings of the name of a state, city, or other location. Forty spellings for Chicago have been located in reputable reference works. Talwrn Court, a street in Iowa City, Iowa, has been spelled in at least 148 different ways. Here are seven variant spellings for CHICAGO and seven for TALWRN:

| | |
|---|---|
| APKAW | CALVIN |
| CHEEGAGO | IOLWIN |
| CHIKKAGO | TALCUM |
| PSCESCHAGGO | TALLWORM |
| SCHUERKAIGO | TLAOLVWERN |
| STKACHANGO | TWITT |
| ZTSCHAGO | TXLWRN |

**geographic transposal**: the name of a city or other location formed by rearranging the letters of a word, phrase, or sentence.

> NERVED = DENVER
> TAN GLOVES = GALVESTON
> PLANES = NAPLES
> PORCUPINE RAT = PORT-AU-PRINCE

**giant synonym square**: a SYNONYM SQUARE of words of twelve or more letters in length.

**glyphic personal name**: a name made with a unique symbol having visual meaning but no pronunciation, e.g., the artist formerly known as "Prince" has for a time gone by "Glyph," "Symbol Man," and "TAFKAP"—an acronym for "The Artist Formerly Known as Prince."

**Goldwynism**: a quote attributed to motion picture magnate Sam Goldwyn.

> "Tell me, how did you love the picture?"
> "No, thanks; coffee isn't my cup of tea."
> "When I want your opinion, I'll give it to you."
> "We're overpaying him, but he's worth it."

**goodbye pun**: a farewell phrase that reveals the personality or occupation of the person saying it by means of a pun.

> FAIR WELL (oil driller)
> TILL NECK'S TIME (Dracula)
> BUN VOYAGE (baker)
> HAVE AN ICE DAY (skater)
> TAKE AIR (lifeguard)
> BE SCENE YOU (movie star)

**grammagram**: a word that, when it is pronounced, sounds like a string of letters. The letterstring is a SYLLABIC REBUS of the word.

> cutey = QT          devious = DVS          anemone = NMNE
> obediency = OBDNC

**grammatical substitution**: the substitution of words of one part of speech for words of another part of speech (e.g. nouns and adjectives, articles and adjectives). Oulipian. See FUNCTION SHIFT, NOUN-ADJECTIVE-ADVERB-VERB MATRIX.

**graphic palindrome**: a letter-unit PALINDROME. "Graphic" distinguishes this form from the PHONETIC PALINDROME, which is based on sound.

**Greco-American graffiti**: the name of an imaginary fraternity or sorority made by putting together words—real and coined—that sound like Greek letters.

CHUGGA LUGGA BREW  I FELTA THIGH
EATA BITA PI  TAPPA KEGGA DAY

**Grelling's paradox**: a paradox that assumes that an adjective is either AUTOLOGICAL or HETEROLOGICAL. *Autological* means that the adjective describes itself; *heterological* means it doesn't describe itself. Since *autological* describes itself, then it is autological. If *heterological* doesn't describe itself, then it is autological. But if it is autological, then it is not heterological and doesn't describe itself. But "not describing itself" means heterological, and thus *heterological* is heterological and does describe itself. And so on.

**-gry place name**: a geographical location ending in the trigram -GRY.

BADAGRY (Nigerian)  EGRY (French)
COGRY (British)  WIGRY (Polish)

**-gry question**: "There are only three words in the English language, all adjectives, which end in –GRY. Two are ANGRY and HUNGRY; the third word describes the state of the world today. What is it?" Bob Grant introduced this controversial question on his talk show on WMCA-AM radio in New York, and it spread around the country. Other media people discussed it on the air or in print. Ann Landers called it a "hoax designed to provoke hours of useless brain racking. . . ." As it turns out, there is no satisfactory answer. The closest is MEAGRY in the *Oxford English Dictionary*.

**-gry surname**: a last name ending in –GRY. Some –GRY surnames that appeared in recent telephone directories include:

ANGRY  KINGRY  GINGRY  UNGRY

**-gry word**: a word ending in the trigram -GRY. The search for –GRY words was set off by the –GRY QUESTION, which was expanded to include any words or names (variant, slang, obsolete, etc.) ending in –GRY and not just adjectives. While there are two commonly known –GRY words, at least 100 lesser-known examples have been found in various sources. In gypsy dialect, for instance, GRY is itself a word, meaning "horse."

AGGRY BEAD       HUGGRYMUGGRY       POTTINGRY
BEGRY               ULGRY                 YMAGRY

**half-switch alphabet**: NOPQRSTUVWXYZABCDEFGHIJKLM, the alphabet rearranged with the first half (A–M) coming after the last half (N–Z). The letters keep the same order within each half.

**halfway word**: a word in which each letter is the same number of ALPHA-BETIC STEPS from the corresponding letters in two other words. In AGE-JIG-SKI, the first letters are nine steps apart (A + 9 = J, J + 9 = S), the second letters are 2 steps apart (G + 2 = I, I + 2 = K), and the third letters are three steps apart (E + 2 = G, G + 2 = I). Here are two longer examples with the numbers of steps in parentheses:

CAPOTE-MERINO-WITCHY    MENTAL-SCORCH-YAPPED
(10, 4, 2, 20, 20, 10)          (6, 24, 1, 24, 2, 22)

**head-to-tail shift**: see CYCLIC TRANSPOSAL.

**head-to-tail sound shift**: a word or phrase becames another when its first sound is moved to the end.

CIAO—OUCH

**heavyweight word**: a word whose letters have the highest AVERAGE LETTER WEIGHT. In general, the average decreases with the length of the word. Here are heavyweight words for four different lengths. The total of the ALPHABETIC VALUES followed by the average letter weight appear in parentheses:

**Herman**: a sentence in which a quote concludes with a name that puns on the quote. The Herman, a spin-off of the TOM SWIFTIE, is named after the first example:

> "She's my woman," said Herman.
> "I'm drawn to you," said Art.
> "Testing—testing," said Mike.
> "I haven't a thing to wear," said Buff.
> "Pass me the binoculars, please," said Seymour.

**Hermanette**: a HERMAN in which the speaker's name completes an overlapping phrase.

> "Out there it's a jungle," Jim said.
> "Hickory Dickory," Doc said.
> "How do you like your eggs?" Benedict said.
> "You're welcome," Matt said.
> "I'm making a hamburger," Patty said.

**Hermione**: a HERMAN in which the speaker's name (and sometimes another word or two) completes another name at the juncture.

> "I tell you he's a saint," Peter declared.
> "Gee, Dad! Thanks! I always wanted a Harley," David's son said.
> "That's my boy!" George said.
> "You're such a grouch! Oh!" Mark said.

**heteroliteral text**: a text in which no two consecutive words have a letter in common. In the phrase NOT A SINGLE WORD, not a single word has a letter in common with the word on either side of it. Here are the first two lines of "The Heteroliteral Raven":

> On a midnight, cool and foggy, as I pondered, light and groggy,
> Ancient books and musty ledgers, not remembered any more, . . .

**heterogram**: see ISOGRAM.

**heterological** (*adj.*): not self-descriptive (said of a word). WRITTEN isn't written, UNFINISHED isn't unfinished, and INVISIBLE isn't invisible. All three are heterological words. See GRELLING'S PARADOX.

**heteronym**: a word with the same spelling as another word but with different pronunciation and meaning.

| | | | |
|---|---|---|---|
| AXES | DRAWER | INCENSE | PALSY |
| BASS | ENTRANCE | MINUTE | TOOTS |

**heteronym poem**: a poem in which pairs of HETERONYMS occur in most or all of the lines. The words from each pair appear near each other to emphasize how words that are spelled the same can differ in pronunciation and meaning. Here are the first two stanzas of "A Hymn to Heteronyms."

> Please go through the entrance of our circus show.
> We guarantee it will entrance you.
> The content will certainly make you content,
> And the knowledge gained sure will enhance you.
>
> A clown moped around when the circus refused
> For him a new moped to buy.
> The incense he burned did incense him to go
> On a tear with a tear in his eye.

**hexagon**: a six-sided form first published in 1883. The letters form words going horizontally left to right and diagonally top to bottom.

```
      C O O L S
    M A R R O W
   S I R N A M E
  M I S D A T E D
 C A R D A M I N E
  O R N A M E N T
   O R A T I N G
    L O M E N T
     S W E D E
```

**hex-word**: a word spelled by three letters that meet at a common vertex formed by on a pattern of hexagonal tiles. Each tile has a letter on it.

**H-graph**: a WORD GRAPH based on a PAVEMENT composed of hexagons.

**hidden middle name**: a given name formed by letters that bridge the gap between the first and last names of an individual. See OVERLAPPING WORD.

ALAN ALDA                    MONA LISA

DA<u>LE</u> <u>EV</u>ANS                    ARISTOT<u>LE</u> <u>ONA</u>SSIS
ABRA<u>HAM</u> LINCOLN                OMAR SHA<u>RIF</u>

**Hidden Words**: a pencil-and-paper game in which the player looks for words that are formed by consecutive letters overlapping two or more words in a sentence. Hidden Words can come in sentences, poems, and stories.

> Impossib<u>le! O, pard</u>on me, by no means.
> Wel<u>l, I o</u>nly <u>got ter</u>rified out of my wits.

Also called BURIED WORDS.

**hideaway number name**: a NUMBER NAME whose letters appear in correct order within a longer number name. There are many trivial examples: e.g., ONE is in TWENTY-ONE and many other numbers. Nontrivial examples are those whose numbers have no digits in common with their host numbers. Three trivial and two nontrivial hideaway number names appear below:

| Number | Digit in Common | No Digit in Common |
|--------|-----------------|--------------------|
| TWO    | TWenty-One      | (none)             |
| THREE  | THiRtEEn        | Two HundREd onE    |
| FOUR   | FOURteen        | Five thOUsand thRee |

**Hieroglyphic Bible**: a type of Bible in which small pictures replaced some of the words in the sentences in order to stimulate children's interest in reading the Bible. The pictures were REBUSES that stood for words or phrases.

**high-contrast spelling set**: a set of two or more words that begin with a different consonant sound spelled with the same letters and that end with the same vowel sound spelled with different letters. In the first set below, TH makes three different consonant sounds, and Y, IGH, and AI make the same vowel sound. In the second set, two different pronunciations of SURE are paired off with two different words spelled SEWER, each having a different pronunciation, too. In each set, the vowel sounds are underlined.

> TH<u>Y</u>—TH<u>IGH</u>—TH<u>AI</u>

> S<u>U</u>RE (shoor)—S<u>EWE</u>R (soor = "drain")
> S<u>U</u>RE (shoh-er)—S<u>EWE</u>R (soh-er = "one who sews")

**high-scoring Scrabble™**: a hypothetical game of SCRABBLE™, in which letters are arranged on the gameboard to show the highest possible score that could be made according to the standard rules.

**homoantonyms**: two words that sound like two other words that are antonyms.

> KNIGHTS, DAZE

**homoconcominyms**: two words that sound like two other words that form a familiar pair.

> HIED, HARE (as in "Neither hide nor hair")

**homoconsonantal sequences**: two sets of words with consonants in the same order, with different vowels. See CONSONYM.

**homograph**: a PUN whose multiple meanings are founded on words with the same spelling and pronunciation, but different meanings. *Homograph* is Greek for "same writing."

> Show me where Stalin is buried and I'll show you a communist plot.

**homolexical substitution**: See DISASSEMBLED POEM, RECONSTRUCTED POEM, VOCABULARYCLEPT POETRY.

**homoliteral text**: a text in which each word has at least one letter in common with the word that comes after it, as in THIS SENTENCE SHOWS HOMOLITERAL TEXT. The shared letters appear in parentheses in this version: THIS (TS) SENTENCE (S) SHOWS (HO) HOMOLITERAL (TE) TEXT. Here is the beginning of "The Homoliteral Raven":

> On one midnight, cold and dreary, while I, fainting, weak and weary,
> Pondered many a quaint and curious volume of forgotten lore, . . .

See DOUBLE HOMOLITERAL.

**homonym**: see HOMOPHONE.

**homophone**: **1.** a word that is pronounced like another word, but is spelled differently and has a different meaning.

**2.** a PUN whose multiple meanings are based on the same pronunciation of words with different spellings. "Homophone" means "same sound" in Greek.

> A man gave his sons a cattle ranch and named it Focus because it was a spot where the sons raise meat.

> Television is like a steak: a medium rarely well done.

**homophonic**: sounding alike; being composed of HOMOPHONES.

**homophonic anagram pair**: a pair of words that are both ANAGRAMS and HOMOPHONES of each other.

| | | |
|---|---|---|
| BEAR—BARE | HOSE—HOES | STEAK—STAKE |
| GREAT—GRATE | PRIDE—PRIED | WEAR—WARE |

Also called "anagrammed homophones."

**homophonic opposites**: two HOMOPHONES with opposite meanings.

| | | |
|---|---|---|
| RAISE—RAZE | RAISER—RAZER | ORAL—AURAL |

**homophonic pair:** a pair of words that are HOMOPHONES of each other.

**homophonic poem**: a poem that uses HOMOPHONES extensively to achieve its effect. There are different ways to do this. The poem "A Bazaar Tail" uses one to five homophones per line. Here are the first two stanzas of the ten-stanza poem:

> One night a knight on a hoarse horse
>   Rode out upon a road.
> This male wore mail for war and would
>   Explore a wood that glowed.

> His tale I'll tell from head to tail.
>   I'll write his rite up right.
> A hidden site our hero found,
>   A sight that I shall cite.

**homophonic sentence**: a sentence made of different words that sound alike. The first example repeats a single syllable, and the second repeats two. Each is followed by an interpretation in parentheses.

> Ay, I eye aye-aye aye. (Yes, I plan to look at this lemur awhile longer.)
> I see icy I.C. (I view frozen Iowa City.)

**homophonic translation**: a translation that uses words that sound (or look) like the original instead of words that approximate the original's meaning.

**homosynonyms**: two words that sound like two other words that are synonyms.

> ROSE, TEARS—ROWS, TIERS

**homovocalic sequences**: two sets of words with vowels in the same order, but with different consonants.

**honorificabilitudinitatibus**: the longest word (27 letters) in Shakespeare's works and later in *Webster's New International Dictionary of the English Language, First Edition*. Its literal meaning, based on medieval Latin, is "with honorablenesses." It appears in *Love's Labour's Lost*, Act V, Scene 1, line 44, spoken by Costard the clown. One anagram of it "proves" that Francis Bacon wrote Shakespeare's plays:

> Hi ludi F. Baconis nati tuiti orbi.
> These plays, F. Bacon's offspring, are preserved for the world.

**horizontal mirror letters**: B, C, D, E, H, I, K, O, and X, the letters that are symmetrical along a horizontal line drawn through the middle of each— the top half is symmetrical with the bottom half. Held upside down in front of a mirror, the letters appear the same as their reflections. See ASYMMETRICAL LETTERS, VERTICAL MIRROR LETTERS.

**horizontal mirror word**: a word spelled with HORIZONTAL MIRROR LETTERS. Held upside-down in front of a mirror, the word looks the same as its reflection.

> CHOICE    ICEBOX    KIDDED    EX-BOOKIE    CHECKBOOK

Also called "mirror palindrome."

**hospitable word**: a word that can change to another word by the insertion of a letter at any position.

CARES—SCARES CHARES CADRES CARIES CARETS CARESS

**hybrid animal name**: an animal name made of two other animal names, such as CATBIRD = CAT + BIRD. Such names can be linked by matching the second half of one name with the first half of another to form a chain. These twelve hybrid animal names begin a chain that can be extended much further:

| | | |
|---|---|---|
| MORAY EEL | BIRD DOG | SWALLOW HAWK |
| EELWORM | DOGFISH | HAWK EAGLE |
| WORM SNAKE | FISH OWL | EAGLE VULTURE |
| SNAKEBIRD | OWL SWALLOW | VULTURE RAVEN |

**hydration**: insertion of a letter at the beginning of a word. This is the reverse of BEHEADMENT.

**hyperhyphenation**: an abundance of hyphens in a single word or sentence.

A draft-dodging, drug-exhaling, sodomy-protecting, shady-dealing, tax-raising, child-exploiting, baby-killing, feminists-pandering, religion-robbing, military-reducing womanizer becomes Commander-in-Chief. (12 hyphens in a single sentence, from the book *The Parched Soul of America* by Clifford Goldstein)

THE WE'VE-ONLY-BEEN-DATING-FOR-A-LITTLE-WHILE-AND-I-DON'T-KNOW-IF-I-WANT-TO-INVEST-THE-TIME-AND-MONEY-TO-GET-A-PERSONAL-GIFT GIFTS (25 hyphens in a single word, from *The Daily Iowan* newspaper)

**iber** (*n. pl.*): more than one SUBER. This plural is perhaps the only one determined by ancient Latin and modern wordplay. A suber is a reverse REBUS. The plural of rebus is "rebi"; thus the plural of suber is rebi in reverse; thus enters "iber."

**ideal word ladder**: see MINIMAL WORD LADDER.

**I-E word**: a word in which the letters I and E appear together. According to this old spelling jingle, the two vowels are pronounced as follows:

> I before *e,*
> Except after *c,*
> Unless sounded as *a,*
> As in neighbor and weigh.

However, the rule doesn't always work. The following I-E words are only a few of the many that violate the letter of the law:

| | |
|---|---|
| ANCIENT | CAFFEINE |
| FANCIER | KALEIDOSCOPE |
| SCIENCE | THEREIN |

**I-invariant**: a UNIVOCALIC with I as the only vowel.

| | |
|---|---|
| PRIMITIVISTIC | WHIRLIGIGS |

**Illôt-Mollo**: A poetry game for three or more players. The players each begin writing anything that comes to mind. After fifteen seconds, one of the players says aloud the word he or she has just written; all the other players must then include this "marker word" in their writing. Every fifteen seconds the process repeats, with a different player calling out a word each time. Also known as "parallel stories."

**imaginary language**: language made entirely of nonsense words. The writer doesn't make up the nonsense words in advance of the writing. Instead, he or she improvises. The poem "Ubble Snop" contains no real words. It begins with this four-line stanza:

> Uv cabble toyoc fezt
> yab sig fovulatic:
> Neppcor-inco fendelism
> ubble snop.

**imperative noun**: a verb-noun compound that can be separated into two words that form a command. The compound and the command are related in meaning. For instance, SAWBONES refers to a doctor because some doctors SAW BONES during operations. Conversely, KILLDEER, a type of bird, doesn't KILL DEER; the word represents the bird's sound. Thus SAW-BONES is an imperative noun, but KILLDEER is not.

DO-NOTHING     PICKPOCKET     SPOILSPORT     TELLTALE

**impromptu writing**: writing without planning any of it in advance. In the nineteenth century, impromptu writing meant making up the lines of a poem to fit the rhymes on a list. The writer didn't know the rhymes ahead of time. In twentieth century, it means making up poetry on the spot—improvising.

**incide word**: a coined word using the suffix –CIDE (denoting "killer" or "killing") in a humorous way. The *OED* records one unintentionally funny example, BOVICIDE ("a butcher"), which inspired the concept. Here are some made-up examples with their deadly definitions:

> CHOP SUEYCIDE: death by overeating at a Chinese restaurant (analogous to the Japanese, SUSHICIDE)
> FLIPCIDE: murder by bashing one over the head with the less-popular side of a record
> OFFCIDE: killing a football player in the middle of a play

**infinite array**: an endless pattern of hexagonal tiles that can be labeled with letters to form HEX-WORDS. In the following example, the tiles form ARE (or EAR or ERA), no matter far they are extended in any direction.

```
E – R – A – E – R – A . . .
 \ / \ / \ / \ / \
A – E – R – A – E – R . . .
 \ / \ / \ / \ / \
R – A – E – R – A – E . . .
```

**infinite sentence**: a sentence that is infinitely long. One example is a sentence that begins "The sentence, "The sentence, "The sentence, . . ." and ends " . . . is infinitely long," is infinitely long," is infinitely long."

**inflationary language**: language in which words that sound like numbers are inflated by one. WONDER, BEFORE, and DECORATE have the sound of 1, 4, and 8 respectively. In inflationary language, they become TWODER, BEFIVE, and DECORNINE.

**inflationary language story**: a story written with an abundance of words translated into INFLATIONARY LANGUAGE. The first paragraph of "Jack and the Twoderful Beans" and its deflated translation appear below.

> Twice upon a time there lived a boy named Jack in the twoderful land of Califivenia. Two day Jack, a double-minded lad, decided three go fifth three seek his fivetune.

> Once upon a time there lived a boy named Jack in the wonderful land of California. One day Jack, a single-minded lad, decided to go forth to seek his fortune.

**insect sign language**: the sign language that Archy the Cockroach (of "Archy and Mehitabel" fame) devised in order to converse with Czar Nicholas of Russia. Each of Archy's six legs represent four letters. By pointing up, down, right, or left with the appropriate leg, he could make 24 letters and "get along without sometimes W and Y."

**insertion**: the process of adding a letter to one word in order to make another word.

ASTRAY = ASHTRAY        REIGN = RESIGN

**insertion-deletion network**: a NETWORK formed by inserting or deleting a letter to change one word to another in all possible cases.

**intercalation**: the insertion of extraneous sounds or words into speech. Although not used universally within a specific locale, the following intercalations have been heard in their respective countries:

| | | |
|---|---|---|
| United States: | UNH | |
| Canada: | UH | U as in must, no N sound |
| Britain: | AH | broad A |
| Mexico: | EH | short E, explosive |
| France: | EH | short E, pronounced with rounded lips |

Also called "embolalia" and "cheville."

**interchangeable letters**: letters that have been used as equally valid substitutes for each other in printed text.

U–V–W      I–J–Y      S–Z      C–K

**interchangeable vowel set**: a set of words resulting from the placement of each of the five vowels at the same point within the same string of letters. The last of the sets below is made of HELLO and four synonyms for it. See VOWELINDROME.

BAG BEG BIG BOG BUG
MATE METE MITE MOTE MUTE
MASSY MESSY MISSY MOSSY MUSSY
HALLO HELLO HILLO HOLLO HULLO

**interior palindrome**: a word, phrase, or name that is palindromic except for one or a few extra letters at both the beginning and the end. The palindrome is completely inside the word. This is a special type of INTERNAL PALINDROME.

F<u>OOTSTO</u>OL      HU<u>LLABALL</u>OO      WM. L<u>LEWELL</u>YN

**inter-language reversal**: a word in one language whose letters in reverse order spell a word in another language. In each of the following, an English word reverses to a foreign word:

RETILED—DÉLITER (French for "to set stones edgewise")
REFINER—RENIFER (Polish for "reindeer")
REPORTS—STROPER (Dutch for "poacher")

**interlocks**: two or more shorter words whose letters can be interwoven to form a longer word.

FIG, REBUS—FIREBUGS

**internal deletion homophone**: a word that becomes its own HOMO-PHONE when one of its internal letters is removed.

| | | |
|---|---|---|
| AUNT = ANT | HOARSE = HORSE | REIGN = REIN |
| BOULDER = BOLDER | MOOED = MOOD | TWO = TO |

**internal palindrome**: a word that has a palindromic string of letters in it.

MILLIMETER          KNITTING          UNDERBRED

**internal tautonym**: a word that has a TAUTONYM in it.

NONSENSE          MISSISSIPPI          SUPERSUPERB
ZENZIZENZIZENZIC

**internal-tautonym sentence**: a sentence in which letters occurring in adjacent words connect to make a TAUTONYM.

John and Mary are brINGING IN GINGer snaps to eat.

**interrupted sentence**: a sentence paused to suggest one meaning and then continued to give the real meaning.

While reprimanding a criminal, the Judge called him a "scoundrel." The prisoner replied: "Sir, I am not as big a scoundrel as Your Honor" here the culprit stopped, but finally added "takes me to be." "Put your words closer together," said the Judge.

**invariant letter**: a letter that occupies the same position in a word as it does in the alphabet. In the word ALPHABET, A is invariant because it begins both the word ALPHABET and the alphabet itself. The first word below has five invariant letters, shown positioned above the alphabet. The second and the third words are the shortest and the longest with a single invariant letter:

A R CH E TY P I CAL     A
A B C D E FG H I J KL     IMMUNOELECTROPHORETICALLY

Also called "alphabet-crashing word."

**invariant sentence**: a sentence written to include as many INVARIANT LETTERS as possible. This sentence has 16 invariant letters:

A BAD EGG HIT KLM WIPERS TWO WAYS.
A BcD E fG HIj KLM noPqRS T u v WxYz

**inverted half-square**: a FORM (second meaning) in the shape of half a square. As in a single square, the words going across are the same as those going down.

```
              F
         T    I
      B  A    R
   T  A  M    E
F  I  R  E    S
```

**inverted pyramid**: a REGULAR PYRAMID upside-down; that is, its longest word is at the top, and its single letter is at the bottom. It spells words across and down. The first appeared in 1883. This is a shorter inverted pyramid:

```
P  Y  R  A  M  I  D
   A  I  D  E  S
      B  O  W
         S
```

**invisible definition**: a dictionary definition that is a blank space on the page. In *Random House Webster's Dictionary*, this word appears as a boldface entry followed by a blank space exactly as it appears here:

**nobody**

**invisible sonnet**: a sonnet that has a title but no lines. The following is one sonnet in a sequence, each of which differs from the others by the number in the title. The fourteen blank lines under the title form the body of the sonnet:

**Invisible Sonnet # 1**

**isogram**: a word having each of its letters used only once. In the previous sentence, A, WORD, HAVING, HAS, EACH, OF, ITS, USED, ONLY, and ONCE are isograms, but LETTER, with two T's, isn't. Here are three 13-letter dictionary examples and one 23-letter coinage:

> ADVENTURISHLY    POSTNEURALGIC
> MUSICOTHERAPY    PUBVEXINGFJORD-SCHMALTZY

Also called "nonpattern word."

**isogrammatic name**: a personal name that uses each letter only once. See THE SCHWARZKOPF CHALLENGE.

**isogram set**: a word or group of words with no repeated letters. The challenge is to find the isogram set having the greatest letter total using one word, two words, three words, etc. The words should come from the same dictionary. These two isogram sets are the largest for one word and the largest for five words in the *Pocket Merriam-Webster's*:

> AMBIDEXTROUSLY (14)
> CHINTZ, PLUMBS, FJORD, GAWKY, VEX (25)

**isolano**: a word that cannot form another word by changing any one of its letters to another letter. See ONALOSI. Twelve three-letter words are isolanos in the *Pocket Merriam-Webster's*:

| | | | | | |
|---|---|---|---|---|---|
| EBB | GNU | ISM | NTH | OHM | URN |
| EMU | IMP | ITS | OBI | OVA | USE |

**isomorph**: a word in a pair or group of words that has the same sequential pattern of letters, as indicated by numbers.

> BARBAROUS—MURMUROUS (123123425)

**Jabberwock** (*v.*): to substitute nonsense words from Lewis Carroll's poem "The Jabberwock" for words in other texts. A Jabberwocked version of Hamlet's famous soliloquy begins with these four lines:

> To be, or not to be, that is the gimble.
> Whether 'tis uffish in the mind to suffer
> The Jabberwock of outrageous fortune
> Or to whiffle against a sea of jubjubs

**Janeism**: a MALAPROPISM, MIXED CLICHÉ, or other comical line spoken by Jane, the scatterbrained wife of Goodman Ace in the 1930s radio program "Easy Aces."

**Mixed clichés:**

Let me tell you, my tar-feathered friend, . . .
Keep a stiff upper cut.
Sitting on pretty street.

**Malapropisms:**

A fly in the oatmeal.
I await your answer with dated breath.
You could have knocked me over with a fender.

**Other:**

I wasn't born yesterday for nothing.
A girl is only young once in a while.
There's a time to and a time not to, and this is it.

**Japanglish TV program title**: a Japanese television show title translated into English.

| "Babbling Music Hall" | "Young Oh Oh" |
| "Welfare Sumo" | "Joyful Map Variety" |
| "Quiz Time Shock" | "Unknown World: 'Toilet Seats of the World'" |

**JKQXZ word**: a word having the five RARE LETTERS in it. The two examples below are coined words based on ZIQ-XHAFEJ, the name of an Albanian village (listed under JQXZ WORD) and on a variant spelling of it:

    ZIQ-XHAFEJLIKE        ZIKXHAFAJESQUE

**joey**: a small word contained in a larger word. See KANGAROO WORD.

**JQXZ word**: a word having the four RARE LETTERS in it. The first example below is a coined word based on ARJUZANX, a town in France listed in *The Times Atlas of the World* (1955). The second is the name of a village listed in *A Gazetteer of Albania* (1946).

    ARJUZANXESQUE        ZIQ-XHAFEJ

**kangaroo word**: a word bearing a smaller word of its own kind inside it. The smaller word, called a JOEY (baby kangaroo), should be related in meaning to the larger; its letters should appear in correct order with at least one extraneous letter breaking them apart; and it should be etymologically unrelated to the kangaroo. For instance CAVERN and CAVE appear to be kangaroo and joey, but they fail for two reasons: The letters of CAVE are clumped together with no letter separating them, and CAVERN and CAVE are related in their linguistic origins. The following are true kangaroos, with their joeys jumping up in capital form:

caLumnIES          destRUctIoN          insTrUcTOR

In some cases, two joeys work together in the same kangaroo. In these examples below, the first kangaroo has TIN + CAN, and the second has HOT + COCOA:

conTaINer          cHOcolaTe
ContAiNer          ChOCOlAte

Also called "marsupial," "multiple deletion."

**key**: a single location used to dial a number on a rotary telephone dial or a touchtone telephone keypad. The individual keys are identified by digits. The 2-key, for instance, is the one labeled 2 / ABC.

**keypunch word**: a word spelled using each key on a telephone dial one time only, exemplified by the word KEYPUNCH itself.

| ADROITLY | FOXTAILS | PLAYTIME | TWANGLES |
|----------|----------|----------|----------|
| 23764859 | 36982457 | 75298463 | 89264537 |

**key-word substitution code**: a CODE formed by writing a keyword down under the first letters of a PLAINTEXT ALPHABET and then writing the alphabet from A to Z, excluding the letters that are already in the key-word.

**K-graph**: a WORD GRAPH using the King's move on an imaginary chessboard. The word is traced one letter at a time in spelling order by moving one square in any direction. If the word has a repeated letter, the path has to be plotted to return and reuse the original letter. Otherwise, the word cannot be K-graphed. The same K-graph can represent different words, and the same word can have different K-graphs. These K-graphs represent IMPOSSIBILITY and MISSISSIPPI:

    L T Y      M I S
    I M P      P
    B S O

The next two words are the shortest that can't be K-graphed and the longest that can:

INSCIENCES (10)
DIAMINOPROPYLTETETRAMETHYLENEDIAMINE (34)

**K-graphable** (*adj.*): able to be placed in a K-GRAPH.

**kidspeak**: language spoken by children that uses a clever variation on the words and grammar of the adult world. A phrase in kidspeak is usually close enough to get across the meaning and far enough to add to it.

> "Could I have some poison berries on my awful?" (boysenberry syrup, waffle) (eight-year-old)

> "The new baby is nine pounds six senses." (five-year-old)

**king's-move pack**: a WORD PACK made by printing one letter after the other in a chessboard-like grid using the king's move. This is based on the K-GRAPH, but it allows a letter to appear more than once if necessary. In this example, the names of the seven colors of the rainbow fit into a grid measuring 5 x 4 letters with only two repeated letters.

```
    V  I  D
  W O  G  N  E
  B L  E  R  A
  U T  Y  O
```

**Knave's English**: written English text composed almost entirely of slang words from various eras and ethnographic groups. The example below, followed by its translation into Standard English, is the first sentence of a story using entries from *The Pocket Dictionary of American Slang*.

> The potato-head cut a rusty on the borax gee-gee, but the kittle-cattle didn't have the oof to carry a lot of weight.

> The stupid person showed off on the gaudy race horse, but the unreliable, undependable group of people didn't have the money to be influential.

**Knight's Tour Letter Puzzle**: an early version of the modern WORD-SEARCH PUZZLE. In the Knight's Tour Letter Puzzle, the player moves the same as the knight in chess to find the words hidden in the square.

**knock, knock joke**: a question-and-answer riddle that is based on a pun and that usually has the following five-line format: "Knock, knock." "Who's there?" "[A name.]" "[A name] who?" "[A name] [the rest of the punning punch-line]." The form became so well known that any word could be substituted in place of a name, and several variations on the form could be used.

Knock, knock.
Who's there?
Sarah.
Sarah who?
Sarah doctor in the house?

**language name**: the name of one of the world's many languages. The following is a small selection of English language names for foreign languages:

| | | |
|---|---|---|
| BZYB | GOTOCOGEGODEGI | NDOGBAND |
| CLACKSTAR | KWOTTO | SALIVA |
| EEELEEREE | LOVE | TTZAE |
| FLUP | MZAB | ZANY |

**language-name palindrome**: a LANGUAGE NAME that is a PALINDROME. This selection comes from a list of 105 language-name palindromes:

| | | |
|---|---|---|
| AULUA | KEYEK | SIIS |
| CIC | MALAYALAM | WARRAW |
| DALAD | OOLOOPOOLOO | YAQAY |

**language-name tautonym**: a LANGUAGE NAME that divides into two or more parts that are spelled the same. See TAUTONYM.

BARABABARABA    GABGAB    KPILAKPILA    KUKUKUKU

**larding**: the practice of inserting one or more sentences between two sentences of a text, and continuing to insert sentences until the desired length is achieved.

**last-half letters**: N, O, P, Q, R, S, T, U, V, W, X, Y, and Z, the last thirteen letters of the alphabet. See FIRST-HALF LETTERS.

**last-half number-name**: a NUMBER NAME spelled with letters from the last half of the alphabet. There is only one: TWO.

**last-half word**: a word spelled with letters from the last half of the alphabet. There are many short words, such as OR or NOT, but not many long ones.

> POPPYWORTS      ZOOSPOROUS      NONSUPPORTS

**leapfrog word**: a word formed by dividing another word into its odd- and even-numbered letters and placing those two sets next to each other. In other words, one set "leapfrogs" out of the original word and lands to the right or left of the other to form the new word.

> FEAST = FAT = FATES = FATES
> FREER = FER + RE = REFER
> HEARTS = HAT + ERS + HATERS
> STEALS = SEL + TAS = TASSEL

**left-sided lettershift pyramid**: a LETTERSHIFT form in the shape of a pyramid.

> L I V I N G
> R O B O T .
> H E R E . .
> D A N . . .
> B Y . . . .
> I . . . . .

**legal palindrome**: a PALINDROME about crime, criminals, and the legal system.

> Sex at noon taxes.
> No on-task lawyer prey walks at noon.
> Tie, tag it. I'll litigate it.
> Emit no liar! Trial on time.
> No, sir. Prison!

**letter-change reversal:** a REVERSAL PAIR that becomes another reversal pair by changing just one letter in each word.

REINED—DENIER  SLOOPS—SPOOLS
| | | | | | | |
SEINED—DENIES  SNOOPS—SPOONS

**letter conundrum:** a rebus-type word puzzle that involves a single letter in either the question or the answer. The letter may be part of a word, or it may be an addition that changes one word to another. The second type is more difficult to construct, and the RARE LETTERS JQXZ are the most difficult to use. Letter conundrums were especially popular from the 1850s to the 1920s. Here are four examples, two of each type:

Why is A like noon? Because it is in the middle of day.
What letter is invisible, yet never out of sight? The letter I.

Why is N like a pig? Because it makes a sty nasty.
What changes a lad to a lady? The letter Y.

**letter distribution:** the number of occurrences of each different letter in a word, regardless of LETTER PATTERN. PASS and TOUT have the same letter distribution (two single letters and one repeated letter), even though they have different letters and letter patterns.

**lettered dice:** see WORD DICE.

**letter kickoff word:** a word that begins with a letter separated by a hyphen or a space from the other letters and pronounced by its letter name. Here is an alphabet of letter kickoff words:

| | | | | |
|---|---|---|---|---|
| A-frame | G-string | M-phase | S-curve | Y-chromosome |
| B-movie | H-bomb | N-type | T-shirt | Z-coordinate |
| C-section | I beam | O-ring | U-turn | |
| D-day | J-bar | P-wave | V-neck | |
| E-mail | K ration | Q-Tip | W-particle | |
| F-stop | L-dopa | R-month | X-ray | |

**letter maze:** a puzzle in which you go from a starting letter to a finishing letter using a specific key that tells you how many letters to move forward or back.

**letter pattern**: the arrangement of letters in a word. DID and BOB have the same letter pattern but different letters.

**letterplay**: WORDPLAY involving the letters of the alphabet and their usage in words without regards to sound or sense.

**letter-plural word**: a word in the singular that sounds like a letter in the plural.

| | | |
|---|---|---|
| SEIZE = C's | GEEZ = G's | TEASE = T's |
| EASE = E's | PEASE = P's | WISE = Y's |

**letter rebus**: a word puzzle in which a word, phrase, or sentence describes a letter of the alphabet. There are four types of letter rebuses: ENIGMATIC REBUS, PHONETIC REBUS, STANDARD REBUS, and SUBER.

**letter riddle**: a riddle that involves a letter of the alphabet. See LETTER REBUS.

**lettershift** (*n*.), also spelled **letter shift**, **letter-shift**: a word whose letters are an equal number of steps along the alphabet from the corresponding letters of another word. BEE is a lettershift of ADD, since the next letters after A, D, D in the alphabet are B, E, E. Most LETTERSHIFT PAIRS are separated by more than a single step. Shifting each letter in COLD three steps along the alphabet results in FROG.

Dmitri Borgmann introduced the concept of lettershifts in his book *Language on Vacation* (1965). The strategy of this form is much different than that of ANAGRAMS, PALINDROMES, and similar forms. Words that are anagrams of each other always have the same letters, but words that are lettershifts may or may not have more than one letter in common.

The lettershift made an appearance on the silver screen in Stanley Kubrick's *2001: A Space Odyssey*. HAL was the name of the computer that controlled the space vessel. Shifting each letter one step gives IBM, the biggest maker of computers at the time. Kubrick claimed that HAL was used because it is a hybrid of the two principal learning systems, Heuristic and ALgorithmic, and not an intended lettershift.

To calculate the steps between one word and another, it is sometimes necessary to use a CIRCULAR ALPHABET, in which the letters are printed in a circle so that Z continues on with A. These two examples of lettershifts include the steps between the words. The column on the right shows how the letters wrap around from Z to A (at FIZZ-GJAA).

| PECAN | F I ZZ |
|-------|--------|
| QFDBO | G JAA |
| RGECP | HKBB |
| SHFDQ | I LCC |
| T IGER | JMDD |
|       | KNEE |

The number of ALPHABETIC STEPS from one word to the other in a lettershift pair is its SHIFT VALUE. PECAN shifts four steps to reach TIGER; thus PECAN-TIGER has a shift value of 4. Going from TIGER to PECAN, however, requires 22 steps forward along the alphabet, giving it a shift value of 22. In this group of lettershift pairs, the shift value of each appears in parentheses.

| | |
|---|---|
| END-FOE (1) | BANJO-FERNS (4) |
| ICE-KEG (2) | CHEER-JOLLY (6) |
| ODD-ZOO (11) | FUSION-LAYOUT (6) |
| OPEN-STIR (4) | UNFIBER-BUMPILY (7) |
| CRIB-LARK (9) | WILIWILI-COROCORO (6) |

**lettershift** (*v.*): to form a LETTERSHIFT.

**lettershift** (*adj.*): composed of letters that are the same number of alphabet steps from a starting word.

**Lettershift Calculator**: a home-made device for generating LETTERSHIFTS of a selected letter string. The Lettershift Calculator consists of a soup can with seven loops of paper wrapped around it. The loops have the alphabet printed on them so that rotating them to spell a word in one row makes 25 parallel letter strings in the other rows.

**lettershift form**: a geometric arrangement of words that are LETTERSHIFTS or PARTIAL LETTERSHIFTS of each other. The words may be placed in any order, but their letters must remain in the position in which they were shifted.

**lettershift multiple**: a LETTERSHIFT SET.

**lettershift pair**: a pair of words that are LETTERSHIFTS of each other. A starting word and its lettershift form a lettershift pair.

**lettershift reversal**: a word formed by reversing a LETTERSHIFT string of another word. THEM shifted ten steps results in the lettershift string DROW, which reverses to the word WORD. WORD is a lettershift reversal of THEM (and vice versa).

| DUNK | HEAR | ALLOY | GHOST |
|------|------|-------|-------|
| EVOL | LIEV | DOORB | STAEF |
| (LOVE) | (VEIL) | (BROOD) | (FEATS) |

**lettershift sentence**: a sentence that is made by shifting the letters of a single word and dividing the resulting letter string into a meaningful statement. INFINITE shifts seven steps along the alphabet to PUMPUPAL, a meaningless string until presented as PUMP UP, AL!

**lettershift set**: three or more words that are LETTERSHIFTS of each other. GOD-OWL-SAP-WET is a lettershift set made of four common words.

**lettershift word**: a LETTERSHIFT.

**lettershift word square**: 1. a WORD SQUARE whose words are LETTER-SHIFTS of the corresponding words in a second square. Each is a lettershift word square of the other.

```
H E R                    R O B
E M U   shifts 10 steps to  O W E
R U T                    B E D
```

2. a WORD SQUARE formed by words that are LETTERSHIFTS of each other having the same SHIFT VALUE. In this square, LAP and APE are 15 steps apart, and APE and PET are 15 steps apart.

```
L A P
A P E
P E T
```

**lettersquare palindrome**: see PALINDROMIC SQUARE.

**letterstring**: a consecutive sequence of letters. A letterstring may be a word or not a word, and it may stand alone or occur as part of a word.

| ALPHABET | SHRDLU | laNGUAge |
|----------|--------|----------|

**letter-unit** (*adj.*): having letters as the basic building blocks of a a wordplay form, such as a "letter-unit ANAGRAM." Also called "letter-by-letter."

**letter-unit palindrome**: a PALINDROME that involves the manipulation of individual letters. While this is usually the case, "letter-unit" is sometimes added to distinguish it from WORD-UNIT PALINDROMES.

**letter-unit transposal**: a TRANSPOSAL that involves rearranging letters instead of words or other units. Usually "letter-unit" is understood, but sometimes it is used to distinguish letter-unit transposals from word transposals. Also called "letter-by-letter transposition."

**letter word**: a word that sounds like a letter.

| | | |
|---|---|---|
| B = BE, BEE | K = QUAY | Q = CUE, QUEUE |
| G = GEE | P = PEA, PEE | Y = WHY |

**Lewis Carroll's alphabet cipher**: a complex substitution CIPHER that makes use of a table of letters in rows and columns. According to Carroll, "each column of this table forms a dictionary of symbols representing the alphabet."

**Liar's Paradox**: an ancient paradox that appears in many forms, the most basic of which is, "If you say, 'I lie,' and in saying it tell the truth, you lie. But if you say, 'I lie,' and in saying it tell a lie, you tell the truth." Also called "Epimenedes's Paradox."

**lightweight word**: a word whose letters have the lowest AVERAGE LETTER WEIGHT for a given word-length. In general, the average increases with the length of the word. Here are lightweight words for four different lengths. The total of the ALPHABETIC VALUE and the weight per letter appear in parentheses.

| | |
|---|---|
| A (1; 1.00) | CABBAGEHEAD (39; 3.55) |
| ABBA (6; 1.50) | COLEOCHAETACEAE (102; 6.80) |

**limergimmick**: a poem that alters the rhyme, rhythm, typography, or other element of the traditional LIMERICK. The most extreme example is this math formula (followed by its translation into words):

$$\frac{12 + 144 + 20 + (3 \times \sqrt{4})}{7} + 5\,(11) = 9^2 + 0$$

A dozen, a gross, and a score
Plus three times the square root of four
    Divided by seven
    Plus five times eleven
Is nine squared and not a bit more.

**Linear Logic**: a system in which logical statements are placed in numbered lines. The reader must read through the lines, change statements to keep the truth value correct, and determine what the lines will say.

**line repetition**: multiple occurrences of a line of poetry in the same poem. Several traditional poetic forms, such as the villanelle and the pantoum, repeat certain lines. Line repetition achieves its apogee in Ron Padgett's sonnet "Nothing in That Drawer," in which all fourteen lines repeat the title.

**line-unit** (*adj.*) having lines of a poem as the basic building blocks of a word-play form.

**line-unit anagram**: a poem whose lines are ANAGRAMS of each other and of the title. For example, "Washington Crossing the Delaware" begins with this stanza:

    A hard, howling, tossing, water scene;
    Strong tide was washing hero clean.
    "How cold!" Weather stings as in anger.
    O silent night shows war ace danger!

**line-unit palindrome**: a poem whose lines read the same from top to bottom and from bottom to top. The words in the first line are the same as the words in the last, and this mirror effect continues through to the middle line(s). The only thing that can change is the punctuation. In this example, each stanza is spoken by a different person:

    "I bought your car.
    I don't know why
    It won't go far.
    It seems to die."

> "It *seems* to die?
> It won't go *far?*"
> I don't know why
> I bought your car!"

**linkade**: a word or phrase is broken into two or more shorter parts that overlap by one letter.

> PHILATELY—PHIL, LATELY        FOREIGN—FOR, REIGN

**lipogram**: a word, sentence, poem, novel, or other text that excludes one or more of the letters most commonly used in writing. The lipogram was invented by Lasus of Hermione in the sixth century B.C. He excluded the letter sigma from two poems. Other ancient lipogrammatists were Pindar, Nestor of Laranda, and Tryphiodorus of Sicily. Tryphiodorus composed a work about Ulysses that consisted of 24 books, each of which omitted one letter of the Greek alphabet.

The letters E and T are the most frequently used in English. In these long examples of words that are lipograms, E doesn't appear in the first, and both E and T don't appear in the second.

> FLOCCIPAUCINIHILIPILIFICATIONS
> PHILOSOPHICOPYSCHOLOGICALLY

In the next example, the 25 commonest letters (A–Y) do not appear:

> ZZZZ

Also called "anti-frequency word."

**lipogrammatic**, also **lipogrammatical** (*adj.*): excluding a specific set of letters from a text; being a lipogram. There are LIPOGRAMMATIC POEMS, LIPOGRAMMATIC NOVELS, and even a LIPOGRAMMATIC INTERVIEW or two.

**lipogrammatic dialogue**: a dialogue in which only predetermined letters are used in spelling the words. In one approach, "Adelaide and Tony," the alphabet is divided between the two characters. Tony's words use letters from the first half, and Adelaide's from the last half. It begins:

> TONY: I'm back, Adelaide!
> ADELAIDE: Ooo . . . your worn sport soup-to-nuts tux!
> TONY: Lambie, I came back. . . .

ADELAIDE: Sorry, Tony. Not now. You run out on us. You run out on your own vows! Now you turn up.

**lipogrammatic interview**: an interview in which the interviewee speaks in words containing only certain letters. In a lipogrammatic interview with Ronald Reagan that begins with the lines below, the former president's answers use just the letters from his name, RONALD WILSON REAGAN:

> INTERVIEWER: What is your reaction to critics of your Presidency? How does a former actor feel about the awesome responsibilities of the Presidency, with all the world his stage?
> REAGAN: Derision or a dressing-down is as degrading as dredging sewage alongside a noose on a gallows ladder. I ignore; no one sees a lone leader's real sorrows.

**lipogrammatic novel**: a novel written entirely with words that omit a specified letter. So far, only two have been published, one in English and one in French. Both omit the letter E, the commonest letter in normal printed text in both languages.

*Gadsby* (1939) by Earnest Vincent Wright was a response to F. Scott Fitzgerald's "negative" novel, *The Great Gatsby*. Wright dedicated the novel to "Youth" and took a "stand against liquor." Unfortunately, its wooden characters overcome adversity in the manner of Horatio Alger heroes. To avoid accidentally using E, Wright removed the E-key from his typewriter. The novel opens with an evening in the life of Mayor Gadsby:

> Gadsby was walking back from a visit down in Branton Hills' manufacturing district on a Saturday night. A busy day's traffic had had its noisy run, and with not many folks in sight, His Honor got along without having to stop to grasp a hand, or talk; for a Mayor out of City Hall is a shining mark for any politician.

*La Disparition* by Georges Perec (DeNoel, 1969) was so well written that several reviewers didn't notice the missing E. It was translated equally E-lessly into English under the title *A Void* (by Gilbert Adair; HarperCollins, 1995). In the spirit of the book, *Time* magazine reviewed it without E's.

**lipogrammatic palindrome**: a PALINDROME using a very limited number of letters throughout. The poem "Palindromic Conversation Between Two Owls" uses only four letters—T, O, H, and W:

> "Too hot to hoot!"
> "Too hot to woo!"
> "Too wot?"

"Too woo!"
"Too wot?"
"To hoot! Too hot to hoot!"

**lipogrammatic pangram**: a text that combines the LIPOGRAM and the PANGRAM by excluding the letter E and by using all the other letters one or more times apiece. This is the first of three stanzas:

> A jovial swain should not complain
> Of any buxom fair,
> Who mocks his pain and thinks it gain
> To quiz his awkward air.

**lipogrammatic poem**: a poem written entirely with words that exclude a specified letter.

**lipogrammatist**: one who writes LIPOGRAMS.

**lipogrammetry**: the practice of writing literary LIPOGRAMS.

**liponymous text**: a text which excludes a particular word or words. In American writer Doug Nufer's 200-page novel *Never Again,* once he used a word, he didn't use it again.

**literary anagram**: an ANAGRAM on a famous line from a poem, a play, or other work by a famous author.

> Dear is the memory of our wedded lives.
>     (from "The Lotus-Eaters" by Alfred, Lord Tennyson)
> Love's treasured word edified my home.
>
> How happy could I be with either? (from *The Beggar's Opera* by John Gay)
> But pray, which do I elope with, eh?

**literary fellow's anagram**: a writer's name anagrammed into a phrase or sentence. See NAME ANAGRAM.

> WILLIAM SHAKESPEARE = He's like a lamp, I swear!
> DANTE GABRIEL ROSSETTI = greatest idealist born
> CHARLES DICKENS = Cheer sick lands.

**literary oxymoron**: an OXYMORON created intentionally. Such oxymora are often found within works of literature:

> HATEFUL GOOD (Geoffrey Chaucer)
> SWEET SORROW (William Shakespeare)
> FAINT PRAISE (Alexander Pope)

**literary tongue-twister**: a TONGUE-TWISTER that uses the name of a famous writer.

> She saw Shelley sell seashells.
> Were Wordsworth's words worth Wordsworth's works?
> All will oil well Orwell's oil well.
> Chaucer's choicest saucer's choice, sir.
> Blake broke bleak bloke.

**locally invariant letters**: letters that are the same distance apart in a word as they are in the alphabet. In INOPERATIVE, there are six locally INVARIANT LETTERS.

> I     NOPE RAT IVE
> ABCDEFGHIJKLMNOPQRSTUVWXYZ

**logocide**: a word murderer.

**logogram**: **1.** a RHYMING PUZZLE that includes both BEHEADMENTS and CURTAILMENTS as clues and/or answers.
   **2.** a LOGOGRIPH.

**logograph**: a puzzle in which a string of letters must be rearranged to form the words of the answer.

**logogriph**: a puzzle formed by short words made of the letters in a single long word. The short words are given as clues in poetry or prose. The object is to figure out the long word. For instance, one poem gives clues for these 13 words: REGAL, AGE, EARL, GEAR, REAL, RAG, RAGE, LAG, EAR, LEG, GALE, and ARE. The letters used are AELGR, which transposes to the answer, LARGE. Also called "logogram."

**logology**: the science of words. Dmitri Borgmann revived this obsolete term listed in the *Oxford English Dictionary* and used it to mean wordplay as an intellectual pursuit.

**logomotive**: a sentence in which a famous name is followed by a HOMO-GRAPH that completes the sentence by punning on the name. The pun gives the sentence two different meanings.

> Was Vincent Price conscious?
> Is Glenn Close up?
> Was Robert Frost bitten?
> Is Koo Stark naked?
> Was Tyrone Power hungry?

**logophile**: a word lover.

**longest word**: the word with the greatest number of letters compared to other words in a specific dictionary, lexicon, or other source, or even compared to all the words in the entire language. Five of the longest words have become part of the lore of wordplay. They are discussed in more detail in their own entries.

> HONORIFICABILITUDINITATIBUS (27 letters)
> ANTIDISESTABLISHMENTARIANISM (28)
> FLOCCINAUCINIHILIPILIFICATION (29)
> SUPERCALIFRAGILISTICEXPIALIDOCIOUS (34)
> PNEUMONOULTRAMICROSCOPICSILICOVOLCANOCONIOSIS (45)

**looping anagram**: see CYCLIC TRANSPOSAL.

**looping anagram progression**: a series of words formed by starting with one word, moving its first letter to the end to form the second word, moving the first two letters of the second word to the end to form the third word, and so on, until returning to the starting word. The longest known progression generates only three different words by moving one, two, and three letters successively:

> TERRAN      ERRANT      RANTER      (TERRAN)

**lost positive**: a word that forms a more well-known word when the appropriate prefix is added.

> NOCENT (INNOCENT)      COUTH (UNCOUTH)

Also called "unce word."

**low-scoring Scrabble™**: an arrangement of letters on a SCRABBLE™ board to represent the lowest possible score in a legal game.

**lucky number name**: a NUMBER NAME spelled with seven letters. There are only three lucky number names:

FIFTEEN                SIXTEEN                SEVENTY

**lucky unlucky equation**: the equation that shows that all three LUCKY NUMBER NAMES add up to the first UNLUCKY NUMBER NAME.

FIFTEEN + SIXTEEN + SEVENTY = ONE HUNDRED ONE
   15    +   16    +   70    =       101

**ludicrous acronym**: an ACRONYM that spells an unusual word, has an unusual meaning, or both. Some are official terms, others are unofficial jokes.

BANANA = Build Absolutely Nothing Anywhere Near Anybody
CREEP = Committee to Re-Elect the President
G.O.D. = Guaranteed Overnight Delivery
DAM = Mothers Against Dyslexia
OINK = One Income, No Kids

**macaronic verse**: poetry that mixes two or more languages. In one type of macaronic verse, the words from each language need to be translated into a common language to make sense. In another type, the entire poem contains real and imaginary Latin words that make sense when respaced and pronounced like English words, as in "A Love Song" by Jonathan Swift:

Apud in is almi des ire,            A pudding is all my desire,
Mimis tres I ne ver re qui re.      My mistress I never require.

| Alo verify findit a gestis, | A lover if I find it, a jest is, |
| His miseri ne ver at restis. | His misery never at rest is. |

**Mad Lib**: a story that leaves some of the words out and replaces them with blanks having the part of speech listed under them to indicate how to make the sentences grammatically correct. The player fills in the blanks. Mad Libs are published in pads by Price/Stern/Sloane of Los Angeles.

**magic sentence grid**: a grid of words that form sentences reading the same across and down. This is similar to a WORD SQUARE POEM.

| The | dog | is | weak |
|-----|-----|-----|------|
| dog | the | fighting | men |
| is | fighting | good | will |
| weak | men | will | fall |

**malapropism**: an absurd, usually humorous misuse of language by the substitution of a word similar in sound, meaning, or logic. The term comes from Mistress Malaprop, a character in Ricahrd Sheridan's play *The Rivals* (1755). The most famous line from the play may be "As headlong as an 'allegory' on the banks of the Nile." These examples aren't in the play:

> If people don't want to come, you can't stop them.
> Posterity is just around the corner.
> Wagner's music is better than it sounds.

**malonym**: a humorous HOMOPHONE or sound-alike mistake.

> In the middle of the field stood a toe-headed boy.
> Our menu is guaranteed to wet your appetite.

**many-sounds-for-the-same-spelling poem**: a poem that uses words that have the same spelling producing a different sound. In the poem, "Tough Slough," some of the words are spelled incorrectly to emphasize the spelling variations. Here are the first two of nine stanzas.

> The wind was rough.
> The cold was grough.
> She kept her hands
> Inside her mough.

And even though
She loved the snough,
The weather was
A heartless bough.

**many-spellings-for-the-same-sound sentence**: a sentence whose words have the same sound spelled in different ways. Here is a 22-word sentence in which each word has a long O sound that is spelled differently in each case.

Although yeomen folk owe pharaoh's vaud bureau's depot hoe oats, chauvinistic Van Gogh, swallowing cognac oh so soulfully, sews grosgrain, picoted brooched chapeaux!?

**"Mary Had a Little Lamb"**: the children's poem that has been rewritten in more wordplay forms than any other work of literature. Usually the rewrite is composed of the first two of the poem's four stanzas. The writer attempts to maintain the meaning, rhyme, and rhythm of the original poem while converting it to the chosen wordplay form. The more restrictive the form becomes, the more difficult it is to keep to the elements of the original. The "Lamb" provides a short, familiar testing ground for comparing the ease or difficult of writing in a variety of different forms.

Ross Eckler wrote the first flock, a group of six LIPOGRAMMATIC "Lambs." Five of them each omit one of the five vowels, and the sixth omits half the alphabet. Other "Lamb" rewrites—and there are dozens—have used a wide range of forms, including ANAGRAM, HOMOPHONE, PALINDROME, PANGRAM, UNIVOCALIC, and others. To fit into the forms, Mary has taken many aliases, such as Marry, Merry, May, Meg, Maria, Marilyn, Ann, Eva, Eve, Polly, and Larry.

The authorship of the original poem is uncertain. Sarah Josepha Hale of Newport, New Hampshire, published it in 1830 in her book *Poems for Our Children*. However, John Roulstone of Sterling, Massachusetts, claims to have written the first three stanzas after witnessing the actual incident there in 1815. The girl in the poem, Mary Sawyer, wrote in a letter in 1879 that Roulstone was the author. Today both towns claim to be the birthplace of "Lamb."

Here is the original version of the first two stanzas, followed by the lipogrammatic version that excludes half the alphabet:

**Mary Had a Little Lamb**

Mary had a little lamb,
Its fleece was white as snow,

And everywhere that Mary went
The lamb was sure to go.

He followed her to school one day,
That was against the rule;
It made the children laugh and play
To see a lamb in school.

**Maria Had a Little Sheep**
*(a lipogram excluding BCFJKPQUVXZ)*

Maria had a little sheep,
As pale as rime its hair,
And all the places Maria came
The sheep did tail her there;

In Maria's class it came at last
(A sheep can't enter there).
It made the children clap their hands;
A sheep in class, that's rare!

**master word**: a word whose letters can be rearranged to form a large number of smaller words. The best master words of different lengths in the *Pocket Merriam-Webster's* appear below, with the number of words that their letters generate shown in parentheses:

| | | |
|---|---|---|
| SAP (6) | SPATE (42) | PIASTER (169) |
| PATE (14) | REPAST (96) | |

**matched homonyms**: HOMONYMS that can form TRANSPOSALS that are also homonyms with a different sound from the original words.

| | |
|---|---|
| MEET | TEEM |
| MEAT | TEAM |

**mathematical English**: a math term given a non-mathematical meaning, usually by means of a DOUBLE SOUND PUN.

The LINE is king of the jungle.
My favorite dessert is cherry PI.
The zoid hunter hoped to TRAPEZOID.

**meaning play**: WORDPLAY involving the meanings of words without regards to letters or sounds.

**melodic pun**: a syllable that sounds like a melody note (DO, RE, MI, etc.) and is sung to that same note in a song. The melodic pun is one of the few wordplay forms that unite the sounds of words with music. In fact, the most obvious example occurs in *The Sound of Music*, the musical in which Julie Andrews sings "DO, a deer, a female deer, / RE, a drop of golden sun. . . ." Many composers have made melodic puns. In Leonard Bernstein's *Mass*, the phrase "me and my soul" is repeated over and over. The words ME and SOUL are sung to the notes MI and SO. In the song "Sodomy," from the 1960s rock musical *Hair*, the word SODOMY is sung to the notes SO, DO, MI. See HOMOPHONE.

**meronym**: a term halfway between two opposites.

> black—GREY—white            convex—FLAT—concave

**mesostich**: an ACROSTIC that spells a word, phrase, or name using letters within the lines of a poem instead of at the beginning. Each letter occupies the same corresponding position from line to line.

**metallege**: a word made by switching two letters in a baseword. The term comes from the field of psychology, in which a metallege is a type of cross-compensation.

> SALVE—SLAVE         GONDOLA—DONGOLA

**metric prose**: prose written with regular rhythm and rhyme. Here is the first paragraph of a letter in metric prose that the poet William Cowper wrote:

> My very dear friend, I am going to send, what when you have read, you may scratch your head, and say I suppose, there's nobody knows, whether what I have got, be verse or not; by the tune and the time, it ought to be rhyme; but if it be, did ever you see, of late or of yore, such a ditty before?

Also called "poetic prose."

**middle of an alphabetic list**: an entry that is located at the center of a reference book or other source in terms of pages. The middle entry in books of names seems to come earlier in the alphabet than the middle entry in dictionaries. These examples are followed by the title of the reference sources they appear in:

> JAHRBUCH            (Boston Public Library serials)

117

| KWIETNIEWSKI | (*Baseball Encyclopedia*, player register) |
| LOVE | (*Bartlett's Familiar Quotations*) |
| MAZARINE | (*Mrs. Byrne's Dictionary*) |
| NOMINAL | (*Oxford English Dictionary*) |

**midpoint of the alphabet**: the point that divides the 26 letters into two equal halves. The midpoint is the "space" between M and N. Since the ALPHABETIC VALUES of M = 13 and N = 14, the alphabetic value of the midpoint is 13.5. See AVERAGE NUMERICAL VALUE OF THE ALPHABET.

**minimal pairing triplet**: a TRIPLET in which two pairs of logically associated words are connected by as few intermediate words as possible. NO changes to YES by means of four intermediate words:

    NO
    NOY
    OY
    OYE
    OYES
    YES

**minimal word ladder**: a WORD LADDER in which one word transforms to another in the fewest number of steps: Each letter in the starting word can change only once in the entire ladder. The number of steps taken is the same as the number of letters in the words. In the first example, made of four-letter words, COLD changes to its near-opposite, WARM. For six-letter words and longer, the beginning and ending words don't have to relate in meaning. At that word length, it is difficult to connect any pair of words in the minimum number of steps.

| | |
|---|---|
| C O L D | B R A V E R |
| C O R D | B E A V E R |
| C A R D | B E A T E R |
| W A R D | B E T T E R |
| W A R M | S E T T E R |
| | S E T T E E |
| | S E T T L E |

**minimum-length pangrammatic ladder**: a PANGRAMMATIC LADDER that uses all the letters of the alphabet in the fewest words possible. For five-letter words, the minimum length is 22 letters.

FAQIR     FATED     HAVES     MALES     CONES

| FAKIR | GATED | HAZES | MULES | CONEY |
| FAKER | BATED | HAJES | MOLES | |
| FAKED | HATED | HALES | POLES | |
| FAXED | HATES | WALES | COLES | |

**mirror letter**: a letter that is symmetrical in shape and thus reflects the same in a mirror. There are three types: DOUBLE MIRROR LETTERS, HORIZONTAL MIRROR LETTERS, and VERTICAL MIRROR LETTERS.

**mirror word**: a word spelled with MIRROR LETTERS. The three types are discussed under DOUBLE MIRROR WORD, HORIZONTAL MIRROR WORD, VERTICAL MIRROR WORD. Also called "mirror palindrome," "lipogrammatic optical trick."

**mischmasch**: a game in which one player provides a set of two or more letters, and the other player tries to find a word containing those letters in the order given (for example, GP, EMO, and IMSE in MAGPIE, LEMON, and HIMSELF).

GP—MA<u>GP</u>IE
EMO—L<u>EMO</u>N
IMSE—H<u>IMSE</u>LF

**misnomer**: an incorrect name, term, or title of something: the wrong name for the right thing, or the right name for the wrong thing.

GUINEA PIGS: not from Guinea, not pigs
DRESSED CHICKEN: naked and featherless
PEANUT: neither a pea nor a nut
ARABIC NUMERALS: from India, not Arabia
INDIA: not India, but Bharat (official Hindu name)

**mixed cliché**: a phrase or sentence that connects two or more well-known sayings to humorous effect. See JANEISM.

**mocking word**: the second part of a two-part dialogue that mocks the first part. The first speaker asks a question of the second speaker. The second speaker replies with a "mocking word," a statement that both responds to the first speaker's question and exemplifies it.

Will you stop asking rhetorical questions!
How can I when I don't know what "rhetorical" means?

You think everything I say is a joke, don't you?
Ha! Ha! That's a good one.

**modified alphabet**: an alphabet in which letters have been added, subtracted, and/or rearranged. These three modified alphabets are REBUSES of the words that follow them:

ABCDEFGHIJKLTNOPQRSTUVWXYZ = for M, a T = FORMAT
ABCDEFGHIJKLMNOPQRSTUVWXZY = shift Y = SHIFTY
ABCDFGHIJKLMNOPQRTUVWXYZ = no S, E = NOSE

**monetary name**: a first or last name that is also the name of any coin or currency in the world. MARK SCHILLING has both.

| $INGULARS | PLURAL$ |
|---|---|
| Jeng YEN | William MARKS |
| Keith KRONER | Kenneth NICKELS |
| Dianna L. PENNY | Heidi PENCE |

**monoconsonantal word**: a word that uses a single consonant one or more times throughout. There are many short ones, such as those in this sentence: BOB, I'LL SEE IF ANNA MAY GO, TOO. The longest monoconsonantal words, one per consonant, in *Webster's Second* and *Third Unabridged*, may not all be familiar, but they are real:

| | | | |
|---|---|---|---|
| BAOBAB | HOIAH | NONANE | OTTETTO |
| COCCACAEA | AJAJA | PIOUPIOU | VEUVE |
| DIIODIDE | KUKUKUKU | QUAEQUAE | WEEWPW |
| FEOFFEE | ALLELUIA | RIRORIRO | OXEYE |
| GEGGEE | MAMMEE | ASSESSEES | ZOOZOO |

**monosyllabic**: having only one syllable. See ONE-SYLLABLE WORD.

**monosyllabic passage**: a section of writing in which each word has only one syllable. The most famous example appears in Alexander Pope's *Essay on Criticism*:

And ten low words oft creep in one dull line.

**monovocalic**: see UNIVOCALIC.

**Morse all-dot pyramid**: a pyramid made of one to ten dots. Going from top to bottom, the pyramid below decodes to E, I, S, H, HE, HI, ESS, SHE, HIS, ISIS.

```
                .
               . .
              . . .
             . . . .
            . . . . .
           . . . . . .
          . . . . . . .
         . . . . . . . .
        . . . . . . . . .
       . . . . . . . . . .
```

**Morse code square**: a WORD SQUARE that uses the dots and dashes of Morse code to make the letters and the words. Morse code squares omit the spaces between the dots and dashes; thus, the same set of Morse symbols can convert to a different different set of letters. This Morse single-six square has at least two possible alphabetic decodings for each row or column. The first row (and column) can mean DO ( _ .. _ _ _ ) or TEAM ( _ . . _ _ _ ).

| | |
|---|---|
| _ · · _ _ _ | DO or TEAM |
| · _ _ · · · | PI or ADE |
| · _ _ · · _ | AX or WIT |
| _ · · · · _ | BET or TEST |
| _ · · · · · | THE or BEE |
| _ · _ _ · _ | YET or TEMA |

**Morse code**: a code consisting of dots and dashes or long and short sounds for transmitting messages. There are two systems, American Morse code and International code. The former is rarely used anymore. The latter, shown below, has been used in communication and in wordplay.

| | | | |
|---|---|---|---|
| A . - | H . . . . | N - . | U . . - |
| B - . . . | I . . | O - - - | V . . . - |
| C . - . - | J . - - | P . - - . | W . - - |
| D - . . | K - . - | Q - - . - | X - . . - |
| E . | L . - . . | R . - . | Y - . - - |
| F . . - . | M - - | S . . | Z - - . . |
| G - - . | | T - | |

**Morse dot-and-dash halfsquare**: a triangle made of alternating dashes and dots that decode into three sets of words in four directions. Across, left to right: TAR, TENT, TEN, K, N, T. Across, right to left: ART, AET, ETA, R., A, E. Down (and up): TOM, IS, TO, S, M, E.

```
_
_  ·
_  · _
_  · _  ·
_  · _  · _
_  · _  · _  ·
```

**multi-generational kangaroo words**: a KANGAROO WORD with a JOEY that is also a kangaroo word with another joey.

```
DISCLOSURE              FRANGIBLE
   CL   U  E            FRA  GI LE
    C    U  E           FRA     I L
```

**multiple charades**: many short words formed by redividing the letters of a single long word.

DISCRIMINATIONAL = DISC + RIM + IN + AT + ION + AL

**multiple embedded number names**: two or more NUMBER NAMES whose letters appear in correct order in the same host number name. For the numbers under 100, SEVENTY SEVEN has the most—12 number names, counting duplicates.

```
SEVENTY-SEVEN
SEVEN
SEVE          N
SEV       E  N
SEV          EN
SE           VEN
             SEVEN
        T  E  N
        T     EN
SEVENT   E  EN
SEVENTY
```

**multiple joeys**: two or more JOEYS inside a larger word, the KANGAROO WORD.

peRAMBuLatE, perAMBuLatE (joeys = RAMBLE, AMBLE)

**multiple kangaroos**: two or more KANGAROO WORDS that have the same shorter word ( JOEY) inside them.

iLlumInaTed, LighT (joey = LIT)

DEceAseD, DEpArteD, DEActivateD, DEcAyeD, DEcimAteD, DEcApitateD, DesiccAted (joey = DEAD)

**multiple number name transposal**: a word that is a TRANSPOSAL of two or more NUMBER NAMES.

ONE FOUR = FORTUNE        EIGHT TEN = TEETHING

**multiple plurals**: two or more plural forms for the same singular.

OCTOPUS = OCTOPUSES, OCTOPI, OCTOPODES
RHINOCEROS = RHINOCEROSES, RHINOCEROTES, RHINOCERI, RHINOCEROS

**multiple singulars**: two or more singular forms for the same plural.

AX, AXIS = AXES        BASE, BASIS = BASES

**multiple transposals**: three or more words that are TRANSPOSALS of the same group of letters. Transposal groups of three, six, and nine letters, with their respective words, are:

(3) APS = ASP PAS SAP SPA
(4) ADEPRS = DRAPES PADRES PARSED RASPED SPARED SPREAD
(5) ACDEINOTU = AUCTIONED CAUTIONED EDUCATION

**multiplicative numerical tautonym**: a word that splits into three groups of letters with ALPHABETIC VALUES whose sums double from the first to the second group and from the second to the third group.

AIRBUS = AI (1+9), RB (18+2), and US (21+19) = 10, 20, 40

**multipuns**: phrases or sentences whose corresponding words sound alike, but have different spellings and meanings.

SONS RAISE MEAT.        SO BEE, TOO, SEES.
SUN'S RAYS MEET.        SEW "B" TO "C's."
                        SOW, BE TWO SEAS.

**musical letter-to-syllable word**: a word formed by changing each musical letter in another word for the musical syllable that signifies the same note. In CRY, C is a musical letter. Change C to its musical syllable, DO, and CRY = DORY.

ELK = MILK    FIR = FAIR    GO = SOLO    CLODS = DOLORES

**musical syllable**: one of the syllables representing the 12 half-tones of the chromatic scale. In the lists below, the alphabetic notes are followed by their musical syllables, traditionally called "*sol-fa* syllables." The natural tones are more widely known. The syllables are used in various forms of wordplay.

| Naturals | Sharps |
|----------|--------|
| C = DO | C# = DI |
| D = RE | D# = RI |
| E = MI | |
| F = FA | F# = FI |
| G = SOL or SO | G# = SI |
| A = LA | A# = LI |
| B = TI | |

**musical syllable poetry**: verse in which MUSICAL SYLLABLES are concealed in the words. In the following poem, the eight syllables representing the natural notes are linked by the letters spelling the words from ARDOR to ORDER.

**Latvian Lover**

You'd fill me with ardor,
Em, if—as, O Lat, I'd order
A dinner—you'll dine
And drink some fine wine.
But did you take note
Of the music I wrote?

**musical syllable-to-letter word**: a word formed by changing each musical syllable in another word for the musical letter that signifies the same note. In READ, RE is a musical syllable. Change RE to its musical letter, D, and READ = DAD.

MARE—MAD    FLAVOR—FAVOR    GRATIS—GRABS

**mutation**: a TRANSPOSAL of a meaningful word, phrase, or sentence into another meaningful word, phrase, or sentence, which is not related to the first.

> MUTATION = ATOM, UNIT

**mynoreteh**: a reverse HETERONYM.

> SATORI—I ROT AS

**N + seven**: a word-substitution method of writing in which every noun in a text is replaced with the seventh noun following it in a dictionary. Oulipian.

**name anagram**: an ANAGRAM of a proper name of a person, place, institution, etc.

> THE CARNEGIE LIBRARY = Be literary—charge in!
> DANTE GABRIEL ROSSETTI = Greatest idealist born
> THE LEANING TOWER OF PISA = What a foreign stone pile!

**name-meaning duplication**: a combination of first and last names that have the same meanings but different linguistic origins. ROY KING is a real-life example, in which "roy" is Anglo-Norman for "king." Here are a few fictitious names that may be real:

> SYLVIA WOODS          NIGEL BLACK          BONNIE GOOD

**name speller**: a personal name whose letters can spell other personal names. No letter can be used more often than it appears in the name speller. The greatest of all is CAROLINE, which spells at least 74 other names. Here are 24 of CAROLINE's offspring:

> CARL    ALEC    RAE    OLIN    LANCE    IAN    NEIL    EARL

CELIA  ALICE  RON  ORA   LENA    ILONA  NICOLE  ELI
CORA   ARLO   RONA  OREN  LOREN  IRA     NORA    ERICA

**names-to-words lettershift**: a well-known person's first and last names that shift to words. The SHIFT VALUES do not have to be the same for both names.

> A N N A    F R E U D       J O H N    L E N N O N
> B O O B    C O B R A       P U N T    B U D D E D

**narrow letters**: a, c, e, m, n, o, r, s, u, v, w, x, and z, the lowercase letters that have no ascenders or descenders in most standard typefaces.

**narrow word**: a word spelled with all NARROW LETTERS. The word *narrow* itself qualifies, as do these longer words:

> overnervousness            overnumerousnesses

**natural oxymoron**: an OXYMORON created for purposes other than making a contradictory term. The contradiction of the parts is an accidental bonus.

> OLD NEWS       RANDOM ORDER
> PRETTY UGLY    STUDENT TEACHER

**neo-adage**: a new proverb formed by collaging parts of old, well-known proverbs. The following neo-adages were formed by arranging the cardboard tiles of a 1960s game, Izzat So, invented by Bob Worgul. Each tile had a cut-up part of a proverb on it. The upright lines delineate the individual tiles:

> Don't put | a gift horse | in one basket.
> The pen | is mightier than | rotten apples.
> A watched pot | killed the cat.
> If the | shoe fits | there is fire.

**network**: an arrangement of words formed by changing one or more letters in each word to generate the next. The change is determined by one or more wordplay operations. This concept expands on the idea of a WORD LADDER, in which one word becomes another through a series of intermediate steps; at each step, a letter is changed in the current word to form the next word. A network, which can be as involved as finding all the links between the words in a single dictionary, is usually composed of a main network linking most of the words, various limited networks, and a few single words isolated from all the others.

**never seen postmark**: a postmark of a made-up town name and the original state postal abbreviation (before the system now in use) to form a well-known word or phrase. In most cases, the never seen postmark achieves its effect by being spoken aloud.

| FAMERINA DEL | INCOME TEX | B-MINOR MASS |
| HITTER MISS | VITA MINN | OOMPAH PA |

**new merology**: wordplay in which letters are assigned numerical values so that NUMBER NAMES add (or subtract) to the numbers they name. This approach to language has roots in ancient GEMATRIA.

**new punctuation mark**: a punctuation mark formed by combining elements of the punctuation marks currently in use: e.g., the interrobang is a combination of a question mark and a exclamation point. Recent new punctuation marks include the questicomma, the hemiperiod, the rotomation point, the prequasiproquestiperiod, and others.

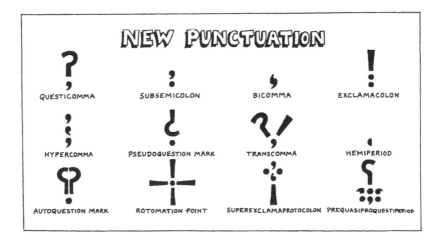

**nine-square**: a WORD SQUARE measuring 9 x 9 letters. The first nine-square was published in 1897:

```
Q U A R E L E S T
U P P E R E S T E
A P P O I N T E R
R E O M E T E R S
E R I E V I L L E
L E N T I L L I N
E S T E L L I N E
S T E R L I N G S
T E R S E N E S S
```

**no-letter poem**: the blank page.

**non-alphabetical order**: any arrangement of the alphabet that doesn't go from A to Z in the traditional way. The result is a SCRAMBLED ALPHABET.

**noncrashing word list**: a set of words in which no letter appears more than once in the same position. In the *Pocket Merriam-Webster's*, a noncrashing word list of 15 six-letter words can be assembled:

| | | |
|---|---|---|
| ASTHMA | GUFFAW | OBLONG |
| BLAZON | HICCUP | SCRUFF |
| CYSTIC | KNOBBY | TOWARD |
| EMBRYO | LENGTH | UPHILL |
| FREEZE | MADDER | WHILST |

**noncrashing word pair**: a pair of words in which no letter occupies the same corresponding position. WORD PAIR is a noncrashing word pair.

```
C O N C E P T U A L I S M     G Y N A E C O M O R P H O U S
E X C E P T I O N A B L Y     D E M U L S I F I C A T I O N
```

**non-overlapping stately word**: a word in which every pair of letters forms a STATE POSTAL ABBREVIATION—the first two letters, the next two, etc. In the word GAME, GA and ME are the abbreviations of Georgia and Maine. (The overlapping middle letters, AM, don't have to form a postal abbreviation.)

CANDID    MEMORIAL    ALKYLAMINE

**nonsense spelling**: spelling that combines letters that usually aren't combined. The poem "The Night That Zrm Elpd the Crfto" contains words with nonsense spelling. Here is the first stanza:

Do you remember avb?
And have you seen the pnf?
They make a lovely jug of wine.
(The avb and pnf are friends of mine.)

See IMAGINARY LANGUAGE.

**nontrivial** (*adj.*): uncommon; significant. A form, example, or problem in WORDPLAY can be nontrivial or TRIVIAL. If it is the only example of a form that is interesting, then it is probably nontrivial. FOUR is the only NUMBER NAME whose numerical value equals the number of letters in its name. It is nontrivial.

**nontrivial transposal**: a TRANSPOSAL in which (1) the words must not be reducible to shorter transposals by removing the same prefix or suffix, and (2) they are not basically interchanged letter sequences. Here are three examples of long nontrivial transposals:

ANTHROPOMORPHIC = CAPTORHINOMORPH
CONTINUEDNESSES = TENDENCIOUSNESS
PRONATIONALISTS = TRANSPOSITIONAL

**non-vicinal**: a word composed of letters, none of which are adjacent in the alphabet. Ironically, VICINAL is a non-vicinal word, but NON-VIC-INAL, with N and O in it, is a VICINAL word.

CAPERINGLY   INTERPENETRATIVELY

**non-vicinal story**: a story composed only of NON-VICINALS. This sentence begins such as story:

Unlyric alto (howler!) vocalizes actively, squealing, squawking and squeaking morceaux in upward octave, as peculiar, drunk clarinet player, certainly reacting, privately quickens, plunges uneasily twice, wrecking carpeting.

**normal word line**: a WORD LINE in which two of the differences between the alphabetic values are 0.

**noun-adjective-adverb-verb matrix**: a table showing the many ways that words can change from one part of speech to another. In the table, the parts of speech in the left column change to the parts of speech in the top row.

For instance, HEAD represents a noun-to-adjective conversion, as in the phrase "head librarian."

|           | Noun  | Adjective  | Adverb    | Verb  |
|-----------|-------|------------|-----------|-------|
| **Noun**      |       | head       | home      | face  |
| **Adjective** | red   |            | well      | muddy |
| **Adverb**    | outs  | in         |           | up    |
| **Verb**      | walk  | transplant | roughshod |       |

**noun of multitude**: a collective noun associated with the specific objects they multiply. Two examples of nouns of multitude for inanimate objects appear below, and some for animate objects appear under ANIMULTITUDE.

   TISSUE OF LIES        CHAPTER OF ACCIDENTS

**no-word alphabet**: a SCRAMBLED ALPHABET in which no words of a specified length can be spelled by selectively reading letters from left to right without repetition. The no-word alphabet below has no four-letter words from the *Pocket Merriam-Webster*.

   HLMNRWBCDFGJKPQTVXZSYEIUAO

**numberdrome 1.** See DIGITAL PALINDROME.
   **2.** See NUMERICAL PALINDROME.

**number grid**: a grid in which NUMBER NAMES are linked together by their letters. The names go horizontally or vertically, and they connect at points where they have the same letter in common. The FIRST grid was the first made:

```
F I R S T           E       S
O     E         S I X T E E N
U     C             G       V
R     O             H       E
T     N     F I F T E E N
T H I R D           E       T
                    E       E
                N I N E T E E N
                        N
```

130

**number lattice**: a NUMBER GRID in which only one letter space separates neighboring lines of letters. This grid uses the same three six-letter NUMBER NAMES across and down:

```
T  W  E  N  T  Y
W     L     W
   E  L  E  V  E  N
   N     V     L
T  W  E  L  V     E
Y     N     E
```

**number name**: one of the words used to signify the counting numbers, e.g., ONE, TWO, NINE TRILLION.

**number-name speller**: a word whose letters can spell a large number of NUMBER NAMES. In each number name, no letter can be used more often than it appears in the name speller. The word INTERCHANGEABILITY spells the names of 11 numbers:

| | | | |
|---|---|---|---|
| THREE | TEN | THIRTY-NINE | NINETY |
| EIGHT | THIRTEEN | EIGHTY | NINETY-EIGHT |
| NINE | THIRTY | EIGHTY-NINE | |

**number-name transaddition**: a word formed by adding one or more letters to a NUMBER NAME and, if necessary, transposing the new set of letters.

NINE + R = INNER     FOURTEEN + CFT = COUNTERFEIT
FIVE + RY = VERIFY   TWENTY + HOOR = NOTEWORTHY

**number-name transposal**: a word that is a TRANSPOSAL of a NUMBER NAME.

ONE—EON     TWO—TOW     THREE—ETHER

**number tree**: a NUMBER GRID in which several NUMBER NAMES are connected to a single number name like branches to a trunk. The number tree below contains terms for children born at the same time to the same mother. The branch names increase in numeric value as they go up the trunk, which has the lowest value.

```
S E X T U P L E T
I
Q U I N T U P L E  T
G
Q U A D R U  P L E T
E
T R I P L E T
O
T W I N
```

**numerical kangaroo**: a word that contains letters in the correct order to spell one or more NUMBER NAMES. At least one number name should have its letters separated by other letters, as a JOEY in a KANGAROO WORD. In these three examples, the first has four different number names using all of its letters; the second has three consecutive number names, and the third has ONE in 16 different combinations in a 16-letter word, including the four combinations shown here.

```
THREONINE        ENLIGHTENED        MONOTONOUSNESSES
THRE     E       E   IGHT           ON              E
    ON  E        N I     NE            O    N        E
       NINE           TEN                  ON      E
  T   E  N                                 O      N    E
```

**numerical near-tautonym**: a word that can be split into three or more parts of the same letter length that have ALPHABETIC VALUE SUMS that increase by 1 or decrease by 1 for each part: e.g., BULLET divides into thirds totaling 23, 24, 25—BU (2 + 21 = 23), LL (12 + 12 = 14), and ET (5 + 20 = 25). In the following two examples, the first has increasing sums and the second has decreasing sums:

> RAKING = RA + KI + NG (19, 20, 21)
> HOMING = HO + MI + NG (23, 22, 21)

**numerical palindrome**: a number whose digits appear the same in both directions. They are much commoner than LETTER-UNIT PALINDROMES. Exactly 100% of all single digit numbers, 10% of all two- and three-digit numbers, and one percent of all four-digit numbers are numerical palindromes. Some numerical palindromes have meaning beyond their numbers:

55 = root beer (*restaurantese*)
343 = first-to-second-to-first double play (*baseball notation*)

Also called "number palindrome," "numberdrome."

**numerical tautonym**: a word that can be split into two or more parts of the same letter length and same ALPHABETIC VALUE SUM. LOVE divides into halves that equal 27 each—LO (12 + 15 = 27) and VE (22 + 5 = 27). Ordinary TAUTONYMS (DODO, PAPA) and PALINDROMES with an even number of letters (DEED, SEES) are trivial cases of numerical tautonyms. In the following nontrivial examples, each word is split into its numerically tautonymic parts. The sum of each part's ALPHABETIC VALUE appears in parentheses.

ANTIDOTE = ANTI + DOTE (43)
NOTION = NO + TI + ON (29)
OVERSECURELY = OVE + RSE + CUR + ELY (42)

**numerical unit**: one of the 49 linguistic units used to spell the NUMBER NAMES used in wordplay. Usually this means the number-names spelling the numbers from 1 to 1000 vigintillion minus 1. They include: ONE to NINE-TEEN (19), the decade number-names from TWENTY to NINETY (8), HUNDRED (1), THOUSAND (1), and the -ILLIONs (20). The number CENTILLION is usually excluded because it is not continuous with the other -ILLIONs.

**numerical wordplay**: wordplay that involves NUMBER NAMES. There are many, many forms. Also called "numerical logology."

**numerical word square**: a WORD SQUARE consisting partly or wholly of numbers. In the square below, ONE and TWO are NUMBER NAMES, and WON is a homophone of ONE. Word squares have used numbers in other ways, too.

T W O
W O N
O N E

**obligatory letter**: a letter that must appear in a text. The obligatory letter may be determined in a variety of ways. In a UNIVOCALIC, the writer decides in advance to use only one vowel throughout the text. In an ANAGRAM, the writer uses all the letters appearing in a given text, but only as often as they occur.

**odd book title**: a real book title that is highly unusual, even inexplicable.

> *New Guinea Tapeworms & Jewish Grandmothers* by Robert S. Desowitz
> *Favorite Flies & Their Histories* by Mary Orvis Marbury
> *How to Cook Husbands* by Elizabeth Strong Worthington

**odd letters**: A, C, E, G, I, K, M, O, Q, S, U, W, and Y, the letters occupying odd-numbered positions in the alphabet.

**odd-letter sentence**: a sentence that uses only ODD-LETTER WORDS.

> Amy says Guy may seek easy wages as a smoky Swiss sea-cook.

**odd-letter word**: a word or name spelled with ODD LETTERS. The second example below is the name of a professional service sorority:

> SEMISUCCESSES    GAMMA SIGMA SIGMA

**odd-numbered letter**: a letter occupying an odd-numbered position in a word or other LETTERSTRING. Odd-numbered letters should not be confused with ODD LETTERS.

**O-invariant**: a UNIVOCALIC with O as the only vowel.

> COMFORTROOTS    CHRONONHOTONTHOLOGOS

**old-style pyramid**: a triangular form in which the lines across spell words and the lines going down the left side, the center vertical, and the right edge also spell words that begin with the top letter. The first was published in 1874.

```
          T
        H E R
      E R A S E
    M I S S I O N
  E N T R E A T E D
```

**onalosi**: a word that can form another word by changing any one of its letters to another letter. This term is used to show its contrasting relationship with ISOLANOS; otherwise, it means the same as FRIENDLY WORD.

  SHORE =   CHORE   STORE   SHARE   SHONE   SHORT

**one-consonant word**: a word having a single consonant and one or more vowels. The challenge is to find the longest such word, which would have many vowels.

  EUAEMIA          EOOAIGEE          UAIUAI-LOI

Compare to MONOCONSONANTAL WORD.

**one-cycle word**: a word whose letters appear in alphabetic order within a single 26-letter cycle in the CIRCULAR ALPHABET. A cycle is considered to start with the first letter of the word and to end with the letter that is 25 steps further along the alphabet, wrapping around from Z to A. For the word TWINS, the cycle would go from T to S, ass shown below. Three other one-cycle words appear below:

```
s
TUVWXYZABCDEFGHIJKLMNOPQR S
T   W           I   N     S
```

BEGORRA      GLOSSAE      SUBFLOOR

**one-letter liporebus:** a REBUS that uses as its clue the alphabet with one letter missing.

  ABCDFGHIJKLMNOPQRSTUVWXYZ = cute (cut E)
  ABCDEFGHIJKLMNOPQRSUVWXYZ = tout (T out)

**one-letter palindrome**: each letter of the alphabet.

**one-letter poem**: a single letter considered as a poem. In 1972, Joyce Holland published *Alphabet Anthology*, which gathered 104 one-letter poems from as many poets. In the index, she listed the totals of the individual letters chosen by contributors as their poems. The most popular was "O." No one submitted "C."

**one-move Scrabble™ score**: the highest score that can be made in a single move in Scrabble™. The move, scoring 1,962 points, was devised in order to see how high a player could score under optimum conditions.

**one-switch reversal**: a REVERSAL in which two letters occupying symmetric positions in a word trade places to form another word.

DRAT = DART     DEIFIER = REIFIED     SNOOPS = SPOONS

**one-syllable word**: a word that has just one syllable. There are lots of short ones, like the ones in this line. Longer spellings usually generate additional syllables. STRENGTHS is a common word with nine letters. Here are some of the longer, more colorful one-syllable words:

SCREETCHED     SPRAUNCHED     STROOTCHED
SCROANCHED     SQUAWTCHED     SPLEEATCHED

**one-to-one triplet**: a TRIPLET that builds up from a single-letter word to a target word and returns to a different single-letter word.

A
AN
RAN
RAIN
TRAIN
STRAIN
ESTRAIN
RESTRAIN
RESTRAINS
RESTAINS
RESTAIN
RETAIN
RETIN
REIN
RIN
IN
I

**one-word anagram**: a word that is an anagram of another word. The two are related in meaning. See ANAGRAM for more discussion.

| | |
|---|---|
| ANGERED = ENRAGED | RAISE = ARISE |
| APT = PAT | SHRUB = BRUSH |
| EVIL = VILE | TAP = PAT |
| MARS = ARMS | TONE = NOTE |

**one-word celebrity anagram**: a single word that is an ANAGRAM of the first and last name of a famous person.

GERMANY = MEG RYAN
COSTUMIER = TOM CRUISE
ASCERTAINS = ISAAC STERN
WATERFALLS = FATS WALLER
NARCOLEPTIC = ERIC CLAPTON

**one-word pangram**: a word having all 26 letters in it. Each letter appears only once. Such a real word is impossible to find, but a word was created to show how it could happen. The word appears at the conclusion of a story about a psychiatric patient with a compulsion to speak only in PANGRAMS. The three doctors and two people assistants name the problem after themselves, calling it "HJELMQVIST-GRYB-ZOCK-PFUND-WAX Syndrome."

**one-word poem**: a single word, real or made up, presented as a poem. In the 1960s, Aram Saroyan wrote the first one-word poems. His poem "lighght" won an $800 prize. In the 1970s, Joyce Holland published *Matchbook*, a magazine of one-inch-square pages stapled inside fully functioning matchbooks. Each issue had nine one-word poems by nine different poets. Here are a dozen one-word poems that appeared in various issues of the magazine:

| | | |
|---|---|---|
| anagramarama | monther | underwhere |
| cerealism | psychasm | whirrrrred |
| electrizzzzz | sixamtoninepm | zoombie |
| hairanoia | tictactile | whhavyagotthasgudtareedare |

**one-word sentence**: a sentence composed of one word. The story "Jack Gets Laid Off" consists of one-word sentences only, beginning with this paragraph:

Wake. Yawn. Stretch. Wash. Dress. Eat. Drink. Leave. Drive. Stop. Go. Stop. Wait. Wait. "Damn!" "HONK!" Accelerate. Pass. "Idiot!" Decelerate. Signal. Turn. Enter. Park. "Slam!" Walk. Climb. Open. Enter. Close. Walk.

**onomastics**: the wordplay of names of all types—personal names, product names, animal names, NUMBER NAMES, chemical names, business names, geographical names, and any other names for members of a real or a conceptual set. Onomastics can involve most, if not all, forms of wordplay—ACROSTICS, ANAGRAMS, PALINDROMES, WORD SQUARES, etc.

The appearance of a name in a wordplay form may or may not make it a good example of onomastics. "DENNIS AND EDNA SINNED" is usually thought of as simply a palindrome, but since it has two names in it, it can also be considered a palindrome in the field of onomastics. Palindromes written to intentionally include names, such as the names of the American presidents, are primary examples of onomastics.

Number names have generated a large amount and variety of new wordplay forms, too. NUMERICAL WORDPLAY, a category of onomastics, has grown to become a major field in its own right.

**ooglification**: the substitution of an OO-sound for another vowel sound to convert a non-slang word into a slang word, or to make a slang word even slangier.

| | |
|---|---|
| SKEDADDLE = SKEDOODLE | GOGGLE = GOOGLE |
| CIGARETTE = CIGAROOT | GUZZLE = GOOZLE |
| DIDDLE = DOODLE | SNOUT = SNOOT |

**opinion oxymoron**: a phrase that may or may not be an OXYMORON, depending on how its parts are interpreted. Its oxymoronic quality depends on the reader's or viewer's beliefs. For instance, BUSINESS ETHICS is an oxymoron only if business and ethics are considered contradictory terms. The opinion oxymoron makes an editorial statement.

| | |
|---|---|
| EDUCATIONAL TELEVISION | IRANIAN MODERATE |
| MILITARY INTELLIGENCE | MORAL MAJORITY |

**orthinology**: word botching—that is, making errors in pronunciation that result in different words with different meanings than the speaker intended. The term is a SPOONERISM of the word *ornithology*. Reverend Spooner received the first honorary degree in orthinology.

**OS-graph**: a word graph based on a pavement composed of alternating octahedrons and squares.

**OUGH**: the combination of letters can be pronounced in seven different ways. The couplet below has all seven OUGHs (O, UFF, OFF, UP, OW, OO, OCK):

> THOUGH the TOUGH COUGH and HICCOUGH PLOUGH me
>     THROUGH,
> O'er life's dark LOUGH my course I still pursue.

**Ouija word**: a word or name that splits apart CHARADE-fashion to produce shorter words that have the same meaning in different languages. *Ouija,* the name of the fortunetelling board, was chosen as the name of the term because it is a Ouija word—OUI (yes) in French is JA in German. These Ouija words use English, French, Latin, Portuguese, and Spanish:

| | | |
|---|---|---|
| ANDY = AND, Y | LATHE = LA, THE | THEO = THE, O |
| YET = Y, ET | HEEL = HE, EL | MIME = MI, ME |
| ORO = OR, O | LETHE = LE, THE | TOAD = TO, AD |

**overlapping stately word**: a word in which every two adjacent letters form a STATE POSTAL ABBREVIATION—letters 1 and 2, letters 2 and 3, etc. For example, in MARINE, MA, AR, RI, IN, and NE all form abbreviations (Massachusetts, Arkansas, Rhode Island, Indiana, and Nebraska). Each abbreviation overlaps the next by one letter.

> CAR     FLAKY     MALARIAL

**overlapping word**: a word formed by connecting the letters ending a person's first name and beginning the last name. See HIDDEN MIDDLE NAME.

> Ez<u>ra P</u>ound          Horatio <u>Ne</u>lson

**oxymoron** (pl., **oxymora**): a figure of speech in which two incongruous, contradictory terms are linked together. OXYMORON is an oxymoron in its own right. It comes from two Greek roots with opposite meanings—*oxys* ("sharp, keen") and *moros* ("foolish"). The best-known American oxymoron is probably the well-known seafood restaurant offering, JUMBO SHRIMP. Oxymora can be divided into three general types: the LITERARY OXYMORON, the NATURAL OXYMORON, and the OPINION OXYMORON.

**oxymoronic** (*adj.*): being an OXYMORON; having the quality of an oxymoron.

**pack** (*v.*): to squeeze letters into a grid as densely as possible to spell words.

**padlock**: a word formed by taking two words, one of which has ending letters that match the beginning letters of the other, dropping those letters, and sliding the leftover letters together.

NOR<u>THER</u> + <u>THER</u>MAL = NORMAL

**pairagram**: a two-word phrase or sentence in which each word is an ANAGRAM of the other.

ACTORS CO-STAR.          MARRIED ADMIRER
AMERICAN CINERAMA        SCAT, CATS!
ELVIS LIVES.             VETO VOTE

**paired-key word**: a word spelled using two telephone KEYS. In these examples, the digits of the two keys are listed in parentheses.

DEFACED (2, 3)   HOGGING (4, 6)   MOMMY (6, 9)
DEMON (3, 6)     LULL (5, 8)      SUSURRUS (7, 8)

**pair isogram**: a word in which each letter occurs twice. The two examples on the left have no special pattern, but the two on the right use all their letters in the first half of the word and repeat them in a different order in the second half:

ARRAIGNING          HORSESHOER
TROMOMETER          INTESTINES

Also called "diplogram." See ISOGRAM.

140

**palindddrome challenge**: the challenge of constructing a PALINDROME having three or more of the same letter at the PIVOTAL POINT. The palindrome should make sense and should exclude initials, odd spellings, strange contractions, etc.

> Warts e<u>bb</u> <u>b</u>est raw.
> Ron, o<u>dd</u> <u>d</u>onor.
> Evade w<u>ee</u> <u>e</u>we, Dave.
> We peer far o<u>ff</u> <u>f</u>or a free pew.
> No rad<u>ii</u>: <u>I</u>, <u>I</u>da, Ron.
> Bu<u>tt</u> <u>t</u>ub.

**palindromania**: **1.** the compulsion to write PALINDROMES.
    **2.** the sense of order found in palindromes.

**palindrome**: a word, phrase, sentence, or other text that spells the same in both directions, such as EVE (word), SEX OF FOXES (phrase), or MADAM, I'M ADAM (sentence).

This ancient and popular form of wordplay was invented in the third century B.C. by Sotades of Maronia (in Thrace). Sotades wrote palindromic poetry satirizing the government. Angered at the satire, Ptolemy II of Philadelphius had Sotades captured, sealed in a chest of lead, and heaved into the sea. The following palindrome represents his last words as he flew through the air:

No sign? Is Sotades' sap won? I—no! I to Maronia? Ptolemy by me? Lot . . . pain . . . or a motion I now passed? A tossing is on.

In English, only a few common words are palindromes, most of which are three to seven letters in length:

| | | | | |
|---|---|---|---|---|
| BOB | BOOB | KAYAK | DENNED | DEIFIED |
| GAG | NOON | REFER | HANNAH | REPAPER |
| MUM | PEEP | SEXES | REDDER | REVIVER |

As word length increases, palindromic words become more difficult to find. Three of the longest are:

MAYALAYAM        SEMITIMES        KINNIKINNIK

The first palindomic sentence in English is credited to John Taylor (1580-1653). It uses an acceptable seventeenth-century spelling of DWELL, and an ampersand:

> Lewd did I live & evil I did dwel.

In the twentieth century, palindromes have proliferated. Eight modern classics appear below. Many authorities regard the first one, by Leigh Mercer, as the finest ever written.

> A man, a plan, a canal: Panama!
> A slut nixes sex in Tulsa.
> Able was I ere I saw Elba.
> Doc, note, I dissent. A fast never prevents a fatness. I diet on cod.
> "Miry rim! So many daffodils," Delia wailed, "slid off a dynamo's miry rim!"
> Red rum, sir, is murder.
> Sit on a potato pan, Otis.
> Straw? No, too stupid a fad. I put soot on warts.

Also called "adreverbum," "anacyclic" (from the French *anacyclique*), "bicephalous phrase," "bifrontal" (from the Italian *bifronte*), "cancrine verse," "carcinoi" ("crabs"), "'drome" (British), "inversion," "pal" (American), "P/D" (British), "PD verse," "reciprocal," "Sotadean phrase," "Sotadean verse," "Sotadic," "versus anacyclici," "versus diabolici," and "versus echoici."

**palindrome pair**: a pair of words that form a palindrome. A palindrome pair can be a DROP-LETTER REVERSAL with its baseword, an INTERNAL PALINDROME with another word, or a REVERSAL PAIR.

> DESSERTS-STRESSED (reversal pair)
> DRAWN-ONWARD (drop-letter reversal with its baseword)
> EMIT-NOONTIME (internal palindrome with another word)

**palindromic** (*adj.*): having the form of a PALINDROME; that is, composed of letters or other units that read the same in both directions.

**palindromic dialogue**: a dialogue in which the characters speak in PALINDROMES. "In Eden, I" is a conversation between Adam and Eve meeting each other for the first time. It begins:

> ADAM: Madam—
> EVE: Oh, who—

ADAM: [No girl-rig on!]
EVE: Heh?
ADAM: Madam, I'm Adam.
EVE: Name of a foeman?
ADAM: O, stone me! Not so.
Eve: Mad! A maid I am, Adam.

**palindromic double square**: a PALINDROMIC SQUARE with one set of words going across and another set going down.

D A B
E V E
B A D

**palindromic initials**: letters that appear in the same order in both directions and that stand for phrases, names of companies, or other things. AMA, SOS, and TNT are three short, well-known examples. These three longer examples are accompanied by their words:

APBPA = Association of Professional Ball Players of America
HMHMH = His Majesty's Household Master of the Horse
MADDAM = Macromodule and digital differential analyzer machine

**palindromic interview**: a dialogue in which the interviewer asks questions in normal sentences, and the interviewee answers in PALINDROMIC SENTENCES. In the dialogue below, the interviewee collects cars and speaks PALINDROMES with the cars' names in them. Here are the first four question-and-answer exchanges:

Q: Hello. You've owned every make of car, haven't you?
A: I had no Honda. Hi!
Q: Which car is the jewel of your collection?
A: A gem? Omega.
Q: But which do you like above all others?
A: Er, a love? Volare
Q: Is there any type of driver you really dislike?
A: Ah, an ass in a Nissan—aha!

**palindromic ladder**: a WORD LADDER whose words, written in a single line, make a PALINDROME. Each word is a REVERSAL of the word equidistant from the middle of the ladder.

```
TRAM
TRAP
TROP
TROT
TOOT
TORT
PORT
PART
MART
```

= TRAM-TRAP-TROP-TROT-TOOT-TORT-PORT-PART-MART

**palindromic name**: an individual's name whose letters read the same in both directions. There are different ways to represent a name in order to make it a PALINDROME. The following examples were invented, but some have since surfaced in telephone directories:

| | |
|---|---|
| MARY BYRAM | Q.S. EGG, ESQ. |
| MARY BELLE BYRAM | GREGORY, ROGER G. |
| N.A. GAHAGAN | REMARKABLE ELBA KRAMER |

**palindromic novel**: a novel that is a PALINDROME from the first letter to the last. The only palindromic novel is *Dr. Awkward in Oslo*, written by Lawrence Levine and published in mimeograph form. It is 31,954 words long.

**palindromic palindrome**: a sentence that is a PALINDROME composed of words that are palindromes. See WORD-UNIT PALINDROME.

Bob sees Nan; Nan sees Bob.

**palindromic pangram**: see PANGRAMMATIC PALINDROME. The first discussion of this form uses the two terms in two successive sentences: ". . . An example of a pangrammatic palindrome can be found in the works of the strange Edwin Fitzpatrick. It will be noted, however, that Fitzpatrick's palindromic pangram. . . ."

**palindromic pattern**: a PALINDROMIC WORD printed in the shape of a square, a diamond, or another form using letters over and over. The word can be traced in different ways by starting at any letter, moving horizontally, vertically, or diagonally to an adjacent letter, and continuing for each successive letter without using the same letter over. The question is, how many different ways can the word be traced? CIVIC can be traced 848 ways in this palindromic pattern:

```
C C C C C
C I I I C
C I V I C
C I I I C
C C C C C
```

**palindromic play**: see PALINDROMIC DIALOGUE.

**palindromic poem**: a poem that is a PALINDROME, that consists of palindromes, or that uses palindromes in some way. Also called "palindrome poem."

**palindromic poetry**: poetry that uses PALINDROMES. In some poems, a single line is a palindrome; in others, each line is a separate palindrome; and in still others, the entire poem, from start to finish, is a palindrome.

**palindromic pun**: a word that sounds like another word, each of which is a PALINDROME in its own right. In these two examples, the first pair of words have no letters in common, and the second pair of words have all letters in common.

I—EYE          ANA—ANNA

**palindromic pyramid**: a set of palindromic words that form a pyramid pattern when written down the page from shortest word to longest. The words are generated by successively removing letters from both ends of the longest word.

| D | TT | PAP |
|---|----|-----|
| ADA | OTTO | REPAPER |
| MADAM | TOTTOT | REREPAPERER |

**palindromic reversal**: 1. a COMPOUND PALINDROME whose parts can switch places to form a new compound palindrome.

PEEPEYE
EYE—PEEP

**2.** a REVERSAL PAIR whose different halves can be spliced together to form a single PALINDROMIC WORD.

```
HAR—HAR
                      =    HARRAH
RAH—RAH
```

**palindromic sentence**: a sentence that is a PALINDROME.

**palindromic single square**: a PALINDROMIC SQUARE with the same set of words going across and down.

```
E  T  A
T  O  T
A  T  E
```

**palindromic slide rule**: a device for making ten thousand PALINDROMES. It works by using eight lists of words, four of which are REVERSALS of the other four. They are printed on four pieces of card stock that are placed one on top of the other. When the cards are moved up and down, the words line up both grammatically and palindromically. Here are three examples:

> Edit deer. Mad pals slap dam, reed tide.
> Spot rail. Straw bats stab warts, liar spot.
> Nab part. Ten paws swap net, trap ban.

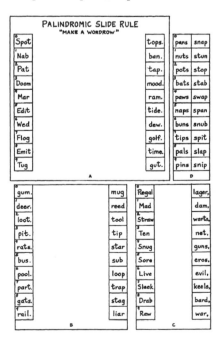

**palindromic square**: a WORD SQUARE composed of words that form a PALINDROME when written in a single line. In 1871, Nellie Jones published the first palindromic square in English. It forms the following palindrome: STEW-TIDE-EDIT-WETS. Hers is a SINGLE SQUARE.

```
S T E W
T I D E
E D I T
W E T S
```

**palindromic tautonymic monoliteral square**: a WORD SQUARE made with the same word spelled with the same letter repeated throughout. The ten-square on the left is univocalic, and the four-square on the right is monoconsonantal. (O-O-O-O-O-O-O-O-O-O represents the cry of the zebra, from *The Last Journals of David Livingstone* (1874). ZZZZ means "to snore," from *The American Thesaurus of Slang*, second edition.

```
O O O O O O O O O O          Z Z Z Z
O O O O O O O O O O          Z Z Z Z
O O O O O O O O O O          Z Z Z Z
O O O O O O O O O O          Z Z Z Z
O O O O O O O O O O
O O O O O O O O O O
O O O O O O O O O O
O O O O O O O O O O
O O O O O O O O O O
O O O O O O O O O O
```

Also called "total palindromic single square."

**palindromic word**: a word that is a PALINDROME. The term "palindrome" used alone can signify a palindromic word.

**palindromist**: a person who writes PALINDROMES.

**Panama parody**: a take-off on Leigh Mercer's famous PALINDROME, A MAN, A PLAN, A CANAL: PANAMA! There are dozens of Panama parodies, making it the most parodied palindrome of all. Here are three that end in the word PANAMA:

> A man, a pallid dill, a Panama.
> A man, a petal, a parade, cedar, a palate—Panama.
> A man, a post, a fare, salad, a laser, a fatso—Panama.

The next three are from a set of 26 Panama parodies. Each concludes in a word beginning with a different letter, and each uses only A's for vowels.

A cab, a tag, a gat: abaca!
A tal, a bag, a Maga: balata!
A lab, a crab, a bar: cabala!

**pangram**: **1.** a sentence in which all 26 letters of the alphabet appear at least once apiece. The goal is to create a perfect pangram, one with normal grammar, common dictionary words, reasonable meaning, and only 26 letters. In 1872, Augustus de Morgan introduced the concept, under the title "Cabala Alphabetica" in his book *Budget of Paradoxes*, and he published the first one:

I, quartz pyx, who fling muck beds.

This landmark line has only 26 letters, but it uses an extra I and U and omits J and V. At that time, those extra letters were considered to be interchangeable with the missing letters: I could be used for J, and U could be used for V. This practice, however, is no longer followed today.

The best-known pangrammatic sentence is a typing exercise, but it uses 35 letters instead of 26:

The quick, brown fox jumps over the lazy dog.

The following high-quality pangrams work in different ways to include all the letters:

Waltz, nymph, for quick jigs vex Bud. (Extra letters)
Mr. Jock, TV quiz Ph.D., bags few lynx. (Abbreviations)
Cwm, fjord-bank glyphs vext quiz. (Obscure words)

Some pangrams have won fame by appearing in *The Guinness Book of Records*, including these two:

Jackdaws love my big sphinx of quartz.
Veldt jynx grimps waqf zho buck.

Since de Morgan introduced the concept, others have invented a wide variety of pangrammatic forms.

**2.** a group of words using all 26 letters once each. In this generalization of the original meaning of pangram (see above), the words don't have to relate in any way. They are simply members of a list.

In the early 1960s, Dennis Ritchie of Bell Telephone Laboratories programmed a computer to compose pangrams. His word stock was an Air Force tape of entries from *Webster's Second Unabridged*. This first experiment in computer wordplay resulted in 3,330 pangrams, including the following three:

> JAB QOPH VEX BLINTZ FARD SKY CWM
> FJELD QURSH VAT ZIG PYX KNOB CWM
> JUNK QOPH VEX BLINTZ FRY DUSK CWM

**pangrammatic** (*adj.*): containing all 26 letters of the alphabet.

**pangrammatic crossword**: a PANGRAM (second meaning) arranged so that the words appear horizontally and vertically as in a CROSSWORD PUZZLE.

```
    Q           V
J U G       W A X
  I     B   S
  C R Y P T
  K         L
F E Z       O H M
  N         D
```

**pangrammatic highway**: a stretch of highway in which the permanent official road signs have all the letters of the alphabet appearing alone or in words. The goal is to find the alphabet in the shortest distance. This set of signs appeared in a .8-mile stretch on the northbound lane of Interstate 287:

> WASHINGTON'S HEADQUARTERS
> NO TRUCKS IN LEFT LANE
> LAFAYETTE AVE.
> EXIT 20 MPH
> BRIDGE FREEZES BEFORE ROAD SURFACE
> INTERSTATE NEW JERSEY 287

**pangrammatic ladder**: a WORD LADDER that contains at least one of every letter of the alphabet. See MINIMUM-LENGTH PANGRAMMATIC LADDER.

**pangrammatic palindrome**: a PALINDROME that uses all 26 letters. The shortest possible would be 51 letters long. Each letter would appear twice except for the center letter. The first pangrammatic palindrome uses 77 letters:

> Oh, wet Alex—a jar, a fag!
> Up, disk, curve by!

Man Oz, Iraq, Arizona, my Bev?
Ruck's id-pug—a far Ajax—elate?
Who?

See PALINDROMIC PANGRAM.

**pangrammatic poetry**: verse that uses all 26 letters in one way or another. Some pangrammatic poems have the letters scattered throughout their lines. In the following quatrain, the lines have an *abab* rhyme scheme, and each line is a 32-letter pangram using the consonants once and the vowels twice.

> Why jog, exquisite bulk, fond crazy vamp,
> Daft buxom jonquil, zephyr's gawky vice?
> Guy fed by work, quiz Jove's xanthic lamp—
> Zow! Qualms by deja vu gyp fox-kin thrice.

Also called "all-alphabet poetry," "pangrammatic rubai," and "pangrammatic verse."

**pangrammatic rebus**: a REBUS using all the letters of the alphabet in any order so that they sound like the words of a sentence. In this pangrammatic rebus, the Z is pronounced by its less-used name "zed."

> O, LN, PJ, IV FEG, W R! MT SA! Y? U C H DK; B XQZ!
> O Ellen, pea jay, ivy effigy, double you are! Empty assay! Why? You see age decay; be excused!

**pangrammatic rebus poem**: a REBUS in the form of a poem using all the letters in alphabetic order. The sounds have to be interpreted as words instead of letters. In this poem, the even-numbered lines rhyme with E.

| **ABC** | **Eh, Bees See** |
| --- | --- |
| ABCD | Abie's seedy. |
| EFG | He hefts—gee!— |
| HIJKL | Age. I, Jake, a hell, |
| MNOP | Am in no pea. |
| QRS | Cue or rest? |
| TUV | Tea? You? Fee |
| WX | Double? You hex, |
| YZ | Wise sea. |

**pangrammatic window**: a segment of published text that unintentionally contains all 26 letters. Windows of 100 letters or fewer are fairly scarce. The shortest discovered so far is a 67-letter sentence found on p. 217 of Sarah Grand's *The Beth Book* (1897). The pangrammatic window appears within the brackets:

> It was an e[xquisitely blue just then, with filmy white clouds drawn up over it like gauz]e.

The shortest found in a classical poem is this 76-letter window in Book I of Milton's *Paradise Lost*:

> Likening his Maker to the gra[zed ox,
> Jehovah, who, in one night, when he passed
> From Egypt marching, equaled with one stroke
> B]oth her first-born and all her bleating gods.

Also called "natural pangrammatic sentence," and "panalphabetic window."

**panoramic number name**: a NUMBER NAME in which the letters also spell ONE through NINE. The examples below show two different ways this can happen. In the first, the letters spelling one number can be reused to spell another; in the second, they cannot. Uppercase indicates letters that are used in spelling the numbers:

EIGHTy-FIVE THOUsaNd SIX huNdREd SEVENty-TWO
EIGHTy-FIVE SEpTENdecIlliON TWELVE THOusaND SIX hundred FOURtEEN
(NINE has to be spelled with N and I in SEPTENDECILLION, N in HUN-DRED, and E in FOURTEEN. TEN has to be spelled with TE in SEP-TENDECILLION and N in FOURTEEN.)

**paratransposition**: a word formed by taking another word, replacing one letter in it with the letter immediately before or after it in the alphabet, and rearranging the resulting letters (e.g., EARTH—EARSH—SHARE). The paratransposition was designed to be a more challenging variation of the SUB-STITUTE-LETTER TRANSPOSAL, which allows any replacement letter. These paratranspositions change different kinds of names to words:

| | |
|---|---|
| MARS—TRAM | CARTER—REACTS |
| SEPTEMBER—PERMEATES | TEXAS—WASTE |
| ROOSEVELT—OVERSLEPT | MONDAY—YEOMAN |

On rare occasions, a paratransposition pair consists of closely related words or names:

Also called "minimum substitute-letter transposal."

**parody**: an imitation of a work or style of art. It is usually a humorous, even satirical, form of literary, cultural, or social criticism. Sometimes the parodist creates in admiration of the original work, and sometimes in contempt. Perhaps for both reasons, "A Visit from St. Nicholas" is the most parodied poem in the English language. In wordplay, parody has an additional purpose: to see what the result would be if a poem or a story were written in a specific wordplay form. Could "Mary Had a Little Lamb" be written without using the letter E? Could Poe's "The Raven" be written in one-syllable words? Yes, and here is how they would begin:

> Mary had a tiny lamb,
>   Its wool was pallid as snow,
> And everywhere that Mary did walk
>   This lamb would always go.

> Once at twelve on one night's drear, 'twas while I, weak and tired, thought
>     here
> On the words in lots of quaint and odd old tomes of mind's lost lore,
> While I dozed, so near a nap, there came but then a soft, quick tap,
> As of one who made a rap, a rap at my front room's closed door,
> "'tis some guest," I spoke, voice low, "who taps at my front room's closed
>     door,
>     Oh just this and not much more."

**parody pangram**: a PANGRAM that is a take-off on a famous pangram. Here is a 26-letter parody of "The quick brown fox jumps over the lazy dog," followed by an interlinear translation of its words, which appear in the *OED*:

> QWYK GLAZ'D VOX JUMPS FERN    BITCH.
> Quick  brown   fox  jumps  ancient  female dog.

**paronomasia**: the art or practice of punning. See PUN.

**partial lettershifts**: words of unequal length that are lettershifts of each other. The shorter word shifts an equal number of steps to a string of consecutive letters in the longer word.

> F R I E N D     . G O O D .      D A Y . .
> . . . F O E     S W E E T S      L I G H T

```
S A D  .  .  .        M O D E L         H O N E Y
. B E I N G          . S H I P         N U T  .  .
E M P T Y  .          .  . T U B        . B A R  .
```

**partially overlapping word group**: a group of words in which every word has exactly one letter in common with every other word, and each letter pair appears in exactly one word. In mathematics, such groups are called "finite projective geometries." The letters ABDEORY form this group:

ADO  ORE  BAR  BOY  YEA  BED  DRY

**partition**: one of two or more mutually exclusive subsets of the alphabet. The letters can be rearranged in any way before dividing them. The purpose is to find PURE WORDS, whose letters fall within a single partition. In the first example below, the alphabet is halved; and in the second, it is divided by the number of Morse dots and dashes (1–4) that represent each letter:

ABCDEFGHIJKLM / NOPQRSTUVWXYZ

ET / AIMN / DGKORSUW / BCFHJLPQVXYZ

**pasquinade**: satirical writing.

**patriotic number**: a number whose NUMBER NAME has USA in it as an unbroken string. Exactly 99.9 percent of all number names are patriotic since they have THO<u>USA</u>ND in them.

**pavement**: the surface of a WORD GRAPH. A pavement is divided into specific geometric shapes in which letters can be placed.

**pencil-and-paper game**: any game or challenge that doesn't involve a board or pieces, just a paper and pencil. The game can be competitive, involving two or more players, or it can be solitaire.

**pentagram**: a set of five letters considered as a single, fixed unit. There are 94,137,056 pentagrams, from AAAAA, AAAAB, AAAAC, . . . to ZZZZX, ZZZZY, ZZZZZ.

**perfect anagrams**: 1. words that are ANAGRAMS of each other and that include at least as many anagrams as there are letters in each word.

**2.** words that are perfect ANAGRAMS as above, but that have the additional requirement that each different letter begins one word (or more).

> ROSE-ROES-ORES-SORE-EROS
> SMITE-MITES-ITEMS-TIMES-EMITS

**perfect palindrome**: a PALINDROMIC SENTENCE composed entirely of palindromic and reversal words. The "Elba" palindrome (Able was I ere I saw Elba) is perfect. ABLE-ELBA and WAS-SAW are REVERSAL PAIRS; I and ERE are palindromes.

**permutable palindrome**: a PALINDROME whose letters can be rearranged to spell another word or set of words. There are four different kinds:

> REFER—FREER (palindrome to non-palindrome)
> TOOT—OTTO (palindrome to palindrome)
> TOOT—TOTO (palindrome to TAUTONYM)
> ANNA—ANAN, NANA (palindrome to REVERSAL PAIR)

**permutation**: an arrangement of a set of different letters without regard for meaning. For a word of $n$ different letters, there are $n!$ permutations. That is, for 2 letters there are 2 permutations, for 3 letters there are 6 permutations, for 4 letters there are 24 permutations, and so on.

**permutation-containing word**: a word (or name) containing all the PERMUTATIONS of a set of letters. Each permutation's letters occur in order within the word, but not necessarily adjacent. For example, all 24 permutations of EGOR, including the four below, appear in the name GEORGE O. GREGORY:

> EORG = GEORGE O. GREGORY
> OGRE = GEORGE O. GREGORY
> GROE = GEORGE O. GREGORY
> REGO = GEORGE O. GREGORY

**permute** (*v.*): to rearrange a set of letters.

**perverse**: see NEO-ADAGE.

**-phobia word:** a word ending in the suffix -PHOBIA, meaning "fear." TRISKADEKAPHOBIA is "fear of the number thirteen." Here are 13 more phobia words, each followed by the thing feared:

ALEKTOROPHOBIA: chickens
BAROPHOBIA: gravity
CHRONOPHOBIA: time
DEXTROPHOBIA: things to the right
GELOPHOBIA: laughter
HEDONOPHOBIA: pleasure
IDEOPHOBIA: ideas
LINONOPHOBIA: string
METROPHOBIA: poetry
ODONTOPHOBIA: teeth
PHILOPHOBIA: love
SIDEROPHOBIA: stars
VESTIOPHOBIA: clothing

**phonetically palindromic sentence:** a sentence that sounds the same when read forwards and backwards.

Madam, I'm Adam.
Did we say you are dead, Bob? Ahaha, Bob, dead, are you? Yes, we did.

**phonetically reversible word:** a word that sounds the same read forewords and backwards.

BABE          KNOWN

**phonetically reversible word pair:** a pair of words, each of which sounds like the other read in reverse. One of the most surprising pairs is WE—YOU.

TEA—EAT          STAR—ARTS          BUT—TUB

**phonetic beheadment:** a form of BEHEADMENT in which the first sound of a word is removed to create a second word.

BASALT—ASSAULT

**phonetic charade:** a form of CHARADE in which the pronunciation remains the same, though the spelling may change.

HAYSTACKS—HASTE, AXE

**phonetic curtailment:** a form of CURTAILMENT in which the last letter of a word or phrase is removed to create a second word or phrase.

CUTE—QUEUE

**phonetic palindrome**: a PALINDROME that sounds the same, but isn't necessarily spelled the same, in both directions.

**phonetic rebus**: a LETTER REBUS that must be sounded out to form a message that reveals the hidden letter. CASEIN means K because it sounds like K SEEN.

> AVOWAL = A VOWEL
> BLACK EYE = BLACK I
> ANNEX = AN X

**phonetic reversal**: a word formed by reversing the units of sound in another word. Sometimes the words have all the letters reversed as well, (MUG=GUM), but not always (TOE=OAT).

> SCOOPS—SPOOKS
> FLESHPOT—TOP-SHELF
> NOWHERE—EREWHON (title of novel by Samuel Butler)

Also called "unit reversal." See PHONETICALLY REVERSIBLE WORD PAIR.

**phonetic terminal deletion**: a form of TERMINAL DELETION in which a word or phrase is changed to another by removing its first and last sounds.

> KWACHA—WATCH

**Phonetic Word Wheel**: a nonsense generator published by Milton Bradley in 1948. It consists of moveable wheels and a pointer. Letters and syllables were printed on the wheels so that when they lined up, they fit together to make real words and nonsense words. According to the instructions, "Drill in nonsense syllables is valuable for older students." Such a device provides an alternative way to explore the possibilities of the English language in creative writing and wordplay.

**phonigmatic rebus**: a combination PHONETIC and ENIGMATIC REBUS.

**phrase pyramid**: a PYRAMID that contains phrases as well as words.

**piano letters**: A, B, C, D, E, F, and G, the letters signifying the musical notes that can be played on a piano (and on other instruments). The term refers to those letters when they spell words, called PIANO WORDS.

**piano sentence**: a sentence made of PIANO WORDS.

Faded baggage, Gabe, caged a beaded face.

**piano word**: a word spelled with PIANO LETTERS.

CABBAGED     DEBADGED     BEADED-EDGE     FACE-BEDDED

**Pig Latin**: an oral language code that many children learn. Pig Latin works by moving the initial consonant sound of a word to the end of it and adding -AY. If the word begins with a vowel sound, -AY is added to the end without changing anything else. Certain words become other words in Pig Latin:

TRASH = ASHTRAY          REX = X-RAY.

**Pig Latin poem**: a poem that uses PIG LATIN in one way or another to achieve a special effect. In this poem, the last word of each odd-numbered line is Pig Latinized into the phrase on the next line. Each stanza has an ABAB rhyme scheme. Here are the first two stanzas:

As I was walking on the beach,
    Each bay
Was sunny, and I tried to reach
    Each ray.

I found some gold. I thought that more
    Ore may
Be hidden. In the ancient lore
    Ore lay

**place-name oxymoron**: a geographic location's name that contains an OXYMORON within its parts.

LITTLE BIG HORN                    OLD NEW YORK

**plaintext**: a message to be put into CODE.

**plaintext alphabet**: the regular alphabet from A to Z, not in CODE. When the letters are coded by substitution of other letters or symbols, the result is a CIPHER ALPHABET.

**playing card anagram**: writing using the 52 letters in the names of the playing cards. The following poem is about the fifty-third card, the Joker.

**Fate**

The Joker's cue:
"In quest I grew."
Can he give in
Even next of kin?

**playing card name sum**: the total number of letters in the names of the 13 playing cards—ACE, KING, QUEEN, JACK, TEN, NINE, EIGHT, SEVEN, SIX, FIVE, FOUR, THREE, and TWO. By the luck of the draw, there are exactly 52 letters, the same as the number of cards in a deck.

**playing card suit sum**: the total number of letters in the names of the four suits—SPADES, DIAMONDS, HEARTS, CLUBS. There are 25, which reverses to 52, the number of cards in a deck.

**PL8 SPEEK**: the language of vanity license plates—i.e., automobile plates containing a special message instead of the state-assigned letters and numbers. Since space is limited to eight characters, drivers have often used wordplay to say more with less. Vanity plates have become so popular that some people make lists of those they have spotted. Collectors of PL8 SPEEK have Internet web sites where they can share their lists.

> 1OSNE1 (sports REBUS, "Tennis anyone?")
> CYCOPTH (scary DELETION, "psychopath")

In 1996, *Parade* magazine held a vanity plate contest that drew more than 7,000 entries. Five of the ten winning plates included:

> IRIGHTI (REBUS, "right between the eyes")
> RUD14ME (number and LETTER REBUS, "are you the one for me")
> HAHAHAHA (coined word, "ha ha ha ha")
> VAN GO (HOMOPHONE, "Van Gogh")
> TI-3VOM (MIRROR WORDS, "move it")

**PL8 SPEEK writing**: a story, poem, or other text using only messages found on vanity plates. The most ambitious piece of PL8 SPEEK writing is an appropriately tinny version of the ancient Greek tragedy by Sophocles, retitled "Oedipus the King (of the Road)." Exactly 154 vanity plate messages make up this fender-bending story, which begins:

ONCEPON ATIME LONG AGO IN THEBES IMKING. OEDIPUS DA-
KING. LVMYMRS. LVMYKIDS. THEBENS THINK OEDDY ISCOOL.
NOPROBS. OKAY MAYBE THEREZZ 1LITL1. MOTHER WHERERU?

After Oedipus learns the truth about his parents, the story reaches its inevitable
collision:

YEGODS WHYMEE? YMEYYME? LIFSUX. IAMBAD.
IAMBADD, IMSOBAD, STOPNOW THIS HEDAKE. FLESH DUZ
STINK. ITZ 2MUCH PAYNE 4ONE2C. TAKEGOD MYEYES! AIEEEEE!

**pneumonoultramicroscopicsilicovolcanoconiosis**: the longest word
(45 letters) in *Webster's Third Unabridged*, meaning "a miners' lung disease
caused by the inhalation of silicate or quartz dust." It first appeared in the
"Addenda" Section of *Webster's Second Unabridged*, where it was spelled with
a K replacing the last C (-KONIOSIS). Broken down into its component
parts, the word means "a disease of the lungs [caused by] dust from volcanic
ash [so fine as to be] beyond the range of [an instrument that sees] very small
[things]." Although it's a medical term, it appears in no medical dictionary.

**poetic prose**: same as METRIC PROSE.

**poetry maze**: a maze in the form of a poem. Each line of the poem is numbered, and each line ends in two more numbers in parentheses. The maze-
traveler chooses one of the two numbers and goes to the line with that number
and repeats the process as often as necessary. The purpose is to go from the
beginning of the maze to the end by finding the grammatically correct path of
lines. "Daedalus's Poetry Maze" begins:

1. You open up the door. (3, 6)
2. As quickly as you dare (17, 24)
3. The shadows tell you more (44, 58)
4. And then you see the chair. (2, 11)

**political issue anagram**: an ANAGRAM of an issue or belief in politics.

AMERICAN DREAM: damn crime area
EQUAL RIGHTS AMENDMENT: ad men requesting a halt
OLLIE NORTH'S DEALS: Tall hero nods, lies.
PANAMA'S NORIEGA: A man? Iron age sap!
TELEVISION: TV is one lie.

**Polybius's checkerboard**: a CODE formed by writing the letters of the alphabet in a 5 x 5 grid. Each letter is represented by the number of the column and the number of the row in which it appears. Since there are 26 letters, two have to share a position. In the arrangement below, 31-11-44 would spell CAT. There are many variants, depending on where the letters are placed.

|   | 1 | 2 | 3 | 4 | 5 |
|---|---|---|---|---|---|
| 1\| | A | B | C | D | E |
| 2\| | F | G | H | IJ | K |
| 3\| | L | M | N | O | P |
| 4\| | Q | R | S | T | U |
| 5\| | V | W | X | Y | Z |

**polyphonic substitution cipher**: a CODE in which several letters are represented by a single letter or symbol. The best-known example is on the telephone dial or keypad, where a single digit represents three different letters. This arrangement, however, means that a seven-digit number may represent several different names. Here is the best arrangement of letters that reduces the amount of duplication:

ADPY / BENZ / CMX / FKTW / GS / HU / ILV / JOQR

Also called "polyphonic cipher."

**possessive celebrity**: a famous person whose last name begins with an S that can be scooted over to join the first name and make it a possessive. In some cases, the last name has to be further divided to give new meaning to the full name. GLORIA SWANSON changes to GLORIA'S WAN SON.

LORETTA SWIT = LORETTA'S WIT
ROBERT STACK = ROBERT'S TACK
SHARON STONE = SHARON'S TONE
SYLVESTER STALLONE = SYLVESTER'S TALL ONE
TOM AND DICK SMOTHERS = TOM AND DICK'S MOTHERS

**presidential anagram**: an ANAGRAM of the name of an American president.

WILLIAM HOWARD TAFT: A word with all—I'm fat.
GROVER CLEVELAND: dang clever lover
HARRY S TRUMAN: rash army runt
THEODORE ROOSEVELT: Loved horse; tree, too.
WILLIAM JEFFERSON CLINTON: Jilts nice women. In for fall.

See FIRST LADY ANAGRAM.

**presidential palindrome**: a PALINDROME using the name of an American president.

> God! Adams is mad, a dog.
> Raw? Tap Marty Van Buren. One rub: Navy tramp at war.
> Now rely. Tyler won.
> Taft: fat.
> To last, Carter retracts a lot.
> I'm a Bush sub, am I?
> Not nil: Clinton.

**presidential pun name**: the name of an American president converted to words that sound like his name.

| | |
|---|---|
| DAMES VIEW CANNON. | James Buchanan |
| HER BIRD-DO FUR. | Herbert Hoover |
| RUN, OLD DRAGON. | Ronald Reagan |
| BILK LEAN TONGUE. | Bill Clinton |

**presidential reversal**: the name of an American president that can form a word, phrase, or other text when reversed.

> HARRISON = NO, SIRRAH!

**progressive half-square**: a FORM that starts with a single letter and adds a letter to the end to form each new line. Going from the bottom to the top, the form is a SUCCESSIVE CURTAILMENT.

```
        T
      T O
    T O G
  T O G A
T O G A S
```

**progressive padlock**: a PADLOCK in which three or more words form an overlapping chain.

> PADRE-RETRENCH-TRENCHANT-ANTHEM-HEMLOCK
> (the lock = PADLOCK)

**progressive terminal deletion**: TERMINAL DELETION involving more than two words or phrases

```
L A M E N T
A M E N
M E
```

**progressive word square**: a WORD SQUARE that starts with a single letter and progresses to a 2-square, 3-square, 4-square, etc. Here are the stages of a progressive word 5-square:

```
                                        R A T A S
                          R A T A       A F A R E
            F A R         A F A R       T A P E R
   P E      A P E         T A P E       A R E A R
A  E A      R E A         A R E A       S E R R Y
```

**pronoun speller**: a word whose letters can be rearranged to spell a large number of pronouns. The letters in SMITHERY can spell at least seventeen pronouns:

| | | | | |
|---|---|---|---|---|
| HE | HIS | ME | THEIRS | YE |
| HER | I | MY | THEM | |
| HERS | IT | SHE | THEY | |
| HIM | ITS | THEIR | THY | |

**prose equivoque**: a prose piece, such as a letter to a friend, in which the words appear in two columns and convey two very different messages. Reading down, column by column, gives one result; and reading across, left column by right column, gives another result. See EQUIVOQUE.

**prose poem**: **1.** a poem written in sentences and paragraphs. It is typically much shorter than a short story.

**2.** a text with accidental rhyme and regular rhythm found in a published prose work. The example below appeared in a nineteenth-century treatise on mechanics by Dr. William Whewell (who grew tired of people constantly pointing it out to him):

> There is no force, however great, can stretch a cord, however fine, into a horizontal line, which is accurately straight.

Also see FOUND POEM.

**pseudo-antonyms**: words that are not opposites, but that are composed of shorter words that *are* opposites. The larger words are not directly related in meaning to each other.

> CATWALK—DOGTROT
> HOTHEADS—COLD FEET
> MATERNITY DRESS—PATERNITY SUIT
> OVERLAY—UNDERSTAND

**pseudo-comparative**: a word to which –ER and –EST can be added to form an apparent comparative and superlative. The three words do not actually relate at all to the true progression, as in SMALL—SMALLER—SMALLEST.

> TEMP—TEMPER—TEMPEST
> BE—BEER—BEEST
> P—PER—PEST

**pseudo-heteronymic pair**: a pair of words that appear to be HET-ERONYMS, but are not because their etymologies are so closely related.

> INSULT (noun)     READ (present-tense verb)   PRIMER (beginner's book)
> INSULT (verb)     READ (past-tense verb)      PRIMER (base coat of paint)

**pseudo-synonyms**: words that have dissimilar meanings, but that are composed of parts that have similar meanings.

> WIND POWER – AIR FORCE
> RAINDROP – WATERFALL
> CENTRAL TIME – MIDDLE AGES
> TALL ORDER – HIGH COMMAND

**pun**: a single word or expression in which two or more ideas are compacted in a way that seems humorous to the person who makes it up. On occasion, a pun can seem humorous to others, too. Some people consider the pun to be the lowest form of humor, but others, including Shakespeare and James Joyce, have elevated it to an art. A pun can be intentional or accidental. It is probably the oldest form of wordplay of all, a prehysterical phenomon that has continued throughout hysteria to the present daze.

Puns abound in newspaper headlines. They can be funny:

SQUAD HELPS DOG BITE VICTIM (The squad helps the victim of a dog's bite; it doesn't help the dog bite the victim.)

Sometimes they can be frightening:

BUSH DROPS TACTICAL NUCLEAR WEAPONS (President George Bush excludes tactical nuclear weapons from the U.S. arsenal; he doesn't use them.)

There are three types of puns—HOMOPHONES, HOMOGRAPHS, and DOUBLE-SOUND PUNS. They appear in their own entries, and they underlie many other wordplay forms.

**pundrome**: a sentence whose words sound the same in either direction. Each word on one side is spelled differently from the corresponding word on the other side. If there are an odd number of words, the middle word stands on its own.

> No eye sees the seas I know.
> Mary, maid missed in mist, made merry.
> Knight, buy Whale's Inn wine or whine in Wales by night.
> Find bee or be fined!

**pun name**: the name of a person expressed in words that sound like his or her name. HEM HILLY TICK IN SUN paints a strange picture, but it is one possible pun name of EMILY DICKINSON.

| | |
|---|---|
| MUD DAWN AWE | Madonna |
| HELL, FUSS! PRESS LEE. | Elvis Presley |
| NAP, O LEE, ON BONY PART. | Napoleon Bonaparte |

**punnery**: the act of making a PUN; the trick of compacting two or more ideas within a single word or expression.

**punning author's name**: an author's name that PUNS on the title of his or her book. In these examples, both author and book are made up. See APTLY NAMED AUTHOR.

> *Cutting It Fine* by Moses Lawn
> *The Corn* by Honor Foot
> *Wine and Women* by Rex Holmes

**punster**: a person who makes up PUNS; a puntificator, a punhandler, a punslinger, a pun pal, a punk.

**pure word**: a word whose letters come from a single partition of the alphabet. For the alphabet divided into first and last halves, the longest word for each partition appears below.

A–M: HAMAMELIDACEAE
N–Z: NONSUPPORTS

**Puritan baptismal name**: a name given to a Puritan baby. The name usually had overt religious significance. In addition, a name might use one or more hyphens to hold itself together. One Puritan maiden, when asked her baptismal name, replied, "'Through-much-tribulation-we-enter-the-kingdom-of-Heaven,' but for short they call me 'Tribby.'" In these ten examples, the last word in each case is the family name, and the rest is the baptismal name.

Kill-sin Pimple
Be-thankful Playnard
Obediencia Cruttenden
Fly-debate Roberts
Faint-not Hewett

Hope-for Bending
Search-the-scriptures Moreton
More-fruit Flower
Fight-the-good-fight-of-faith White
Meek Brewer

**pyramid**: a FORM in a triangular shape. See REGULAR PYRAMID.

**Q-graph**: a WORD GRAPH based on a PAVEMENT composed of squares. Q stands for "quadrature."

**Q-not-followed-by-U word**: a word that does not obey the orthographic rule of English that stipulates that Q is followed by U. The best-known is the country name IRAQ. Below are 12 uncapitalized dictionary words, each with

Q followed by a different letter (A, D, E, F, H, I, L, O, R, Q, or S), or by no letter. All appear in the *Unabridged Merriam Webster* except for QOBAR (in *Funk & Wagnalls*) and FIQH (in *Random House*).

| | | | |
|---|---|---|---|
| BUQSHA | MIQRA | QIVIUT | TALUQDAR |
| COQ | QANEH | QOBAR | WAQF |
| FIQH | QERE | TAQLID | ZAQQUM |

**quadrisogram**: a set of four words in which no letter is repeated.

PUNCHWORKS, GADFLY, VEXT, ZIMB

See ISOGRAM.

**quadruple homophone**: a quartet of words that are HOMOPHONES of each other.

| | |
|---|---|
| AIR—ERE—ERR—HEIR | RIGHT—RITE—WRIGHT—WRITE |
| OAR—O'ER—OR—ORE | T'S—TEAS—TEASE—TEES |

**-quake word**: a word ending in -QUAKE, which usually means "a shaking or trembling." (The first –QUAKE word below is a garden plant, not a bovine upheaval.)

| | | |
|---|---|---|
| COWQUAKE | MOONQUAKE | WATERQUAKE |
| EARTHQUAKE | SEAQUAKE | WORLDQUAKE |
| HEARTQUAKE | STATEQUAKE | |
| ICEQUAKE | SUNQUAKE | |

**quasi-antonyms**: words that look like opposites, but are not opposites. Instead, they have the same meaning:

BURN UP—BURN DOWN
FAT CHANCE—SLIM CHANCE
IRREGARDLESS—REGARDLESS
LOOSEN—UNLOOSEN

**quaternade**: a word that can be broken up into four sequences of every fourth letter to form four shorter words.

```
PANTALOONERY
P     A     N
   A     L     E
   N     O     R
      T     O     Y
```

Also called "quadade." See ALTERNADE, QUINADE, TRINADE.

**QU-followed-by-a-consonant word**: a word in which QU is followed not by another vowel, but by a consonant. Such words are rarer than Q-NOT-FOLLOWED-BY-U WORDS. Here are six, each with QU followed by a different consonant (H, R, B, D, G, and M). All appear in the *Unabridged Merriam Webster,* except for SQUG in *Funk & Wagnalls.*

PIQURE   QUBBA   QUHILK   SQUDGY   SQUG   ZAQQUM

**quick-change word**: a TELEPHONE WORD in which each letter appears on a different keypad from the previous one. This is slightly more restrictive than prohibiting DOUBLED LETTERS.

ELECTROENCEPHALOGRAPHY
35 3 2 8 7 6 3 62 3 7 4 2 5 6 4 7 2 7 4 9

**quinade**: a word that can be broken up into five sequences of every fifth letter to form five shorter words.

```
  PARAMELACONITES
  P      E      N
   A      L      I
    R      A      T
     A      C      E
      M      O      S
```

See ALTERNADE, QUATERNADE, TRINADE.

**quintisogram**: a set of five words in which no letter is repeated among them.

THUMBING, FROWZLY, JACKS, VEX, PDQ

See ISOGRAM.

**qwaint**: a word spelled (or mispelled) in such a way that it refers to its meaning. The term is a Middle English spelling of *quaint*, but most people would see it as a quaint spelling of *quaint*, which makes *qwaint* a qwaint, too. The word *lithp* is a qwaint that first appeared in the sixteenth century. It has appeared in plural form, too, as *lithpth*. Some contemporary qwaints include:

DECEMBRRR          NEVERENDIN          EXXXCESS

**QWERTY keyboard**: a typewriter or computer keyboard using the standard arrangement of letters, so called because Q, W, E, R, T, and Y are located at the top left. See TYPEWRITER KEYBOARD.

**radio call letter word**: a four-letter word coincidentally spelled with the letters that the FCC has assigned to an AM radio station.

KEEP—Twin Falls, ID      WARM—Scranton, PA
KILT—Houston, TX      WHEE—Martinsville, VA
KITE—Terrell Hills, TX      WINK—Fort Myers, FL
KNEW—Oakland, CA      WOOF—Dothan, AL
KNOW—Austin, TX      WORD—Savannah, TN

**rare doubled letters**: X and Y, the letters least commonly occurring twice in a row in a word.

HAJJI      HOOQQA      WAXXENN      SNARLEYYOW

See CONSECUTIVE-IDENTICAL-LETTER WORD.

**rare letters**: 1. J, Q, X, and Z, the four least commonly used letters. 2. J, K, Q, X, and Z, the five least commonly used letters.

**Reaganagram**: an ANAGRAM of the name of former U.S. President Ronald Reagan. A computer search using the letters in RONALD WILSON REAGAN resulted in hundreds of thousands of sets of words, many of which can be rearranged to form provocative anagrams. At a much slower rate, humans have done their own anagramming of all three names and of the name RONALD REAGAN. Also called "Reagan anagram."

**real word square**: a WORD SQUARE made up of words separated into fragments that are themselves words.

CLIP    PER    MAN
PER    CENT    AGE
MAN    AGE    LESS

See BIGRAM-FRAG SQUARE.

**rebade**: a REBUS in which the clue generates two or more words whose alternate letters form a two-word answer. A rebade, as its name indicates, is a combination rebus and ALTERNADE. In this example, APT is the clue, and ATRIP/FEAST is the answer:

APT = AFTER    A    IS    PT
          A    T    R          I    P
             F    E    A    S    T

**rebus**: a form of WORDPLAY in which letters, numbers, syllables, words, or other symbols represent a letter, a word, or a longer message. Rebuses can be interpreted by sounding out letters, interpreting locations of letters in relation to other letters, or "reading" words in other special ways that result in a letter, a word, or a longer message. See LETTER REBUS, STANDARD REBUS, SYLLABIC REBUS.

**rebus poem**: a poem that uses SYLLABIC REBUSes. They can occur among the words, or they can form a poem on their own. "The Farmer" (1903) is a poem that uses one two-letter REBUS in each line. Its first stanza reads:

The farmer leads no EZ life,
   The CD sows will rot;
And when at EV rests from strife
   His bones all AK lot.

**reciprocal automynorcagram**: a pair of texts, each of which is an AUTO-MYNORCAGRAM of the other.

**reconstructed poem**: a poem made by rearranging the words (and not the individual letters) of another poem. Also called "reconstruction." See DISASSEMBLED POEM, VOCABULARYCLEPT POETRY.

**redivide** (*v.*): to separate the letters of a word, phrase, or sentence to form a different text that is a CHARADE of the original; to CHARADE a text.

**redivider**: a synonym for CHARADE. The term was recently coined to replace *charade*, which can be confused with the older riddle form and with the modern parlor game. However, most books of wordplay in the last 50 years have used the term *charade*. *Redivider*, a palindromic word, was chosen to emphasize the relationship of the form to the PALINDROME.

**redundancy**: a well-known phrase or other short text that is repetitive and repetitious. One of the most redundant of all is: THE TRUTH, THE WHOLE TRUTH, AND NOTHING BUT THE TRUTH.

| | |
|---|---|
| AND PLUS | OVER-EXAGGERATE |
| FINE AND DANDY | TIME CLOCK |
| HE-MAN | TOO EXCESSIVE |
| MANUAL DEXTERITY | UNEXPECTED SURPRISE |
| OLD GEEZER | YOUNG CHILD |

**redundant place name**: a place name that has parts whose meanings are repeated.

TABLE MESA ("mesa" means "table" in Spanish)
GREENWICH VILLAGE ("Greenwich" means "green village")
MURDERKILL (a river in Delaware; "kill" is Dutch for "creek" or "stream")

**redundant quote**: a quote that is a REDUNDANCY originating accidentally or intentionally with the speaker.

"careful caution"—US Secretary of State Alexander Haig
"I will try not to repeat myself, as I said . . ."—David Dimberly (BBC1)
"Money is better than poverty, if only for financial reasons."—Woody Allen

**reflexicon**: a word list that describes its own letter count. A reflexicon is similar to a SELF-ENUMERATING SENTENCE, but the reflexicon omits all extraneous words. There are only two in English, including this one:

fifteen E's, seven F's, four G's, six H's, eight I's, four N's, five O's, six R's, eighteen S's, eight T's, four U's, three V's, two W's, three X's

**regular pyramid**: a triangular arrangement of letters in which the rows and the columns spell different words. The first, shown here, was published in 1874:

```
        D
      E R E
    S L A V E
  C O M M E N D
```

**repeated key-pattern word**: a TELEPHONE WORD with letters appearing on keys whose digits occur in repeated sequences. Here are examples of words that repeat two, three, and four digits:

| TRUSTS | MURMUROUS | LIMPKINS |
|--------|-----------|----------|
| 878787 | 687687687 | 54675467 |

**repeated letter change**: a word that becomes another word when a specific letter is changed to another letter in all occurrences.

MONOCLE—MANACLE

**repeated letter deletion**: a form of DELETION that involves the removal of all instances of the same letter in a word or phrase to create a new word or phrase.

BASSIST—BAIT

**restaurauntese**: the slang lexicon of waiters, waitresses, and cooks in diners and other road-side restaurants. The terms stand for orders of various foods and prepared dishes. In classic diner tradition, the restaurant workers shout the orders back and forth. The best-known term is "ADAM AND EVE ON A RAFT," meaning "poached eggs on toast."

BOSSY IN A BOWL = beef stew
CHOCKER HOLE AND MURK = donut and coffee
GARIBALDI = Italian hero sandwich
GIMME A SHIMMY = give me an order of Jell-O
WHISTLEBERRIES AND HOUNDS, A PAIR = beans with two franks

**retronym**: an adjective-noun pairing brought on by a change in the noun's meaning, usually because of technology. To give one example, what used to be called books (which always had hard covers) are now called hardcover books to distinguish them from the more recent paperback books.

GUITAR—ACOUSTIC GUITAR (to distinguish from the electric guitar)
SOAP—BAR SOAP (to distinguish from powdered and liquid soap)

**reversal**: a word or phrase that spells another word or phrase in reverse; a word or phrase spelled by reversing the letters of another word or phrase. Given the mirror nature of the form, it is appropriate that both definitions have been used. "Reversal" is sometimes modified by another word, and it sometimes modifies another word. See REVERSAL SENTENCE.

DESSERTS—STRESSED

This wordplay form has had more names than any other. "Anagram," oddly enough, was the original term. Other terms include "ananym," "antigram," "drow," "half-palindrome," "heterodome," "inversion," "palinode," "recurrent palindrome," "retronym," "reversagram," "reversal pair," REVERSAL SENTENCE, "reversible," "reversible anagram," "reversion," "sentence reversal," "semordnilap," "sotadic palindrome," and "word reversal."

**reversal charade**: a CHARADE formed by reversing a word and then redividing its letters.

Leno—One "l"

**reversal double square**: a REVERSAL SQUARE with one set of words going across and another set going down. Each set, written in a single line, reverses to a different set of words, as in:

```
P A R     Across: PAR—ITA—NET = TEN—ATI—RAP
I T A     Down: PIN—ATE—RAT = TAR—ETA—NIP
N E T
```

**reversal lettershift**: a LETTERSHIFT WORD that is a reversal of the starting word—e.g., GNAT shifts 13 steps to form TANG.

**reversal pair**: a pair of words that are REVERSALS of each other. See PALINDROME PAIR.

SPACER—RECAPS   DELIVER—REVILED   GATEMAN—NAME TAG

**reversal pseudonym**: an author's or artist's first and last name with the letters in reverse. In 1968, a famous singer/pianist cut an album with his first name and last name in regular order and the letters of each name in reverse order:

EIVETS REDNOW = STEVIE WONDER

See ANANYM.

**reversal sentence**: a sentence that spells another sentence in reverse.

Eva, can I stab one man's dog?
Gods name no bats in a cave.

Rail at natal bosh, aloof gibbons!
Snob! Big fool! Ah, so blatant a liar!

See SENTENCE REVERSAL.

**reversal single square**: a REVERSAL SQUARE with the same set of words going across and down. When the set is written in a single line, it reverses to a different set, as shown here:

P A T      PAT–ARE–TEN = NET–ERA–TAP
A R E
T E N

**reversal square**: a WORD SQUARE composed of words that form a reversal set—i.e., when the words going in the same direction are written in a single line, their letters spell different words in reverse. In this square, the reversal set is SLAP-LANA-ANAN-PANS, which reverses to SNAP-NANA-ANAL-PALS. It is also a SINGLE SQUARE.

S L A P
L A N A
A N A L
P A N S

**reverse alphabet**: ZYXWVUTSRQPONMLKJIHGFEDCBA, the alphabet with its letters arranged in reverse alphabetic order. Some call this the "witch alphabet."

**reverse alphabetically-ordered AEIOU word**: a word in which the five vowels appear once each in reverse alphabetic order.

DUOLITERAL        UNORIENTAL        SUBCONTINENTAL

**reverse alphabetically-ordered consonant word**: a word whose consonants appear in reverse alphabetic order.

    TRINOMIALLY     TETRAPOLOIDIC

**reverse alphabetically-ordered number name**: a NUMBER NAME whose NUMERICAL UNITS occur in reverse alphabetic order. At most, 13 units can be put in reverse in a number name.

    TWENTY-THREE SEXDECILLION SEVENTY-SEVEN QUATTUOR-DECILLION ONE NONILLION NINETY-NINE MILLION EIGHTY-EIGHT

**reverse alphabetic sequence**: an ALPHABETIC SEQUENCE with its letters arranged in reverse order in the CIRCULAR ALPHABET. They may be separated by other letters in a word, or they may be adjacent, as in these words:

    <u>FED</u>       BLAC<u>KJ</u>ACK       N<u>UTS</u>       L<u>AZY</u>

**reverse alphabetic word**: a word whose letters occur in reverse alphabetic order. SOME is one, and ONE is, too.

    YOLKED    SPONGED    ZYXOMMA    SPOON-FEED

**reverse-alphabetized number names**: the NUMBER NAMES spelled in reverse and placed in alphabetic order according to the reverse spelling. The first and the last reverse-alphabetized number names in the number system are:

THREE HUNDRED (DERDNUH EERHT)

SIX HUNDRED SIXTY VIGINTILLION SIXTY SEPTILLION SIXTY SEXTILLION SIXTY (YTXIS NOILLITXES . . .)

**reverse alphomic word**: see REVERSE ALPHABETIC WORD.

**reverse bialphabetic word**: a word whose letters are in reverse BIAL-PHABETIC ORDER. The letters can be divided into two reverse ALPHABETIC SEQUENCES (second meaning). Here are two ways to divide the same word:

    SPRINGHEAD     SPRINGHEAD
    S R NG  A      SP  I G  E D
      P I   HE  D       R N H  A

Also called "reverse dialphabetical order."

**reversed beheadment**: the BEHEADMENT of a word followed by the REVERSAL of the remaining letters to make a new word.

PETAL—LATE

**reversed curtailment**: the CURTAILMENT of a word followed by the REVERSAL of the remaining letters to form a new word.

STINKY—KNITS

**reversed deletion**: the DELETION of a letter in one word, followed by the REVERSAL of the remaining letters to create a new word.

ESPALIER—RELAPSE

**reversed head-to-tail shift**: the movement of the first letter of a word to the end followed by the REVERSAL of all the letters to make a new word.

FLATCAR—FRACTAL

**reversed letter change**: the substitution of one letter for another followed by the REVERSAL of all the letters to form a new word.

TWANGER—REGNANT

**reversed letter shift**: the movement of one letter to a new position followed by the REVERSAL of all the letters to create a new word. (Note that "letter shift" here does not mean the same as LETTERSHIFT.)

IGNITED—DIETING

**reversed terminal deletion**: the DELETION of the first and last letters of a word followed by the reversal of the remaining letters to make a new word.

REBIRTH—TRIBE

**reverse invariant sentence**: a sentence whose letters occupy as many corresponding positions in the REVERSE ALPHABET as possible:

mY oWl? iT is uPON My agInG FEDorA.

**reverse-keyboard word**: a word whose letters occur from right to left in the TYPEWRITER KEYBOARD ALPHABET.

**reverse parallelism**: a literary device in which the first half of a sentence switches words in the second half to turn the meaning around.

> "Ask not what your country can do for you. Ask what you can do for your country."—President John F. Kennedy.

> "Suit the action to the word, the word to the action."—William Shakespeare.

**reverse trinade**: a word that can be reversed and then broken up into three sequences of every third letter to form three shorter words.

```
ASTRONOMICAL =    LACIMONORTSA
                  L   I   N   T
                  A   M   O   S
                    C   O   R   A
```

See TRINADE.

**reversible inverted half-square**: an INVERTED HALF-SQUARE that spells one set of words horizontally (left to right) and vertically (bottom to top), and another set of words when read in the opposite directions.

```
N A M E T A G
  L A M I N A
    D I M I T
      T I M E
        D A M
          L A
            N
```

**reversible tautonym**: a TAUTONYM formed by reversing the individual parts of another tautonym.

```
TOM-TOM = MOT-MOT
```

**reversible word ladder**: a WORD LADDER that begins with a word and ends with its reversal.

```
RAT     TRAM
RUT     TEAM
RUN     TEAT
RAN     PEAT
```

```
TAN        PERT
TAR        PART
           MART
```

**R-graph**: a WORD GRAPH based on the rook's move in chess.

**rhetorical irony question**: a question that uses words in normal fashion except that two of the words have double meanings that make them opposites.

> Can a bride groom herself?
> Can cats dog one's footsteps?
> Do harts have hindquarters?

**rhopalic sentence**: **1.** a sentence that begins with a one-syllable word and adds a syllable to each succeeding word. HE COUNTED SYLLABLES RELENTLESSLY is a short rhopalic sentence. Here is an 11-word example:

> Some people completely misunderstand administrative extemporization—idiosyncratical antianthropomorphism undenominationalizing politico-ecclesiastical honorificabilitudinity.

**2.** a LETTER-UNIT rhopalic sentence. Usually this is called a SNOWBALL SENTENCE.

**rhopalic verse**: a poem composed of rhopalic lines that begin with a one-syllable word and add a syllable to each word in succession. The following is a four-line poem, each line a four-word rhopalic:

> May eagles lacerate eternally
> Your liver, overproud Prometheus!
> Your fiery offering, predictably,
> Has rendered humankind vainglorious.

**rhymatic writing**: prose writing in which every two words rhyme. "Rhymatic Fever" is a story beginning with these sentences:

> Free, we drive. I've passed fast highways, byways—soaring, roaring.
> Then when we see a way, space, place for car, I try stopping, hopping out.
> Route shows rose flowers, towers blooming, looming over clover. . . .

**rhyming puzzle**: any of several types of RIDDLES or ENIGMAS in the form of a rhyming poem.

**riddle**: a question with its answer disguised in metaphor, personification, or other form of wordplay. The modern riddle is usually a prose question, such as "What is black and white and red all over?" (Answer: "a newspaper," "an embarrassed zebra," etc.) Originally, the riddle was a statement in prose or poetry.

The riddle is the oldest form of oral word game. It shows up in every culture and in every era. One of the earliest, from ancient Babylonia, refers to a chest of silver and a casket of gold. The answer is "an egg." The English nursery rhyme, Humpty-Dumpty, is also a riddle whose answer is "an egg." In 1511, Wynkyn de Worde published the first collection of English riddles, called *Demaundes Joyous*. It contained 54 riddles, 29 taken from a French book.

**riddle-contest**: a challenge in which a person has to answer a RIDDLE or lose something valuable, such as his or her life. These occurred in the ancient Hindu Vedas and in the twelfth-century Old Norse Eddas.

**riddle of the Sphinx**: an ancient Greek RIDDLE that has survived the ages. Oedipus saved the city of Thebes by solving it. In Thomas De Quincey's retelling of the story, the riddle goes like this:

> "What creature is that which moves on four feet in the morning, on two feet at noon-day, and on three toward the 'going down of the sun'?" Oedipus, after some consideration, answered that the creature was Man, who creeps on the ground with hands and feet when an infant, walks upright in the vigour of manhood, and leans upon a staff in old age.

**ring**: a sequence of words in which each word is connected to the next and the last word is connected to the first by a common property. WORD CYCLES and WORD RINGS are two examples.

**Rochester transaddition**: a TRANSADDITION in which a word with no repeated letters is turned into a series of other words by doubling each letter and transposing the results.

SCARE—CARESS, SCARCE, CAESAR, RACERS, CREASE

**roller-coaster word**: a word whose letters go up the alphabet (toward Z), turn on a single letter, and then go down the alphabet (toward A)—or vice versa. For instance, the letters of INTONED go up, turn on T, and then go down; and the letters of WONDERS go down, turn on D, and then go up.

**roller-coaster word chain**: a WORD CHAIN in which every two adjacent words (or parts of words) slide together to form a new word that is one letter longer than the previous pair of adjacent words. In the chain below, the word pairs begin by forming AA, ADO, DOES, and end by forming MARKET-PLACES.

A-A-DO-ES-CAR-PAL-MIST-EACH-WHERE-AFTER-MARKET-PLACES

**Roman numeral letters**: C, D, I, L, M, V, and X, the letters used to make Roman numerals. The numeric values are:

| | | | |
|---|---|---|---|
| M = 1000 | C = 100 | X = 10 | I = 1 |
| D = 500 | L = 50 | V = 5 | |

**Roman numeral palindrome**: a palindromic word (see PALINDROME) spelled with Roman numeral letters only.

| | | | |
|---|---|---|---|
| DID | XXX | CIVIC | MILLIM |

**Roman numeral part-word**: a word that contains an unbroken sequence of Roman numeral letters as well as other letters.

MILLIMICRON          BACILLICIDIC          MILLIMILLINARY

**Roman numeral word**: a word composed entirely of Roman numeral letters.

| | | | | |
|---|---|---|---|---|
| MIMIC | ILICIC | CIMICIC | DIVI-DIVI | DIDIL DIDDIL |

**Romantic equation**: an equation in which two or more ROMANTIC NUMBERS have Roman numerals and Arabic numbers that sum up to the same amount. The first three Romantic numbers are the only consecutive numbers that do so:

```
f IV e + s IX + se V en
  5  +  6 +   7      = 18
 IV  +  IX +  V
  4  +  9 +   5      = 18
```

**Romanomagic square**: a square of nine numbers in which each row, column, and diagonal has the same sum of Arabic numbers, the same amount of letters, and the same sum of embedded Roman numerals. In this example, each row, column, and diagonal has an Arabic sum of 216, a letter amount of 25, and a Roman sum of 15.

| | | |
|---|---|---|
| sIXty-two | eIghty | seVenty-four |
| eIghty-four | seVenty-two | sIXty |
| seVenty | sIXty-four | eIghty-two |

**Romantic number**: a number having a well-formed Roman numeral embedded within its name. Romantic numbers go from fIVe (IV = 4) to forty-four thousanD nInety-nIne (DII = 502).

| | |
|---|---|
| eIght (I = 1) | seVenty-nIne (VI = 6) |
| twenty-fIVe (IV = 4) | one thousanD sIX (DIX = 509) |

**Romantic word**: a word having a well-formed Roman numeral embedded within its name. The ROMAN NUMERAL LETTERS may or may not occur consecutively, but they must make a Roman numeral when read from left to right. CONSECUTIVELY, with CCIVL (not a Roman numeral), is not a Romantic word, but CONSECUTIVE, with CCIV (204), is.

| | | |
|---|---|---|
| It | (I = 1) | eXhIbItIon (XIII = 13) |
| IbIs | (II = 2) | eXpLetIve (XLIV = 44) |
| InhIbIt | (III = 3) | LoVe-InspIrIng (LVIII = 58) |
| gIVe | (IV = 4) | LuXurIatIon (LXII = 62) |
| eVe | (V = 5) | eXCaVatIonIst (XCVII = 97) |

**Rorschach word pair**: a dictionary entry consisting solely of an incomprehensible boldface word or phrase separated by a colon from another incomprehensible word or phrase. The following appear in the S section of *Webster's Second* or *Third*:

SADDLEQUERN : METATE
SMEAR DOCK : GOOD-KING-HENRY
SAMBUCA : TRIGON

SCHABZIEGER : SAPSAGO
SHOTCRETE : GUNITE
SPHEX : CHLORION
SRANAN TONGO : TAKI-TAKI
SYMPHYTA : CHALASTROGASTRA

**rotary telephone word**: a TELEPHONE WORD requiring a rotary phone for its effect.

**same-initial shiftgram**: a SHIFTGRAM that begins with the same letter as the starting word.

EGGCUP + 24 = ceeasn = ENCASE
PACING + 2 = rcekpi = PICKER

**same-length isogram set**: a set of words from a single dictionary that have the same number of letters, none of which are repeated. Here are the best examples using three- and seven-letter words from the unabridged *Merriam-Webster*.

NTH VEX JUG RIP ADZ SKY FOB CWM
JACKBOX FRESHLY DUMPING

**SATOR square**: the oldest word square in the world. It is discussed in more detail under WORD SQUARE.

**Schwarzkopf Challenge, The**: the challenge of finding or making up a PANGRAMMATIC full name around SCHWARZKOPF, the 11-letter ISO-GRAMMATIC last name of General Norman Schwarzkopf of Gulf War fame. In combination with the abbreviation of his rank, GEN. SCHWARZKOPF has 14 letters. Coined names exceeding this include:

EMILY JUNG SCHWARZKOPF (20 letters)
BIG MEL TY SCHWARZKOPF, JUN. (22 letters)
BENJY GIL Q.T. "MUD" SCHWARZKOPF, XV (26 letters)

**Scrabble™**: a board game in which wooden letter tiles are placed in squares to spell words horizontally or vertically. Each letter tile has a point value printed on it, except for the blank tile, and the board has squares that double or triple the point value of a letter or a word. While there are many other board games involving words, Scrabble is the most popular of all time.

Alfred Butts, an unemployed architect living in New York, invented the game during the Great Depression. Butts originally called it "Lexico," then "It," and then "Criss-Cross." He privately produced and sold the game for several years. In 1948, a friend of his, James Brunot, helped mass-produce and mass-market the game under the name "Scrabble." The game sold only 2,000 sets in the first year. In 1952, the owner of Macy's store ordered the game, and other toy stores jumped on the bandwagon. Sales took off, and the game became a success. In 1953, Selchow and Righter bought the rights to the game.

Due to its great popularity, Scrabble has become a household word. Its intricate mix of letters, letter values, rules, and board has made it a wordplay vehicle unlike any other board game. Among other challenges, wordplay writers have tried to find the highest possible scores that can be made under special conditions. The Scrabble dictionary has become one of the most respected sources for words used in all forms of wordplay. See HIGH-SCORING SCRABBLE, ONE-MOVE SCRABBLE SCORE.

**Scrabble™-friendly word square**: a WORD SQUARE made of words found in the two Scrabble dictionaries, *Official Scrabble Words* and *Official Scrabble Players Dictionary*. The largest squares found so far are EIGHT-SQUARES.

**Scrabble™ sentence**: a sentence made by transposing all 100 Scrabble tiles.

COUNTRYMEN, I AM TO BURY, NOT EULOGIZE, CAESAR; IF EVIL LIVES ON, BEQUEATHING INJURY, GOOD OFT EXPIRES: A PALSIED, AWKWARD DEATH!

**Scrabble™ value**: the numeric value of a given letter in Scrabble™, used to score the players' words. The number appears on the bottom left corner of each tile. In this list, the Scrabble value is followed by the letter or letters that have that value:

```
0 = blank
1 = A E I L N O R S T U
2 = D G
3 = B C M P
4 = F H V W Y
5 = K
8 = J X
10 = Q Z
```

Also called "letter value," "score value."

**scrambled alphabet**: the alphabet rearranged in any order. There are 403,000,000,000,000,000,000,000,000 arrangements possible. Several word-play problems use scrambled alphabets: for instance, which arrangement of letters spells the most words from left to right? The following arrangement spells 398 words in *Merriam-Webster's Pocket Dictionary*, more than six times the number spellable in normal alphabetic order:

```
BSFPWCHJQMOAVUIRNGLKTDZEXH
  S P         A    N
    W  H      A      L      E
(etc.)
```

See NO-WORD ALPHABET, —FRIENDLY ALPHABET, —UNFRIENDLY ALPHABET.

**second-order reduplication**: a word with nearly identical halves. One letter in the first half differs from the corresponding letter in the second half. If both halves were the same, it would be a first-order reduplication, better known as a TAUTONYM.

MISHMASH     KNICKKNACK     HERKIMER-JERKIMER

**self-contradictory word**: a word with parts that have conflicting meanings.

MONOPOLY (MONO-, POLY-, meaning "one" and "many")
UNDEROVERLOOKER (UNDER, OVER)

**self-descriptive crossword**: a CROSSWORD containing phrases such as "five f" or "twelve e" that count all the letters within the whole and allow letters to do double duty at the points where two words cross. If presented as a list instead of a crossword, however, the counting doesn't add up. See REFLEXICON.

**self-descriptive number name**: a NUMBER NAME whose letters have ALPHABETIC VALUES summing up to the number itself. There is no self-descriptive number name of that kind in English. The problem becomes, What assignment of numerical values to letters produces the number names whose letters add up to the numbers themselves? There are different ways of answering this question, including these three:

(1) The letters of the alphabet can be rearranged and reassigned values based on their new positions. The rearrangement below produces 37 self-descriptive number names, beginning with 50, 60, 80, 90, 201. The dots indicate "wild card" positions in which any of the nine remaining letters can be placed. The new values are E = 2, S = 3, . . . N = 26:

.ESIV.F.WR.Y.UD..H.TXOLG.N

(2) The letters can be assigned any positive or negative whole number values so long as no letters have the same value. The following assignment makes ONE through TWELVE self-descriptive:

| E | F | G | H | I | L | N | O | R | S | T | U | V | W | X |
|---|---|---|---|---|---|---|---|---|---|---|---|---|---|---|
| 3 | 9 | 6 | 1 | -4 | - | 5 | -7 | -6 | -1 | 2 | 8 | -3 | 7 | 11 |

(3) The letters can be assigned fractional values. The next assignment uses the numbers 1 through 13 with divisors of 6 to make ONE through SIX self-descriptive:

| E | F | H | I | N | O | R | S | T | U | V | W | X |
|---|---|---|---|---|---|---|---|---|---|---|---|---|
| 1/6 | 4/3 | 7/6 | 11/6 | 1/3 | 1/2 | 5/6 | 2 | 2/3 | 3/2 | 5/3 | 1 | 13/6 |

Also called "perfect number name."

**self-enumerating book**: a book in which each page after the first enumerates the letters on its predecessor. The first page starts it off with an "x," and the next three pages continue building up the "plot." The text recycles every 155 pages.

Page 1: x
Page 2: one x
Page 3: one e, one n, one o, one x
Page 4: five e's, five n's, five o's, one x

**self-enumerating sentence**: a sentence that correctly states the quantities of one or more of its parts.

> This sentence contains five words.
> This sentence contains thirty-six letters.
> In this sentence there are sixteen words, eighty-one letters, one hyphen, four commas, and one period.

**self-invariant word**: a word that has none of its letters occupying the same corresponding position as any of its own letters when they are arranged in alphabetic order. EARTH is self-invariant, but UNIVERSE, because of the I, isn't.

```
EARTH          UNIVERSE
AEHRT          EEINRSUV
```

**self-referential** (*adj.*): referring to itself. TRUTHFUL NUMBERS are self-referential numbers. See SELF-REFERENTIAL.

**semantic rhyming word set**: a collection of words that rhyme and that also connote a similar meaning or feeling. The 20 words in this set suggest action, vigor, and violence:

| | | | | |
|---|---|---|---|---|
| BASH | DASH | HASH | FLASH | SPLASH |
| BRASH | FLASH | LASH | RASH | STASH |
| CLASH | GASH | MASH | SLASH | THRASH |
| CRASH | GNASH | PASH | SMASH | TRASH |

**semordnilap**: a synonym for REVERSAL. This term is the word *palindromes* spelled in reverse.

**sentence reversal:** a sentence that another sentence spells in reverse.

> Snob! Big fool! Ah, so blatant a liar!
> Rail at natal bosh, aloof gibbons!
>
> God's name no bats in a cave.
> Eva, can I stab one man's dog?

See REVERSAL SENTENCE.

**sequential word squares**: WORD SQUARES that have different words except for one that appears in each different position from square to square. In the sequential word squares below, SEE occupies different horizontal and vertical positions. The first sequential words squares, measuring 7 x 7 letters, were published in 1895 by "Sphinx."

```
S E E        A S P        H I S
E R A        S E E        I R E
E A T        P E T        S E E
```

**set-up pun**: a PUN that concludes a story developed for the purpose of making the pun at the end. The punch line in the story below puns on the famous musical line, "Pardon me, Boy, is that the Chatanooga Choo-Choo?"

> Roy Rogers went bathing in a creek. Along came a mountain lion and began nibbling on one of Roy's new shoes. Dale Evans entered the scene, pulled out her trusty rifle, and shot the lion. She turned to her husband and asked: "Pardon me, Roy, is that the cat that chewed your new shoe?"

**seven seas**: the seven seas located within the five oceans. In true wordplay fashion, the "seas" are "C's" floating in the oceans' names:

ANTARCTIC    ARCTIC    ATLANTIC    INDIAN    PACIFIC

**seven-square**: a WORD SQUARE measuring 7 x 7 letters. The first was published in 1877:

```
C A M A R G O
A T O N E R S
M O T I V E S
A N I L I N E
R E V I V A L
G R E N A D E
O S S E L E T
```

**sex change charade**: a two-word phrase or sentence made out of a single word starting with the prefix EX-. The letter S is added to the beginning and ending of the original word, and the resulting LETTERSTRING is separated into SEX and a second word. For instance, EXCHANGE plus the two S's produces SEXCHANGES, which divides into SEX CHANGES. Here are a few more:

EXACT = SEX ACTS                    EXPOSE = SEX POSES
EXANIMATE = SEX ANIMATES            EXPRESS = SEX PRESSES
EXPULSE = SEX PULSES
EXCOMMUNICATE = SEX COMMUNICATES

**Shakespearean coined word**: a word that first appeared in Shakespeare's plays or poems. He is credited with coining more than 1,700 words, one out of every ten in his published works. Shakespeare did not coin them all himself. Many were in use in speech, but he was the first to put them in print. Here is a selection of 17 words—about one percent:

| | | |
|---|---|---|
| amazement | foppish | monumental |
| bump | gnarled | obscene |
| courtship | hoodwinked | premeditated |
| dislocate | invulnerable | road |
| dwindle | leapfrog | suspicious |
| exposure | misplaced | |

**Shakespearean palindrome**: a line from one of Shakespeare's plays or poems that is a WORD-UNIT PALINDROME. The words (not the letters) read the same in both directions. Here are two from *Macbeth*:

Tomorrow and tomorrow and tomorrow

Fair is foul, and foul is fair

**Shakespearean pangrammatic sonnet**: Sonnet 27, "Weary with toil, I haste me to my bed." All 26 letters appear at least once among its lines, making it the only PANGRAM (first meaning) out of all 154 of Shakespeare's sonnets. See PANGRAMMATIC POETRY.

**Shakespearean pun**: a pun that appears in a play by William Shakespeare. In *Shakespeare's Wordplay*, M. M. Mahood estimates that the Bard of Avon uses about 3,000 puns in his plays. After her first murder, Lady Macbeth makes this pun on *gilt /guilt*:

If he do bleed,
I'll gild the faces of the grooms withal;
For it must seem their guilt.

**Shakespearean reversible sonnet**: Sonnet 66, "Tir'd with all these, for restful death I cry," which can be read when the words are reversed from last word to first (see REVERSAL). Here is how the last two lines of the original become the first two in reverse:

(Forward)    Tir'd with all these, from these would I be gone,
                  Save that to die, I leave, my love, alone.

**shaped poetry**: poetry written in a shape related to the topic or theme of the poem. Simmias of Rhodes, a Greek poet living in the fourth century B.C., wrote the earliest known shaped poems. His three take the shape of an egg, a hatchet, and a pair of wings. In the seventeenth century, George Herbert wrote the first shaped poems in English, including one called "Easter Wings" in the shape of wings. In the nineteenth century, Lewis Carroll wrote the best-known—"Mouse's Tale" in *Alice's Adventures in Wonderland*—in the shape of a mouse's tail. Guillaume Apollinaire's calligrammes are well-known twentieth-century examples. Shaped poetry is one branch of CONCRETE POETRY, possibly the most radical poetry movement of the twentieth century.

**shape-shift** (*v.*): to change from one shape to another. One letter can shape-shift to another through a series of intermediate drawings. Each drawing looks less like the starting letter and more like the ending letter. A line may grow longer, shorter, break apart, or disappear. If the shapes are printed one per page on a tablet, the result is an animated cartoon, an ALPHATOON.

**shift** (*v.*): to move an equal number of steps along the alphabet for each letter in a word, in order to generate a LETTERSHIFT of that word; to LETTERSHIFT (*v.*) a word.

**shiftgram**: a word formed by shifting the letters of another word an equal number of steps along the alphabet and then transposing the new string into a word. LAD-MBE-NCF-ODG = DOG. A shiftgram is a combination LETTERSHIFT and ANAGRAM.

> MUSIC + 8 = UCAQK = QUACK
> OVERLEANED + 4 = SZIVPIERIH = VIZIERSHIP

**shift pair**: a LETTERSHIFT PAIR.

**shift-quadruple**: a LETTERSHIFT SET of four words.

**shift-triple**: a LETTERSHIFT SET of three words.

**shift value**: the number of ALPHABETIC STEPS along the CIRCULAR ALPHA-BET that one letter is from another. Also called "step size."

**shift-word,** also spelled **shiftword**: see CYCLIC TRANSPOSAL. The term "shift-word" should be avoided because of its similarity to LETTERSHIFT WORD.

**"Siamese" pyramid**: a PYRAMID that combines two half-squares. The half-squares can be read across and down and then slid together to form the pyramid. This three-in-one form was first published in 1961. Here is a short example:

```
       C            C                         C
      H A          A H                      H A H
     L I T        T E R                   L I T E R
    P O T S      S H O T                P O T S H O T
```

**silly subject heading**: a library reference direction that, for one reason or another, is funny—and in some cases inexplicable.

AMERICAN GIANT CHECKERED RABBIT
BANKRUPTCY—POPULAR WORKS
DENTISTS IN ART
FANTASTIC TELEVISION PROGRAMS
FOOD, JUNK
ODORS IN THE BIBLE
SEWAGE—COLLECTED WORKS
SICK—FAMILY RELATIONSHIPS
WASPS (PERSONS)

**singing with words**: a solitaire game linking the letters of a word to the lyrics of a song. The player picks a song and a short word and guesses which letter the word will wind up on the last syllable of the song. Then he or she sings the song and counts out the word's letters over and over on the song's syllables to find out if the song ends at the chosen letter. It's similar to using a rhyme such as "Eenie Meenie Miney Moe" to make a choice. This example shows DOG used with the first two lines of the sung version of "Mary Had a Little Lamb":

```
Ma- ry had a  lit- tle lamb, lit- tle lamb, lit- tle lamb,
 D   O  G  D    O   G         D    O   G     D    O   G     D
```

Ma- ry had a lit- tle lamb; it's fleece was white as snow.
O    G    D    O    G    D    O    G    D    O    G    D    O

**single-key word**: a word spelled with each of the three letters on a single telephone KEY. The first three words are perfect since they use each letter once; the last three are imperfect since they lack a letter and/or use a letter more than once.

| CAB | FED | GHI | DEEDED | HIGH | NOON |
|-----|-----|-----|--------|------|------|
| 222 | 333 | 444 | 333333 | 4444 | 6666 |

**single-letter difference pair**: a pair of words that are spelled the same except for one letter. See VOLATILE WORDS.

| AERO-ZERO | QUARTO-QUARTZ |
|-----------|---------------|
| WAFER-WAXER | DUALITY-QUALITY |

**single-shift code**: a CODE in which each letter from A through Y is replaced by the letter to its left in the alphabet, and Z is replaced by A. Then A becomes B, B becomes C, and so forth, as shown below. The word CAT is represented as DBU.

A B C D E F G H I J K L M N O P Q R S T U V W X Y Z
B C D E F G H I J K L M N O P Q R S T U V W X Y Z A

**single square**: a WORD SQUARE in which the words going across are the same as the words going down: A single set of words makes a single square. Constructing a single square is easier than constructing a DOUBLE SQUARE of the same size. The following single square took less than 30 seconds to make:

X R A Y
R A R E
A R E A
Y E A R

**single-step pair**: a pair of words spelled the same except for a single letter that differs by one alphabetic step, e.g., WORD and WORE. In the first three examples below, one living creature turns into another. In the last example, three types of creatures are connected in a WORD STEPLADDER.

| GNAT | LOUSE | LICE | BASS |
|------|-------|------|------|
| GOAT | MOUSE | MICE | BATS |
|      |       |      | CATS |

**single transposal square**: a TRANSPOSAL SQUARE in which the columns and the rows transpose to the same set of words. On first glance, the letters look like random strings in a grid, but each row's letters can be rearranged to form a different word, and each column's letters can be rearranged to form the same word as in the corresponding row (first row and first column have the same word, and so on).

**single-word oxymoron**: a word that can be divided into two parts that have contradictory or incongruous meanings.

| | |
|---|---|
| BRIDEGROOM | FIREWATER |
| WHOLESOME | BITTERSWEET |

See OXYMORON.

**singular plurals**: two words, each of which in plural form looks like the singular of the other. The only known example of such a spelling phenomenon is the pair of words that follow. XENIA is "the supposed influence of foreign pollen upon the pollinated," and XENIUM is "a present given to a guest or stranger."

| Singular | Plural |
|---|---|
| XENIA | XENIUM |
| XENIUM | XENIA |

**666**: the Biblical "Number of the Beast," referred to as "Six Sixty-Six" or "Six Six Six." Some scholars think that it was a numerical transformation of the letters in the name of the Roman emperor, Nero. Others have noted that the Roman numerals in use at the time of Christ, DCLXVI, add up to 666. There are several websites that show some of its unusual numerical properties. In modern wordplay, the number has appeared in different ways, usually humorous. Here the Beast is shown to be a FOX since its three letters have ALPHABETIC VALUES whose digits sum up to six in each case:

FOX = F (6), O (15 = 1 + 5 = 6), X (24 = 2 + 4 = 6) = 666.

**six-square:** a WORD SQUARE measuring 6 x 6 letters. The first American six-square was published in 1871:

```
S C I O N S
C A T N I P
I T H A C A
O N A G E R
N I C E S T
S P A R T A
```

**six-vowel translation word pair**: a pair of words that come from two languages, that have the same meaning, and that contain all six vowels and no consonants. There are two English-French pairs made of words meaning YES:

AYE—OUI          YEA—OUI

**six-vowel word**: a word that uses all six vowels once apiece.

AUREOMYCIN          BUOYANCIES

**skewed word line**: a WORD LINE in which none of the successive differences between the ALPHABETIC VALUES is 0.

**slanted word line**: a WORD LINE in which one of the differences between the alphabetic values is 0.

**slenderizing**: the removal of a specific letter from all occurrences in a text to generate a new text (preferably, one that makes sense).

He plans to blank out when the blinding clash comes.
He pans to bank out when the binding cash comes.

**sneeze word**: a word that signifies the sound of a sneeze in a language. English has several variations, including AH-CHOO! and KER-CHOO!

HAN-CHEE! (Chinese)          ITUSH! (Hebrew)
KYCHNUTI! (Czech)            WA-HING! (Indonesian)
A-TCHOUIN! (French)          AP-CHI! (Russian)

**snowball/melting snowball sentence**: a sentence that begins with a one-letter word, adds a letter to each successive word, reaches a midpoint, and then subtracts a letter from each successive word till reaching a one-letter word again. In this sentence, MANIPULATION is the midpoint:

Q is the very first letter mystics disclose, involving infrequent puzzleistic manipulation; cryptograms contradict prevalent judgment; solving expert shows this may be X.

**snowball sentence**: **1.** a sentence that begins with a one-letter word and adds a letter to each word in succession. I AM THE WORD is a short snowball sentence. Here is a 20-word snowball sentence that ends in a 20-letter word:

> I do not know where family doctors acquired illegibly perplexing handwriting; nevertheless, extraordinary pharmaceutical intellectuality, counterbalancing indecipherability, transcendentalizes intercommunications's incomprehensibleness.

Also called "rhopalism," "prose rhopalic," "rhopalic prose," "rhopalic sentence."

    **2.** a syllable-unit snowball sentence. Usually, this is called a RHOPALIC SENTENCE.

**solid cluster five-vowel word**: a word in which the five major vowels appear together with no consonants between them.

    MIAOUED          AIAOUEZ

**sound change**: the change from one sound to another in a word to make a second word.

    TUNGSTEN—TONGUESTER

**sound shift**: the movement of one sound in a word to a new position in order to make another word.

    UMBER—BUMMER

**soundplay**: WORDPLAY involving the sounds of words without regards to letters or meanings.

**specialty definition**: a definition followed by a made-up term that is a word spelled differently to match the meaning.

> Eskimo cement: IGGLUE
> Quill injury: PORCUPAIN
> Spelling wager: ALPHA-BET

Warehouse of literary falsehoods: LIE-BRARY
Whisky-flavored pastry: BOURBUN

**spell-checker Jabberwocky**: a rewrite of Lewis Carroll's nonsense poem "Jabberwocky" using a computer spell-checker. Since there are numerous made-up words in the poem (*brillig, slithy,* etc.), the spell-checker "corrects" them by search for words in its dictionary that are closest in spelling. Different spell-checkers give different rewrites. Here is the opening stanza of the original poem and the first spell-checker version of the same:

| | |
|---|---|
| 'Twas brillig, and the slithy toves | Teas broiling, and the silty tomes |
| Did gyre and gimble in the wabe; | Did gyrate and gamble in the wave; |
| All mimsy were the borogoves, | All misery were the boroughs, |
| And the mome raths outgrabe. | And the mime rashes outraged. |

**spelled-out letter**: a letter that has its own name (other than the letter itself) listed in any dictionary. *Webster's Second* spells most of the letters (BEE, CEE, DEE . . .), and *Webster's Third* spells almost half (BE, CE, DE . . .). Both dictionaries differ in all of their spelled-out letters (DOUBLE-U vs DOUBLE-YOU). *Webster's Second* has two spellings for Z (ZED, ZEE), while *Webster's Third* has none.

**spelling bee**: a contest in which participants take turns spelling words. If a contestant misspells a word, he or she drops out until only one person is left—the winner. The first spelling bee was held in 1875 in Philadelphia. Forty men and forty women, most of them schoolteachers, participated. Some of the groundbreaking misspelled words include CHLOROFORM, DUELLIST, GOURMAND, and MUSKETEER.

Spelling bees became a craze for a while, and when the craze died down, they never went away. They are especially popular in schools. Variations on the concept emerged, including spelling the word backwards or spelling the word by having each person say one letter. Lord Palmerston of England tested the spelling skills of eleven Cabinet Ministers by asking them to spell the words in the sentence below, but none of the gentlemen was able to spell all of the words correctly:

It is disagreeable to witness the embarrassment of a harassed peddler gauging the symmetry of a peeled potato.

**spiraling alphabet**: the alphabet written in a clockwise spiral over and over, starting with A and going outward. One purpose is to find words that appear in a single line. The spiral below could be continued indefinitely. One horizontal and one vertical word are highlighted, but other words can be found.

```
Q  R  S  T  U  V  W
P  U  V  W  X  Y  Z
O  T  G  H  I  J  A
N  S  F  A  B  K  B
M  R  E  D  C  L  C
L  Q  P  O  N  M  D
K  J  I  H  G  F  E
```

**split definitive**: a word given a new definition by breaking it into two shorter words and using their meanings.

ADAMANT: the first insect
BEWILDER: act more uncontrollably
FRIENDSHIP: love boat
LEGEND: ankle

NOTICE: water or steam
QUARTERBACK: coin return
SEEKING: Elvis lives!
ZITHER: female's pimple

**spoonergram**: a word or phrase that is a SPOONERISM of another word or phrase.

VISITATION—'TIS EVASION
OPTIMISTICALLY—MISTY OPTICALLY
TINY SHOE!—SHINEY, TOO!
RUNNING CAT—CUNNING RAT
BEER NIGH?—NEARBY.

Also called "spannergroom," "spammergroon," "groonerspam."

**spoonergram opposites**: two SPOONERGRAMS that have opposite or contrasting meanings.

BACKING LOSERS—LACKING BOOZERS
CHARRED HILLS—HARD CHILLS

**spoonerick**: a LIMERICK that uses one or more SPOONER-RHYMES, such as this untitled example:

Some kids nowadays, it is said,
Are too fond of stopping in bed.
But according to Spooner
The Forties lot sooner
Enjoyed themselves bopping instead.

**spoonerism**: an unintentional transposition of sounds in words. The term was named after Rev. William Archibald Spooner. Many spoonerisms were attributed to him, but few were spoken by him. Here are a few that he is credited with saying:

> Mardon me, padam, but you are occupewing the wrong pie. May I
>     sew you to another sheet?
> I have in my bosom a half-warmed fish.
> It is kisstomary to cuss the bride.
> Is the bean dizzy?
> Our queer old Dean.

**spoonerism equation**: an equation in which two or more NUMBER NAMES on one side of the equal sign switch their initial consonants to form two or more non-numeric words on the other side.

> NINE + FIFTY = FINE + NIFTY
> SIX + FIVE + THREE = FIX + THRIVE + SEE

**spoonerism poem**: a poem in which the word or words ending one line are made into a SPOONERISM that serves as a rhyme in the next line. "Knives, Forks, and Spoonerisms" begins with these lines:

> When Sandy sees a flying crow,
> It makes her weep.  The crying flow
> Runs down her nose and lips and cheeks
> Into a cup that chips and leaks.
> Outside the house, her parking spot
> Is lit up by a sparking pot . . .

**spooner-rhyme**: a rhyme formed by spoonerizing a set of words. The two are spooner-rhymes of each other.

| Mabel Tanners | shortcake |
|---|---|
| table manners | court shake |

Sometimes spelled "spoonerhyme." See SPOONERGRAM.

**square & diamond inside**: a WORD SQUARE that has a DIAMOND in it.

```
O B E S E
B R A W L
E A V E S
S W E D E
E L S E S
```

**squaring the circle**: constructing a WORD SQUARE that has the word CIRCLE in it. This challenge refers to the age-old geometry problem of constructing a square whose area is exactly the same as that of a given circle. In the nineteenth century, Ferdinand von Lindemann proved it to be impossible for geometry, but an anonymous word-square constructor proved it to be possible for wordplay.

```
C I R C L E
I C A R U S
R A R E S T
C R E A T E
L U S T R E
E S T E E M
```

**standard rebus**: a LETTER REBUS in which a word or phrase must be respaced to form a message that reveals the hidden letter. BASIS refers to the letter B because it's B AS IS.

```
IAMB = I AM B
DISAPPEARING = D IS APPEARING
SEESAW = SEES A W
```

**Star of David**: a symmetric pattern in the shape of a six-pointed star created with hexagonal letter tiles for spelling HEX-WORDS. In the example, the pattern of 13 different letters on the left has 12 triangles in it. The letters on each triangle form one of the words in the list at the right. All 13 letters spell UNPREDICTABLY.

```
              D
            /   \
    C — L — I — N          LID   PIT   PER
     \ / \ / \ /           LAC   TIN   PET
      A — P — T            LAP   RAY   BET
     / \ / \ / \           LIP   RAP   RUE
  Y — R — E — B
         \ /
          U
```

**star's name**: the name that a movie star uses instead of their original given name. In each of these examples, the star's name appears first:

CHARLES BRONSON—Charles Bunchinsky
CHER —Cherilyn LaPierre
W.C. FIELDS—William Claude Dukenfield

JUDY GARLAND—Francis Gumm
STEVIE WONDER—Steveland Morris
DORIS DAY—Doris von Kappelhoff

**starter**: a word that starts a NETWORK.

**state double four-square**: a STATE SQUARE measuring 4 x 4 letters and forming one set of abbreviations across and another set down.

```
M I N V
T N M A
N C O K
V A K Y
```

**state double three-square**: a STATE SQUARE measuring 3 x 3 letters and forming one set of state postal abbreviations across and another set down. The following is the only state square of any size that doesn't repeat an abbreviation.

```
N M N
C O H
A R I
```

**stately word**: a word whose letters form a string of STATE POSTAL ABBRE-VIATIONS. There are two types: NON-OVERLAPPING STATELY WORDS and OVERLAPPING STATELY WORDS.

**state name word-weight group**: a group of two or more U.S. states having the same WORD-WEIGHT. The largest group includes only two states, but there are ten of them. Here are four, with their common word-weights.

FLORIDA, KANSAS (65)    CALIFORNIA, MARYLAND (88)
DELAWARE, TEXAS (69)    NEW MEXICO, NEW YORK (111)

**state palindrome**: a PALINDROME that contains the name of one of the fifty U.S. states.

No Delaware raw ale, Don.
He yawned: "Lost Idaho had its olden way, eh?"
Tie USS Illinois? Simple help mission! I'll issue it.
'Tis Iowa law! O, is it?
I made Kansas, as naked am I.
"Not New York," Roy went on.

**state postal abbreviation**: a pair of letters designated by the U.S. Post Office as the abbreviation for the name of one of the 50 states. They appear in various wordplay forms, including STATELY WORDS. In this list, the state names are omitted.

| AK | CO | HI | KS | ME | MT | NJ | OK | SD | VT |
|----|----|----|----|----|----|----|----|----|----|
| AL | CT | IA | KY | MI | NC | NM | OR | TN | WA |
| AR | DE | ID | LA | MN | ND | NV | PA | TX | WI |
| AZ | FL | IL | MA | MO | NE | NY | RI | UT | WV |
| CA | GA | IN | MD | MS | NH | OH | SC | VA | WY |

**state postal abbreviation ambiguity problem**: the problem of finding a systematic set of rules that would result in a single, unique two-letter abbreviation for each of the fifty states. At present, 16 of the abbreviations are ambiguous; they could stand for 31 incorrect states. For instance, NE (Nebraska) could stand for Nevada. The goal is to formulate rules that, given the name of a state, would generate one and only one abbreviation—or to come as close to that goal as possible.

**state single four-square**: a STATE SQUARE measuring 4 x 4 letters and forming the same set of STATE POSTAL ABBREVIATIONS across and down.

```
I  N  C  A
N  M  O  R
C  O  H  I
A  R  I  A
```

**state square**: a square of letters in which each pair of adjacent letters forms a STATE POSTAL ABBREVIATION across and down. For instance, the letters N, M, N, and V would link three abbreviations, NM, MN, and NV. No abbreviation may be used more than once in the same direction, but repetition is allowed from one direction to the other.

**stereowords**: two words printed so that they become a third word when viewed the right way. The letters of the first two words merge and form different letters. They are similar to the early-twentieth-century stereopticons, which gave the illusion of three-dimensionality to pictures.

**stinky pinky**: a two-word rhyming phrase, e.g., FLOWER POWER.

**stinky pinky buzzword**: a real-life STINKY PINKY allegedly used as jargon in certain occupations. Although presented as real, the examples below may be fabricated. Each gives the stinky pinky, the speaker's occupation, and the meaning.

> SLOPPY COPY (adwriter): badly worded press release
> YELL BELL (car salesman): car theft alarm
> NERD HERD (high-school teacher): honor society
> SHABBY ABBY (beauty pageant director): poorly outfitted contestant
> BUMPER HUMPER (trucker): tail-gater

**strike-out**: a word that results from deleting the even letters of another word.

> | | | | |
> |---|---|---|---|
> | B U O Y A N T | B R I S T L E | F E A S T | P R E S T O |
> | B - O - A - T | B - I - T - E | F - A - T | P - E - T - |

**strike-out poetry**: verse that includes STRIKE-OUTS in its lines. In the strike-out poem "Girls I've Struck Out With," female names are deleted to shorter words. The first stanza goes:

> SALLY I find much too S-L-Y
> ANNETTE just raised the A-N-T-E
> CLAIRE is wary in my C-A-R
> DIANNE must serve her D-A-N tea

**strike-out sentence**: a sentence containing a STRIKE-OUT and the word it comes from.

> Few people find BEAUTY in a B-A-T.
> She may no longer wear a B-R-A, but it's still in her BUREAU.

**string**: **1.** a LETTERSTRING. **2.** a WORD STRING.

**suber**: a LETTER REBUS that must be respaced like the STANDARD REBUS and read in reverse to form the message. (*Suber* is *rebus* in reverse.) KENO signifies K because in reverse it can be read ONE K.

> BOLOS = SOLO B
> DENOTES = SET ONE D
> ONWARD = DRAWN O

**subletter**: a new letter intended to represent an actual sound made with the upper respiratory system. (Dictionary words such as MOAN do not qualify.) A subletter is represented by a capital letter in brackets. It can appear at the beginning, middle, or end of a word, or it can stand alone. When a letter is repeated within brackets, the subletter's sound is drawn out longer. Here are 15 subletters followed by three sentences using some of them:

| | | |
|---|---|---|
| [A] belch | [F] moan | [K] sniffle |
| [B] cough | [G] pant | [L] snore |
| [C] gasp | [H] shriek | [M] snort |
| [D] hiccup | [I] snarl | [N] spit |
| [E] kiss | [J] sneeze | [O] yawn |

"Hey, punk, [I] what are you doing [M] on this side of town [N]?"
"I rea[K]lly caught a bad[B] case of the flu[K][B][K]."
"Great food! [AAAAA]! Excuse me!"
"I [O] can hard[OO]ly keep awa[OOO]ke [L][LL][LLL]. . . ."

**substitute-letter transposal**: a word formed by changing one letter to another in a different word and then transposing those letters to form a new word: RACE – E + S = RACS = CARS.

THURSDAY = SATURDAY
ENIGMATOGRAPHY = PYTHAGOREANISM

**substitute-letter word chain**: a series of words formed by the successive SUBSTITUTE-LETTER TRANSPOSAL of each word to form the next. The words in this chain are names of trees:

| | | | | |
|---|---|---|---|---|
| ROWAN | MANGO | MAPLE | PECAN | ALDER |
| GORAN | ALMON | APPLE | PEACH | BELAR |
| BONGA | ALAMO | PLANE | CAPER | ROBLE |
| NOGAL | PALMA | ASPEN | CEDAR | BOREE |

**substitution code**: a CODE in which each letter is replaced by a different letter or symbol.

**subtransposition**: a word whose ALPHABETIC VALUES multiply to the same product as the product of the alphabetic values of another word—e.g., AND (1 x 14 x 4 = 56) and HAG (8 x 1 x 7 = 56) are subtranspositions of each other. The most common product appears to be 300, shared by the first line of words below. The longest known subtransposition pair, also shown below, has a common product of 1,866,240,000 and no letters in common.

ALEE BEEF ABBY CEDE DACE DOE EEL JOB LAY LEE ODE TO
PRECEPTOR   DILLYDALLY

**subtransposition group**: one of nine groups, labeled by a single digit, into
which SUBTRANSPOSITIONS can be placed. The digit is determined by
repeatedly summing the digits in the product of the ALPHABETIC VALUES of
the subtranspositions. FIVE and LOCK have a common product of 5940, and
$5+9+4+0 = 18 = 1+8 = 9$, which means they belong into the 9-group. Most
words belong in that group.

**successive beheadment**: the consecutive removal of one letter at a time
from the beginning of a word to make a series of words (see BEHEADMENT).
The series ends with one letter.

> ASPIRATE
> SPIRATE
> PIRATE
> IRATE
> RATE
> ATE
> TE
> E

**successive beheadment sentence**: a sentence that uses the words resulting from the SUCCESSIVE BEHEADMENT of a single word. In this case, THIS
is the word:

> IS THIS HIS "S"?

Also called "reductive anagram," "subtractive anagram."

**successive bigram beheadment**: a SUCCESSIVE BEHEADMENT of two
letters at a time. In this example, NG is a common Asian surname:

> DELIBERATING
> LIBERATING
> BERATING
> RATING
> TING
> NG

**successive buildup reversal**: a series of words formed by three or more consecutive BUILDUP REVERSALS.

> Elbert : treble
> Delbert : trebled
> Adelbert : trebled A
> Adelberta : a trebled A

**successive curtailment**: the consecutive removal of one letter at a time from the end of a word to form a series of words ending at a single letter. See CURTAILMENT.

> PASTERNS
> PASTERN
> PASTER
> PASTE
> PAST
> PAS
> PA
> P

Also called "apocope," "paragoge."

**successive curtailment sentence**: a sentence that uses the words resulting from the SUCCESSIVE CURTAILMENT of a single word. In the first sentence below, H means the eighth question in a series; and in the second sentence S signifies the school grade "satisfactory."

> Is HE HER HERO, HEROD? HEROD'S reply is silence.
> S? SO SOL, SOLO, SOLOS.

**successive deletion**: the consecutive removal of one letter at a time from the interior of a word to generate a series of words. The series ends with two letters and no interior. See DELETION.

> STARTLINGS
> STARTINGS
> STARINGS
> STRINGS
> STINGS
> SINGS
> SINS
> SIS
> SS

**successive terminal deletion**: the consecutive removal of two letters at a time, one from each end of a word, to form a series of words. See TERMINAL DELETION.

> A W A K E N E R S
> W A K E N E R
> A K E N E
> K E N
> E

Also called "successive terminal elision."

**successive transaddition**: the consecutive addition of a letter and TRANSPOSAL of the remaining letters to generate a series of words.

**successive transdeletion**: the consecutive removal of a letter and TRANSPOSAL of the remaining letters to generate a series of words, called a TRANSDELETION CHAIN, ending with a single letter. The resulting words can be placed in a TRANSDELETION PYRAMID.

**sumgrams**: two or more words whose letters have SUMWORD VALUES that add up to the same amount.

> TEE $(9 + 13 + 13 = 35)$
> QUIZZICAL $(0.4 + 3.3 + 7.3 + 0.1 + 0.1 + 7.3 + 3.5 + 8.5 + 4.5 = 35)$

**sum word**: **1.** a word formed by adding the ALPHABETIC VALUES of the adjacent letters in another word and converting the sums to the letters that have those alphabetic values. If a sum is greater than 26, then 26 is subtracted and the remainder is used as the alphabetic value. Here is how CAN generates the sum word DO:

| C | A | N | (starting word) |
|---|---|---|---|
| 3 | 1 | 14 | (alphabetic values of letters in CAN) |
| | 4 | 15 | (sums of adjacent alphabetic values ) |
| | D | O | (letters having alphabetic values of 4 and 15) |

Also called "'can do' word."
    **2.** a word considered as the sum of its letter FREQUENCY VALUES. Those values are based on the number of times a letter occurs in every hundred letters of English prose. A appears 8.5 times, B 1.5 times, and so on. The challenge is to the sum word with the lowest value and that with the highest value for each letter length.

TEE (9 + 13 + 13 = 35)          ZUZ (0.1 + 3.3 + 0.1)

**sumword value**: the value assigned to a letter based on the amount of times it appears in every hundred letters of English prose.

| | | | | |
|---|---|---|---|---|
| A = 8.5 | F = 3 | K = 0.5 | P = 3.1 | U = 3.3 |
| B = 1.5 | G = 1.3 | L = 4.5 | Q = 0.4 | V = 1 |
| C = 3.5 | H = 6 | M = 2.5 | R = 7 | W = 2.3 |
| D = 4 | I = 7.3 | N = 7.5 | S = 6.5 | X = 0.3 |
| E = 13 | J = 0.2 | 0 = 8 | T = 9 | Y = 2 |
| | | | | Z = 0.1 |

**supercalifragilisticexpialidocious**: the most well-known nonce word to come out of the movies. It made its film debut in the musical *Mary Poppins* (1964), where it meant "wonderful" and where it was described as "the biggest word you ever heard." It made its court debut in 1965–66, when songwriters Parker and Young unsuccessfully sued the makers of the musical for copyright infringement. The two men claimed that they wrote the word in 1949 in an unpublished song, in which they spelled it "supercalafajalistickespialadojus." In order to simplify the hearing, the court ruled that "supercalifragilisticexpialidocious" could not be repeated, and that, "All variants of this tongue-twister will hereinafter be referred to collectively as 'the word.'" For a while, "supercalifragilisticexpialidocious" and "the word" were legal synonyms.

**super-charade**: a long word that can redivide into many shorter words of at least two letters in length. The number of words is important; their meaning isn't. Here is the greatest super-charade of all:

ANTIDISESTABLISHMENTARIANISM =
ANT ID IS ES TAB LI SH MEN TARI AN ISM

**supersentence**: a single sentence that includes at least one example of each of the seven phrases and subordinate clauses in English grammar: 1) adverb clause, 2) adjective clause, 3) infinitive phrase, 4) noun, 5) gerund phrase, 6) participial phrase, and 7) prepositional phrase. The shortest example uses 11 words:

[4]Whoever rebels, [6]daring [3]oppose [7]by [5]fighting [1]when oppressed, [2]which overcomes, conquers.

**super title**: a refashioned name for a person's job, a piece of clothing, etc., that disguises or softens the meaning of the original name.

BEAUTY CAKE = BAR OF SOAP
UNDERFASHIONS = UNDERWEAR
UNFOUNDED STATEMENT = LIE
CANINE CONTROL OFFICER = DOG CATCHER
PRE-OWNED VEHICLE = USED CAR

**superultramegalosesquipedalia**: the class of extremely long words. Any word having 1,000 or more letters would certainly qualify. Most words of that length are chemical terms, like the three described below. If the third word were typed out in a single row of ten-point letters, it would measure one-tenth of a mile. The longest word ever published with correct spelling appeared in *Word Ways* (May, 1980, p. 118). Its 3,644 letters identify the Bovine Glutamate Dehydrogenase protein. Two parts are underlined to indicate uncertainties in the chemical analysis of the protein:

alanylaspartylarginylglutamylaspartylaspartylprolylasparaginylphenylalanylphenylalanyllysylmethionyl-
valylglutamylglycylphenylalanylphenylalanylaspartylarginylglycylalanylserylisoleucylvalylglutamylas-
partyllysylleucylvalylglutamylaspartylleucyllysylthreonylarginylglutaminylthreonylglutaminylglutamylg
lutaminyllysylarginylasparaginylarginylvalylarginylglycylisoleucylleucylarginylisoleucylisoleucyllysyl-
prolylcysteinylasparaginylhistidylvalylleucylserylleucylserylphenylalanylprolylisoleucylarginylarginylas-
partylaspartylglycylseryltryptophanylglutamylvalylisoleucylglutamylglycyltyrosylarginylalanylgluta-min
ylhistidylserylhistidylglutaminylarginylthreonylprolylcysteinyllysylglycylglycylisoleucylarginyltyro-
sylserylthreonylaspartylvalylserylvalylaspartylglutamylvalyllysylalanylleucylalanylserylleucylme-
thionylthreonyltyrosyllysylcysteinylalanylvalylvalylaspartylvalylprolylphenylalanylglycylglycylalanylly-
sylalanylglycylvalyllysylisoleucylasparaginylprolyllysylasparaginyltyrosylthreonylaspartylglutamylas-
partylleucylglutamyllysylisoleucylthreonylarginylarginylphenylalanylthreonylmethionylglutamylleucy-
lalanyllysyllysylglycylphenylalanylisoleucylglycylprolylglycylvalylaspartylvalylprolylalanylprolylaspara-
ginylmethionylserylthreonylglycylglutamylarginylglutamylmethionylseryltryptophanylisoleucylalany-
laspartylthreonyltyrosylalanylserylthreonylisoleucylglycylhistidyltyrosylaspartylisoleucylasparaginy-
lalanylhistidylalanylcysteinylvalylthreonyllysylprolylglycylisoleucylserylglutaminylglycylglycylisoleu-
cylhistidylglycylarginylisoleucylserylalanylthreonylglycylarginylglycylvalylphenylalanylglycylhis-
tidylisoleucylglutamylasparaginylphenylalanylisoleucylglutamylasparaginylalanylseryltyrosylme-
thionylserylisoleucylleucylglycylmethionylthreonylprolylglycylphenylalanylglycylaspartyllysylthreo-
nylphenylalanylalanylvalylglutaminylglycylphenylalanylglycylasparaginylvalylglycylleucylhistidylseryl-
methionylarginyltyrosylleucylhistidylarginylphenylalanylglycylalanyllysylcysteinylvalylalanylvalylgly-
cylglutamylserylaspartylglycylserylisoleucyltryptophanylasparaginylprolylaspartylglycylisoleucylaspar-
tylprolyllysylglutamylleucylglutamylaspartylphenylalanylalanyllysylleucylglutaminylhistidylglycylthre-
onylisoleucylleucylglycylphenylalanylprolyllysylalanyllysylisoleucyltyrosylglutamylgly-
cylserylisoleucylleucylglutamylvalylaspartylcysteinylaspartylisoleucylleucylisoleucylprolylalanylalanyl-s
erylglutamyllysylglutaminylleucylthreonyllysylserylasparaginylalanylprolylarginylvalyllysylalanylly-
sylisoleucylisoleucylalanylglutamylglycylalanylaspartylglycylprolylthreonylthreonylprolylgluta-
minylalanylaspartyllysylisoleucylphenylalanylleucylglutamylarginylasparaginylisoleucylmethionylvaly-
lisoleucylprolylaspartylleucyltyrosylleucylasparaginylalanylglycylglycylvalylthreonylvalylseryltyro-
sylphenylalanylglutaminylleucyllysylasparaginylleucylasparaginylhistidylvalylseryltyrosylglycy-
larginylleucylthreonylphenylalanyllysyltyrosylglutamylarginylaspartylserylasparaginyltyrosylhistidyl-
leucylleucylmethionylserylvalylglutaminylglutamylserylleucylglutamylarginyllysylphenylalanylgly-
cyllysylhistidylglycylglycylthreonylisoleucylprolylisoleucylvalylprolylthreonylalanylglutamylpheny-
lalanylglutaminylaspartylarginylisoleucylserylglycylalanylserylglutamyllysylaspartylisoleucylvalylhisti-
dylserylglycylleucylalanyltyrosylthreonylmethionylglutamylarginylserylalanylarginylgluta-
minylisoleucylmethionylarginylthreonylalanylmethionyllysyltyrosylaspartylleucylglycylleucylas-
partylleucylarginylthreonylalanylalanyltyrosylvalylaspartylalanylisoleucylglutamyllysylvalylphenyla-
lanylarginylvalyltyrosylasparaginylglutamylalanylglycylvalylthreonylphenylalanylthreonine

206

Here are some others:

**1,913 Letters.** The chemical term for Tryptophan Synethetase A was the longest ever published in *The Guinness Book of Records* (1971).

**3,644 Letters.** The Bovine Glutamate Dehydrogenase protein was printed out, but misspelled as a 3,641-letter word in the *National Biological Research Foundation* (1976), cited but not printed in *The Guinness Book* (1976), and summarized in three-letter amino acid abbreviations in the *Journal of Biomedical Research* (1979).

**66,000 Letters.** A 5,386-element nucleotide sequence of Deoxyribonucleic Acid Bacteriophage OX 174 was reported in the *Journal of Molecular Biology* (1978). If molecules were named by their nucleotide sequences and not by three-letter amino acid abbreviations, the resulting word would be about 66,000 letters long.

**syllabic rebus**: a REBUS in which letters and/or numbers are sounded out to form syllables.

> NRG = energy
> 280 = "too weighty"
> I12CU = "I want to see you."
> I00204I80 = "I ought not to owe for I ate nothing."
> LMN = a lemon
> XPDNC = expediency

**symmetric crash group**: a group of words, each of which CRASHES exactly once with every other word. Each letter in every word participates in one and only one crash. For three-letter words, there are four words in the crash group. The first, second, and third letters of one word crash with the first letter of one other word, the second letter of another, and the third letter of another.

> PEN POT SET SON

**synonym chain**: a series of synonyms that go from the starting word to its opposite.

> BLACK-DARK-OBSCURE-HIDDEN-CONCEALED-SNUG-
> COMFORTABLE-EASY-SIMPLE-PURE-WHITE

**synonymic reversal**: a REVERSAL whose meaning is similar to that of the original word.

> PAT = TAP (both mean "to touch lightly")
> STATE = ÉTATS (French for "states")

Also called "synonym reversal."

**synonymic transdeletion**: the deletion of one letter in a word followed by transposing the remaining letters to create a new word that is similar in meaning to the original: DRIVE – V = DRIE = RIDE.

> NEGLECTING = NEGLIGENT
> RIDICULOUS = LUDICROUS

**synonym square**: a WORD SQUARE consisting of a baseword and words related in meaning or belonging to the same class. The related words form the rows, and the baseword forms one of the columns. The other columns don't necessarily spell words.

```
s   p   a   C   e
f   a   v   O   r
f   o   r   U   m
d   a   i   R   y
g   a   r   T   h
```

**Syzygy**: a word puzzle in which one word changes into another through a series of intermediate words. Each word has some letters in common with the preceding word (and not just one letter, as in a WORD LADDER). This puzzle never caught on because it was too complex. In the following Syzygy, the player was told to "Send MAN on ICE."

> MAN
> PERMANENT
>      ENTICE
>        ICE

**tag**: a published reference work other than the most generally accepted dictionaries. Atlases, specialized dictionaries, and telephone directories are examples of tags.

**tall writing**: writing that uses imponderably erudite linguistic alternatives to the commonplace diurnal jargon in order to state that which, had it been expressed less ornately, could have achieved greater intercommunicative cognizance without the unnecessary blather. The following lines begin "The Domicile Erected by John," a tall writing version of "This Is the House that Jack Built":

> Behold the Mansion reared by dædal Jack.
>
> See the malt stored in many a plethoric sack,
> In the proud cirque of Ivan's bivouac.
>
> Mark how the Rat's felonious fangs invade
> The golden stores in John's pavilion laid.
>
> Anon, with velvet foot and Tarquin strides,
> Subtle Grimalkin to his quarry glides,—
> Grimalkin grim, that slew the fierce rodent
> Whose tooth insidious Johann's sackcloth rent.

**tautogram**: a text in which every word begins with the same letter.

**tautonym**: a word or words made of two or more parts that have the same spelling. MAMA and PAPA are tautonyms.

> YATATA YATATA
> BOUNCY-BOUNCY          PER SECOND PER SECOND

Also called "reduplication," "two-part tautonym."

**tautonymic ten-square**: a TEN-SQUARE that uses TAUTONYMS and allows repetition of words. The first tautonymic ten-square was published in 1921:

```
O R A N G U T A N G
R A N G A R A N G A
A N D O L A N D O L
N G O T A N G O T A
G A L A N G A L A N
U R A N G U T A N G
T A N G A T A N G A
A N D O L A N D O L
N G O T A N G O T A
G A L A N G A L A N
```

**telepalindrome**: a TELEPHONE WORD spelled with letters whose digits on the keys form a NUMERICAL PALINDROME.

| EDUCATED | SUNSPOTS | EVAPORATE |
|----------|----------|-----------|
| 33822833 | 78677687 | 382767283 |

**telephomnemonic**: a word or phrase spelled by the letters corresponding to the digits in a telephone number. When the following words were dialed in various locales, the phone started ringing. This was in 1981, before such usage became common.

SEX PLAY  NEW YORK  HOLY PIG

**telephone answer**: a word, phase, or sentence used to greet the caller on a telephone. Alexander Graham Bell, the alleged inventor of the phone, suggested that people answer by saying "Ahoy." The customary greeting in each of seven countries appears below, in English translation:

"Hello." (US)
"Are you there?" (England, Portugal)
"Here is Mr. So-and-so." (Germany)
"What is it?" (Spain)
"I'm listening." (Russia)
"Say, say!" (Japan)

**telephone double-digit word**: a word or words that can be dialed with only two digits.

| BABOON | DEIFIED | DEMON |
|--------|---------|-------|
| 2 2 2 6 6 6 | 3 343433 | 3 3 6 6 6 |
| JACKAL | FAÇADE | HIGH NOON |
| 52 2 525 | 3 2 22 3 3 | 4 44 4 6 6 6 6 |

**telephone grid**: the grid on a touch-tone phone consisting of 10 numbered keypads. Each digit from 2 to 9 is accompanied by a set of three consecutive letters (excluding Q) placed in a 3 x 3 grid. The 1 has no letters. Many telephones have a fourth row with 0 and OPER (for "operator") in the middle and other symbols on either side. The pattern of numbers, letters, and keypads looks like this:

| 1 | 2 ABC | 3 DEF |
|---|-------|-------|
| 4 GHI | 5 JKL | 6 MNO |
| 7 PRS | 8 TUV | 9 WXY |
| * | 0 OPER | # |

**telephone isogram**: a word or words that can be dialed without repeating a digit. WORD (9673) works, but PHONE (74663) uses 6 twice. The maximum length for a telephone ISOGRAM is eight letters, one per digit.

| POLICE | EARTHLY | SODALITY | MAPLE + IVY |
|--------|---------|----------|-------------|
| 7 6542 3 | 3 2 78 45 9 | 7 6 3 2548 9 | 6 2 753  4 89 |

**telephone letters**: A, B, C, D, E, F, G, H, I, J, K, L, M, N, O, P, R, S, T, U, V, W, X, and Y, the letters on a telephone dial or touch-tone keypad. (The letters Q and Z are excluded.) Recently some telephone manufacturers have added the two missing letters to the dial/keypad so that 7 = PQRS and 9 = WXYZ. This break with tradition is generally ignored in wordplay.

**telephone reversal**: a word whose telephone number is the reverse of another word's telephone number, but whose letters are not the reverse of the other word's letters.

| 3456 7 | (reverses to) | 76 543 |
|--------|---------------|--------|
| FILMS | (doesn't reverse to) | SOLID |

**telephone value**: the numeric value of a letter based on the telephone digit with which it appears on the dial or the keypad.

|            |           |           |
|------------|-----------|-----------|
| ABC = 2    | JKL = 5   | TUV = 8   |
| DEF = 3    | MNO = 6   | WXY = 9   |
| GHI = 4    | PRS = 7   |           |

**telephone word**: a word spelled with TELEPHONE LETTERS. Since most words qualify, telephone wordplay must do more. A telephone word combines the letters and digits on the telephone dial or keypad in ways that are unique to their letter/number relationships.

**telestich**: an ACROSTIC poem or puzzle in which the last letters of the lines spell out a word, phrase, or name going down the page.

**ten-square**: a WORD SQUARE measuring 10 x 10 letters. A ten-square composed of ten words listed in standard references is the goal of modern formists. It hasn't been achieved yet.

**terminal:** the first or last letter of a word.

**terminal deletion**: the removal of the first and the last letter of a word to generate another word or words. This form combines BEHEADMENT and CURTAILMENT.

| HEART | KNIGHTLINESS | REVOLVER |
|-------|--------------|----------|
| EAR   | NIGHT LINES  | EVOLVE   |

Also called "terminal elision."

**terminal man**: a man or a woman whose surname, beginning with two or more Z's, is the last entry in a telephone book. Most of these names were probably coined for the purpose of coming in last. The examples below were selected from a list of 45 terminal men (40 with two Z's and 5 with three Z's) found in phonebooks published from 1972 to 1974.

| ZZYMITH, Zola         | ZZZYANDOTTIE, Archimedes I. |
|-----------------------|-----------------------------|
| ZZYYNIK, William      | ZZZYD, Vladimir             |
| ZZYZYZKOFF, Zander Z. | ZZZYH, Z.Z.                 |
| ZZYZZ, Z.             | ZZZYPT, Robert              |
| ZZYZZX, Hero          | ZZZYZZITT, Robert           |

Zachary ZZZZRA, with the first reported four-Z surname, was listed in the 1974 *Guinness Book of Records*. In 1979, *Time* magazine reported that

ZZZZRA was zapped out of last place by Zelda ZZZZWRAMP. In response, ZZZZRA expanded his surname to ZZZZZZZZZRA and won his position back. He was actually Bill Holland, a painting contractor, who used the name as an advertising gimmick.

The 23-letter surname ZZZZZZZZZZZZZZZZZZZZZZZ, probably the longest all-Z name ever, appeared in the 1993 Queens, New York, phone directory. Its purity was unsullied by a first name or initial.

**terminal switch**: a TRANSPOSAL in which the first and the last letters of a word exchange places to form another word; a type of METALLEGE.

DESERVER = RESERVED          LASCAR = RASCAL

**tetragram**: a set of four letters in a specific order considered as a single unit. There are 456,976 tetragrams, from AAAA, AAAB, AAAC . . . to ZZZX, ZZZY, ZZZZ.

**T-graph**: a WORD GRAPH based on a PAVEMENT composed of triangles.

**"the" country**: a country whose name is preceded by the definite article *the*.

the Congo          the Sudan
the Netherlands          the Ukraine

**thedom**: puzzledom. The word may come from *thedom* (*theedom, thedam*), which in medieval times meant "thriving" or "prosperity."

**Thinglish**: a tall, thin form of printed English used in certain visual puzzles. The letters are so tall and thin that they are challenging to read.

**thousand-words problem**: the challenge of finding a MASTER WORD whose letters can be used to spell a thousand other words of equal or lesser length. This problem was suggested by the saying, "a picture is worth a thousand words." The word PICTURE yields only 46 *Pocket Dictionary* words. The word PIASTER generates a little over 1,000 words from several sources.

**three-letter body part**: a part of the human body that is spelled with three letters. The concept first appeared in a *Reader's Digest* quiz: "Can you name ten parts of the human body (no slang words) that have only three letters?"

The following 20 are listed in *Webster's Collegiate*. LAP is questionable because it disappears when a person stands up.

| | | | | |
|------|------|------|------|------|
| ARM | GUT | LAP | MAW | SAC |
| EAR | HAM | LEG | PAP | TIT |
| EYE | HIP | LID | RIB | TOE |
| GUM | JAW | LIP | ROD | VAS |

**three-letter switch**: a TRANSPOSAL in which three letters in one word change places to form another word; a type of METALLEGE.

DECIMATION—MEDICATION

**three-square**: a WORD SQUARE measuring 3 x 3 letters.

T O P
O N E
P E T

**threenodials**: verse using only the letters in the word *threnodials*, the only 11-letter word that uses the 11 most common letters in English. See ETAOIN SHRDLU POETRY.

**tic-tac-toe board letters**: F, H, I, L, and T, the letters that can be super-imposed on the lines of an upright tic-tac-toe board.

**tic-tac-toe board palindrome**: a PALINDROME composed of TIC-TAC-TOE BOARD LETTERS.

Till I fit it, I fill it.

**tic-tac-toe board word**: a word spelled with TIC-TAC-TOE BOARD LETTERS.

I      HI      LIT      TILL      FILTH

**tic-tac-toe word**: a word spelled with only "O's" and "X's." There are only five in *Webster's Third Unabridged*. They frequently show up in tic-tac-toe games.

O      OO      OX      OXO      X

**Timely neologism**: a new word appearing in *Time* magazine. *Time* has a reputation for introducing new words into the English langue. Occasionally,

Timely neologisms become mainstream words, and some are recognized by lexicographers. Here is a timeless selection from the cornucopia of *Time*:

BRAWNSTORM            FEET-ON-THE-GROUND
CO-RESPONSIBLE        MACHO-MINDED
DROOPY-EARED          NOSEBLOW
TALKED-TO             ECOFREAKS
OUTPOLLUTE            WORDPLOY
SCANDAL-SNIFFING      PRESLEYMANIA

**timely poem**: a poem that uses clock times that sound like some of the words. This poem is a variation of "Thirty days hath September," retitled "Poem for Twelve Months," or:

### Poem 4:12 Months

4:30 days lasts September,
April, June, and November.
The rest all last 4:31
Except for February alone,
Which lasts 4:28 in fine,
In leap year, lasts 4:29.

**Tom Swiftie**: a sentence that has a quote attributed to Tom Swift (or anyone) and that ends with an adverb punning on the quote. Tom Swift was a character appearing in a series of books by Edward Stratemeyer in the 1920s. Tom sometimes spoke sentences of this type:

"I'll try to dig up a couple of friends," said Tom gravely.
"I got the first three wrong," she said forthrightly.

Sometimes spelled "Tom Swifty." Also called "adverbial pun." See CROAKER, DOUBLE CROAKER, HERMAN.

**tongue-twister**: a sentence or poem that is difficult to pronounce quickly. Tongue-twisters became popular when several books published the poem below. It is an earlier version of "Peter Piper Picked a Peck of Pickled Peppers":

Peter Piper pick'd a peck of pepper:
Did Peter Piper pick a peck of pepper?
If Peter Piper pick'd a peck of pepper,
Where's the peck of pepper Peter Piper pick'd.

Short tongue-twisters such as those below are supposed to be spoken five or six times without making a mistake. *The Guinness Book of Records* listed the last one below as the most difficult of all.

> A knapsack strap.
> She sells sea-shells.
> Rubber baby buggy bumpers.
> The sixth sick sheik's sixth sheep's sick.

**tongue-twister limerick**: a TONGUE-TWISTER written in the form of a LIMERICK, using the same rhythm and the same rhyme scheme.

**tongue-twister palindrome**: a PALINDROME that is also a TONGUE-TWISTER. It reads the same with equal difficulty in both directions.

> Top step's pup's pet spot.

**tongue-twister sobriety test**: a test allegedly used by police to determine whether a person is sober or drunk. The suspect had to recite this twister:

> The Leith police dismiss us.

**top**: a word FORM shaped like a top (or an arrow pointing down), in which words are spelled across and down.

```
          A C T
          B O A
          S N L
          E V E
          N E B
          T,R E
          A S A
      P R O T A R S U S
        E D I T I O N
          D O I N E
          N O G
          N
```

**touch-tone telephone word**: a TELEPHONE WORD requiring a touch-tone keypad for its effect. Each of the following words is typed on one triple-key line (horizontal, vertical, or diagonal) on a keypad.

Middle row (456): NONILLION  Right column: MONEYED
Bottom row (789): SYRUPY  Minor diagonal: SLEEPLESS
Middle column (258): CUTBACK

**town-state word**: a word formed by connecting the name of a town with its two-letter STATE POSTAL ABBREVIATION. The two on the left are real, and the rest are made by transporting a town from its home state (listed in parentheses) to another state:

AVA IL          ALMO ND (not ID)      MAY OR (not ID)
JACK AL        DOLPH IN (not AR)     SUN NY (not CA)

**transaddition**: the addition of a letter to a word followed by the TRANSPOSAL of all the letters to make a new word.

WORD + E = WORDE = ROWED.

**transade**: the separation of a word into two or more shorter parts followed by the TRANSPOSAL of the letters in each part to make two words.

SOLUTION—SOUL, INTO

**transbeheadment**: the BEHEADMENT of a word followed by the TRANSPOSAL of the remaining letters to create a new word.

POEMS - P = OEMS = SOME

**transcurtailment**: the CURTAILMENT of a word followed by the TRANSPOSAL of the remaining letters to form a new word.

POETRY - Y = POETR = TROPE.

**transdeletion**: the DELETION of a letter followed by the TRANSPOSAL of the remaining letters.

SONNET - N = TONES

Also called "transposed deletion."

**transdeletion chain**: a set of words formed by the SUCCESSIVE TRANSDELETION of a word to a single letter. REPRESENTATIONAL begins a 16-letter transdeletion chain:

REPRESENTATIONAL, TRANSPERITONEAL, PRESENTATIONAL, SEPTENTRIONAL, STEPRELATION, INTERSEPTAL, ETERNALIST, REINSTATE, INTEREST, ENTRIES, INSERT, REINS, RISE, SIR, IS, I

**transdeletion pyramid**: the arrangement of a TRANSDELETION CHAIN into a triangular shape from long word to single letter. In this series of words, SERIES is the transdeleted word:

```
S E R I E S
 S I R E S
  R I S E
   S I R
    I S
     I
```

**translingual lettershift**: a foreign word that is the LETTERSHIFT of an English word having the same meaning.

YES + 16 = OUI ("yes" in French)

**transmute** (*v*.): see TRANSPOSE (*v*.).

**transposal** (*n*.): the rearrangement of the letters in one text to form another text. The two texts don't have to be related in any way. The earliest transposal may have appeared as the answer to a puzzle published under the name "Matilda" in the July 16, 1796, issue of *Weekly Museum*, a New York magazine.

> An insect of the smallest kind
> If you transpose, you soon will find
>   That from all mortals I do quickly fly;
> When gone, my loss in vain they'll mourn,
> In vain will wish for my return,
>   Tho' now to kill me, ev'ry art they try.

The answer is MITE / TIME.

Technically, a transposal and an ANAGRAM are the same, except that, according to some authorities, an anagram should be related in meaning to the original word.

See TRANSPOSITION.

**transposal** (*adj.*): composed of a set of letters that rearrange to form another set of letters; formed by transposing a set of letters; related to TRANSPOSAL (*n.*).

**transposal form**: a FORM, such as a WORD SQUARE, which permits the use of TRANSPOSALS.

**transposal group**: a set of TRANSPOSALS of a well-known group of words.

EAST, WEST, SOUTH, NORTH—SATE, STEW, SHOUT, THORN

**transposal index**: the number of letters that must be added to a word before it can be transposed. The fewer letters needed, the more transposable the word. These three words show decreasing transposability.

|                            |   |
|----------------------------|---|
| MONDAY = DYNAMO            | 0 |
| SUNDAY + H = UNSHADY       | 1 |
| THURSDAY + LI = HYDRAULIST | 2 |

**transposal name**: a person's full name in which the first name and the last name are transposals of each other. The four transposal names below are from a list of about ninety million names on a national CD-ROM telephone directory. The number in parentheses shows how many listings turned up for each The first transposal name is by far the most common:

| | |
|---|---|
| GARY GRAY (544) | DEBRA BEARD (31) |
| RONALD ARNOLD (147) | AMY MAY (29) |

**transposal poetry**: See ANAGRAMMATIC VERSE. Also called "transpositional poetry."

**transposal pseudonym**: a pen name that an author has made by rearranging the letters in his or her real name. Here are three transposal pseudonyms followed by the real names.

R'HOONE = HONORÉ (de Balzac)
ACOFRIBAS NASIER = FRANCOIS RABELAIS
REDBARN WASH = (George) BERNARD SHAW

**transposal rectangle**: a rectangular array of letters arranged so that each row and column can be transposed to form a word; a type of TRANSPOSAL FORM.

```
A  B  C        Across: CAB, FED, GHI, LON
D  E  F
G  H  I        Down: GLAD, BEHN, COIF
L  N  O
```

**transposal sentence**: a sentence made of words or phrases that are TRANS-POSALS of each other.

> Selma lames Salem males!
> Gander ranged garden—danger!
> Minnesota nominates most inane men, o saint!

**transposal square**: a WORD SQUARE in which each row and column has a set of letters that can be transposed into a word; a type of TRANSPOSAL FORM.

**transposal system**: a group of mutual TRANSPOSALS in which each letter appears at the beginning of at least one of the transposals.

> TIME = ITEM = MITE = EMIT

**transpose** (*v.*): to rearrange one set of letters into another set.

**transposition**: a TRANSPOSAL. Thes two terms usually have the same mean-ing and are used interchangeably. In most cases, this dictionary uses "trans-posal." The only exceptions are terms in which the term "transposition" or any variation of it doesn't mean "transposal." For an example, see SUB-TRANSPOSITION.

**transpositional** (*adj.*): TRANSPOSAL (*adj.*). For consistency, the adjective "transposal" is used in this book instead of the adjective "transpositional."

**triad**: a three-word phrase that forms three well-known two-word phrases by combining first and second words, second and third words, and first and third words:   LAST MINUTE WALTZ = LAST MINUTE, MINUTE WALTZ, and LAST WALTZ. These two phrases work the same way:

> SILVER SAND DOLLAR                WHITE LIGHT HOUSE

**trianagram**: a trio of words that are ANAGRAMS of each other and that read as a sentence.

Discounter introduces reductions.

Also called "triplet."

**trictionary**: the challenge of making a sentence that includes five consecutive dictionary words. The reader opens the dictionary randomly and points to a boldface main entry. Using that word and the next four different main entries in order of occurrence, he or she uses them all in a sentence.

FOLDAWAY, FOLDBOAT, FOLDER, FOLDEROL, FOLDING DOORS

The foldaway bed on the foldboat was strewn with folders full of folderol about folding doors.

**tricycle**: a WORD CYCLE of three words. Each adjacent pair of words, including the last-first pair, forms a familiar compound word or two-word expression: SAW HORSE POWER = SAWHORSE, HORSEPOWER, and POWER SAW. See BICYCLE, UNICYCLE.

**trigram**: a set of three letters considered as a single, fixed unit. There are 17,576 possible trigrams, from AAA, AAB, AAC . . . to ZZX, ZZY, ZZZ. s

**trigram-positioned word**: a word in which the letters occupy the same position in their corresponding telephone TRIGRAMS. For instance, MAD is composed of the first letters in the trigrams MNO, ABC, DEF

| | |
|---|---|
| AM (1st letter) | MAGMATA (1st letter) |
| BE (2nd letter) | BUNKER (2nd letter) |
| BEEN (2nd letter) | ISOCYCLIC (3rd letter) |
| IS (3rd letter) | |

**trilingual synonymic anagram**: a trio of words, each from a different language, that are synonyms and anagrams of each other.

MINE (English)
MIEN (French)
MEIN (German)

**trinade**: a word that can be broken up into three sequences of every third letter to form three shorter words. See ALTERNADE.

ABOMINATE                    PACIFICATORY

```
A   M   A          P   I   C   O
B   I   T          A   F   A   R
O   N   E          C   I   T   Y
```

**trio isogram**: a word in which each letter occurs three times. See ISOGRAM.

DEEDED          GEGGEE

**tripartite color rhyme**: verse whose major purpose is to rhyme PUR-
PLE, ORANGE, and SILVER. See COLORFUL RHYME.

> Wyatt Earp'll
> Shoot till he's purple,
> Then carefully chill ver–
> Mouth in a silver
> Cup, which he'll pour, inj–
> Ecting an orange.

**triple acrostic**: an ACROSTIC poem or puzzle in which the first letters of
the lines spell out a text going down the page, the last letters spell out another,
and the middle letters spell out a third.

**triple charade sentence**: a PALINDROMIC sequence of words that can be
redivided to make two palindromic CHARADES, neither of which repeats a
word in the other nor in the starting sequence.

> DIAS, EN, NA, ANN, ES, A, ID
> "DI, A SENNA," ANNE SAID.
> DIASENNA, ANNE'S AID

**triple homophone**: a trio of words that are HOMOPHONES of each other.

BALD = BALLED = BAWLED     HEAL = HEEL = HE'LL
CITE = SIGHT = SITE          PRAISE = PRAYS = PREYS

**triple internal tautonym**: a word with a LETTER STRING that is repeated
three times in a row.

SHEHEHEYANU          LOGOGOGUE

**triple oxymoron**: a phrase having three words, each of which forms an
OXYMORON with the word next to it.

**triplet**: a method of linking words of different lengths by adding or subtracting a letter at each step. The name refers to Lewis Carroll's invention, the DOUBLET, which has come to be known as a WORD LADDER. This triplet links SAND to SAND to form an hourglass shape:

```
S A N D
A N D
A N
A
A D
S A D
S A N D
```

**triple tautonym**: a word made of three parts having the same spelling. Of these examples, only the first is a dictionary word:

AIAIAI          CHA-CHA-CHA          DELTA -DELTA-DELTA

Also called "three-part tautonym."

**triple transposal**: a trio of words that are mutual TRANSPOSALS. In other words, they are spelled with the same letters in different order. Here are two of the longest:

CECROPIA MOTHS = PHOTOCERAMICS = COMPOSITE ARCH (13)
UNISON INTERVALS = NONUNIVERSALIST = INVOLUNTARINESS (15)

Also called "triplet."

**triplets-in-parallel**: two or more TRIPLETS that connect two or more words in the same number of steps. This example connects two well-known PALINDROMES:

| LIVE | NOT | ON | EVIL |
|------|-----|------|-------|
| LIE | NO | ONE | VIL |
| LE | O | DONE | VI |
| E | AO | DOE | I |
| EN | A | OE | IN |
| ENS | HA | E | INN |
| DENS | HAD | EA | INNE |
| DENIS | AD | ENA | INNED |
| DENNIS | AND | EDNA | SINNED |

**trisogram**: a set of three words in which no letter is used twice.

> FANCYWORKS, BLIGHTED, JUMP

See ISOGRAM.

**trivial** (*adj*.): commonplace; insignificant. A WORDPLAY form, an example of the form, or a problem using the form can be trivial or nontrivial. For instance, the solution to a wordplay problem is trivial when it is one of many related, unremarkable solutions. THREE is the first of many number names that end in a double vowel. Others include TWENTY-THREE, THIRTY-THREE, ONE MILLION THREE, etc. THREE is the real solution, and the others are simply THREE preceded by other number names. THREE is nontrivial; all the others are trivial.

**true riddle**: a RIDDLE that describes an object or a creature in an obscure way.

> What goes up when the rain comes down? An umbrella.
> What goes to sleep with its shoes on? The milkman's horse.

**truthful number**: **1.** a number that counts the letters in its name. FOUR is the only truthful number in English. FOUR has four letters.

    **2.** in a general sense, a number that counts one of the verbal, visual, or other elements in its name. ONE counts itself as a single word, a single syllable, a single digit; it counts its consonant, its even letter, its first-half letter. It is truthful in many ways. Here are some other numbers that are truthful for different reasons:

> TEN: 10 raised dots in Braille
> TWELVE: 12 points in Scrabble
> FIFTEEN: 15 dots and dashes in International Morse Code
> TWENTY NINE: 29 straight lines in its letters

**Turkey Irish**: an oral language code similar to PIG LATIN. In Turkey Irish, the sound "*ub*" (with a short "*u*") is placed before each vowel in a word. Here are two words that become nonsense in Turkey Irish, and two that become other words:

> SPEAK = SPUB-EAK          DULL = DOUBLE
> LANGUAGE = LUB-ANG-UB-AGE     HE = HUBBY

**twenty-consonant poetry**: a form of writing in which each of the twenty consonants is used exactly once before being repeated. Y is always treated as a vowel. Although it is called "poetry," twenty-consonant poetry can include prose, drama, and other genres.

> I quit my job; a crazy wage slave, dead hunk of pox.

An additional convention allows repeating a consonant as many times as desired as long as no other consonant intervenes:

> I asked Bill for a waxy TV quip. Oh, gaze in my juice.

**twenty-one-consonant poetry**: the same as TWENTY-CONSONANT POETRY, except that Y can be counted as a consonant or a vowel each time it is used.

**twinned reversal**: a REVERSAL PAIR that becomes a different reversal pair by rearranging its letters.

> STRAPS—SPARTS     DRAWER—REWARD
> SPRATS—STARPS     WARDER—REDRAW

**two-headed headline**: a newspaper headline that has one meaning intended as the title of the news story and another meaning that, because of a pun, gives an entirely different story of its own.

> THUGS EAT THEN ROB PROPRIETOR
> SAFETY EXPERTS SAY SCHOOL BUS PASSENGERS SHOULD BE
>     BELTED
> MEAT HEAD FIGHTS HIKE IN MINIMUM PAY
> HERSHEY BARS PROTEST
> QUEEN MARY HAVING BOTTOM SCRAPED
> NEW AUTOS TO HIT FIVE MILLION
> STUD TIRES OUT

**two-letter alternation poem**: a poem in which two letters alternate from start to finish to form the words. Here is the first stanza of "Isis," in which I and S alternate:

> Sis, is Isis Isis?
> Is Isis I, Sis? I?
> Sis, is Isis I, Sis?
> Isis is I, Sis, I!

**two-letter word:** a word spelled with just two letters. They range from common words like ME to uncommon words like CA. In many wordplay problems of word length, the lower limit is a two-letter word.

AM   BY   DO   HE   IF   ME   OH   PA   TO   WE

**two-square**: a WORD SQUARE measuring 2 x 2 letters.

N O
O N

**two-syllable word**: a word that has only two syllables. AA and IO are among the shortest. Two of the longest include:

STRENGTH-GRAINED        SQUAITCHED-MOUTHED

**type-collection**: a list of words that represent all possible occurrences of a specific arrangement of letters. An extremely simple type-collection to assemble is that of words beginning with each letter of the alphabet, from A to Z. A much more difficult one is that of words beginning with each letter doubled, from AA to ZZ. There are many other types of type-collections.

**type-collection of bigrams**: a list of words containing each of the 676 possible BIGRAMS. Assembling this TYPE-COLLECTION is one of the classic challenges of LOGOLOGY. It took at least three decades and several contributors to fill in all the blanks. Here are the first ten words for bigrams beginning with E and the first ten for those beginning with Q:

yEAr, basEBall, bECause, usED, bEEn, bEFore, bEGan, bEHind, thEIr, rEJected

tariQA, ShuQBa, QCepo, taluQDar, QEre, cinQFoil, IraQGate, fiQH, QIviut, FeQJakuqe

**typewriter keyboard**: the keyboard with letters arranged in the standard order shown below. It is also called the QWERTY KEYBOARD after the first six letters at the top left. In touch-typing, each finger is used to type a specific set of letters, numbers, etc. Numerous forms of wordplay involve the arrangement of letters on the keyboard:

Q   W   E   R   T   Y   U   I   O   P
A   S   D   F   G   H   J   K   L
Z   X   C   V   B   N   M

**typewriter keyboard alphabet**: QWERTYUIOPASDFGHJKLZX-CVBNM, the alphabet with its letters arranged in order of appearance on a TYPEWRITER KEYBOARD, going from left to right and then down.

**typewriter-keyboard order word**: a word whose letters occur from left to right in the TYPEWRITER KEYBOARD ALPHABET.

QUIPS　　　　TOPAZ　　　　WERTUALL

**typewriter sentence**: a sentence typed with a specific set of letters on the TYPEWRITER KEYBOARD. The following sentence, including punctuation, can be typed entirely with the right hand when the shift key is locked in position for capital letters:

IN JULY, OH MY KILLJOY JOHNNY, I'LL LOOK IN UPON MY JUMPY POLO PONY UP IN HILLY HONOLULU.

**typewriter word**: a word typed with a select group of letters on the TYPEWRITER KEYBOARD. There are several kinds of typewriter words, based on letter location and/or on the hand or the finger that strikes the keys in touch-typing. Some of the different types of typewriter words appear below.

Top row keys: TYPEWRITER
Middle row keys: FLAGFALLS
Bottom row keys: BZZZBZZZ

Left hand: AFTERCATARACTS
Right hand: JOHNNY-JUMP-UP

Right index finger: HUMMUM
Left middle finger: DEEDEED

**ugliest word**: a word that someone considers to be extremely unpleasing in its meaning and/or in its sound. Different people may name ugliest words based on personal experience. Here are three candidates for ugliest word:

PHLEGM          KAKKAK          UGLIEST

**U-invariant**: a UNIVOCALIC with U as the only vowel.

UNTRUSTFUL          UNTRUTHFUL

**ultimate transposal set**: a set of letters that can be transposed into an extreme number of different words, names, or phrases found in published sources. These sets of letters are especially transposable:

ACERST          AEGINRST          ACEINORST

**unattractive opposites**: two antonyms that do not have any letters in common.

HUSBAND-WIFE          DAY-NIGHT
ADAM-EVE          TRUTH-LIE
FATHER-SON          FOR-AGAINST
BOY-GIRL          GOOD-EVIL

**undergrounder**: a word that exists on two levels: the surface level, where meanings are found in dictionaries; and the subterranean level, where a different meaning appears when the word is treated as a compound made of two shorter words. The best-known undergrounder solves the riddle, "When is a door not a door?" Answer: "When it is AJAR."

AGATE: a moveable barrier closing an opening in a fence or a wall
CARMEN: male humans seated in automotive vehicles

HANDSOME: possessing one or more hands
MOTHER: someone occupationally involved with moths
REPAIR: to cause animals to mate again

**undominated alphabetic sequence**: an ALPHABETIC SEQUENCE found in a word that doesn't appear in a longer sequence in any other word. SIGH has the sequence GH, but SIGHING has a longer sequence, GHI, which includes GH. GHI is an undominated alphabetic sesquence for words having letters adjacent and in order, but GH isn't.

**unfolded Platonic solid**: one of the five Platonic solids (tetrahedron, cube, octahedron, dodecahedron, and icosohedron) labeled at its vertices with different letters of the alphabet so that words can be formed at the vertices of each face. In the example below, a tetrahedron is labeled so that each triangle in it forms one of the four words on the right.

```
        S              EAT SAT SEA SET
       / \
      E — T
     / \ / \
    S — A — S
```

**_____-unfriendly alphabet**: a CIRCULAR ALPHABET in which no set of adjacent letters of the same length can be found in a dictionary word. A BIGRAM-unfriendly alphabet is impossible, but a TRIGRAM-unfriendly alphabet has been assembled:

... VGIQAOJYUWLCDRHPMNZSBTXEFK ...

See SCRAMBLED ALPHABET.

**unicycle**: a two-syllable word in which the syllables can be reversed to form another two-syllable word with the syllables retaining their original pronunciation.

| | |
|---|---|
| MANGER = GERMAN | PANTRY = TRYPAN |
| CALMER = MERCAL | MINTER = TERMIN |

See BICYCLE, TRICYCLE.

**unidigital word**: a word whose letters have ALPHABETIC VALUES using a single digit throughout.

| Letters: | K | A | K | K | A | K |
|----------|---|---|---|---|---|---|
| Alphabetic values: | 11 | 1 | 11 | 1 | 11 | 1 |

**unit**: the basic part of language to be manipulated in a PALINDROME. Usually the letter is the unit, but other units can be and have been used: BIGRAMS, TRIGRAMS, syllables, morphemes, words, phrases, sentences, lines of poetry, paragraphs, stanzas. When the limit of the literary form has been reached—when the unit becosmes the whole poem, story, etc.—then the work can't be a palindrome.

**Universal Letter**: a single symbol in which all the letters of the alphabet can be found. In the example below, most of the letters appear upright, but G, J, and Q appear sideways. For proper viewing of those three, the symbol must be rotated 90° counterclockwise.

**univocalic**: a word that uses only one of the six vowels. The vowel can appear one or more times. LETTER, WORD, and SENTENCE are univocalics. Here are longer examples for each vowel:

ARCHCHARLATANS          COMFORTROOTS
DEFENSELESSNESSES       UNTRUTHFUL
PRIMITIVISTIC           GYPSYFY

Also called "vocalic invariant." See A-INVARIANT, E-INVARIANT, I-INVARIANT, O-INVARIANT, U-INVARIANT, Y-INVARIANT.

**univocalic haiku**: a haiku that uses only one vowel throughout the text. This poem is titled "The Haiku of Eyes":

In twilight this spring
Girls with miniskirts will swim
In string bikinis.

**univocalic palindrome**: a PALINDROME using only one vowel through-out. The poem "Palindromic Conversation Between Two Owls" uses O only (it appears under LIPOGRAMMATIC PALINDROME).

**univocalic poetry**: verse that uses one and the same vowel in all of its words. E is the easiest to use; I and U are the hardest. Here are the first two lines of an I-only poem:

> I'm living nigh grim civic blight;
> I find its victims, sick with fright.

**unlucky letter**: B, which can be sliced vertically to form the "unlucky number" 13.

**unlucky number name**: a NUMBER NAME spelled with thirteen letters. Here are the first and the last of very, very many:

> ONE HUNDRED ONE        NINE DECILLION

**unparagraph**: a paragraph written using only UN- words. "UnSherlock Unbound" is an unparagraph that begins:

> Unworldly unreason unmasks unknown unconcerns, unbuilds unsafety, uncages uncertainty. Unintelligence uneasily uncrowns unreality. . . .

**unquote**: a text containing a famous quotation taken out of its original context in order to parody the original. The following unquote gives new meaning to Neil Armstrong's immortal words spoken on the first moon walk:

> "With such a tiny foot, THAT'S ONE SMALL STEP FOR A MAN. ONE GIANT LEAP FOR MANKIND would take a size-twelve shoe."

**unspeakable sentence**: the following sentence, which can be written but not spoken because the word SLOUGH has three different pronunciations:

> There are three ways to pronounce "slough."

**UN- word**: a word beginning with the prefix UN-. Some of the UN- words, such as these in the *OED*, are undeniably unusual:

| | |
|---|---|
| UNDAY | UNHOUSEHOLD-NAME |
| UNDINING-ROOM | UN-IN-ONE-BREATH-UTTERABLE |
| UN-DO-WITHOUT-ABLE | UNMOTHERHOOD |

UNDRYUPABLE          UNTALKABOUTABLE
UNFURNACE            UN-TO-BE-IMITATED

**unwritable sentence**: the following sentence, which can be spoken but not written, because the word that sounds like TU has three different spellings:

> There are three ways to spell (to, two, too).

**upside-down letters**: H, I, N, O, S, X, and Z, the letters that look the same upside down.

**upside-down palindrome**: a word or sentence made of UPSIDE-DOWN LETTERS that read the same in both directions. In the two PALINDROMIC SENTENCES below, the "Nixon" PALINDROME has different spacing when it is turned upside down, while the "Ho (Chi Minh)" palindrome keeps the same spacing:

> NOON          SOHOS          TUT-TUT          TAT-TAT-TAT
>
> NO X IN NIXON.
> OH NO SIX XIS ON HO

Also called "four-way palindrome."

**upside-down word**: a word spelled with UPSIDE-DOWN LETTERS. NIXON is the only upside-down presidential name.

**verb-adverb paradox**: the contradiction found in the meanings of different adverbs modifying the same verb, or of the same adverb modifying in different ways the same verb. These sentences show some of the possible paradoxes:

> A house burns up and down at the same time.
> We chop down a tree and then chop it up
> We fill in a form by filling it out.
> After we set up a table, we can upset it.

**verb hypertense**: a new verb tense that goes beyond current tenses such as Past, Present, Future, Future Perfect, etc. Here are some sentences using verb hypertenses:

> He will does walked. (Future Present Past)
> He will will walk. (Double Future)
> He could can walk. (Unconditional Present)
> She is being doing walking. (Obsessive Progressive)
> She did will was have walked. (Refractive Future Perfect)
> She might be having been about to be walking. (Superjunctive)

**vertical mirror letters**: A, I, M, O, S, T, U, V, W, X, and Y, the letters that are symmetrical along a vertical line drawn through the center of each—the left half is symmetrical with the right half. The letters and their reflections appear the same when they are held in front of a mirror. Also called "mirror palindrome." See ASSYMETRICAL LETTERS, HORIZONTAL MIRROR LETTERS.

**vertical mirror palindrome**: a PALINDROME made of VERTICAL MIRROR WORDS. The two examples below are vertical mirror palindromes, but the second one keeps the same spacing in the mirror, too:

AHA! MAY I MAIM A MIAMI YAMAHA?
TOOT IT A TI TOOT

**vertical mirror word**: a word spelled with VERTICAL MIRROR LETTERS (see HORIZONTAL MIRROR WORD). Held in front of a mirror rightside up, a vertical mirror word printed horizontally has correctly formed letters appearing in reverse order. If the word is printed vertically, however, the letters appear in correct order. IVY MOUTH WAX, a fictitous brand of toothpaste, contains all 11 vertical mirror letters once apiece. In the examples below, the first two are real words and the third is a coined word:

MYOMOTOMY       HOITY-TOITY       AUTOMOTIVATIVITY

**"V-14" problem**: the problem of finding 14-letter words and names that begin with V- and that alternate consonants and vowels. There are only two V-14 words in the *Pocket Merriam-Webster's*:

VERISIMILITUDE          VITUPERATIVELY

**vicinal**: a word in which each letter has an ALPHABETIC NEIGHBOR. That is, each letter in the word occupies a position in the alphabet next to another letter that appears in the word. THIS is a vicinal whose letters pair off as HI and ST, but THAT isn't a vicinal. One of the longest vicinals appears below with its letters (one of each) arranged in groups of alphabetic neighbors.

ANTIDISESTABLISHMENTARIANISM = AB DE HI LMN RST

**vicinal story**: a story composed entirely of VICINALS. Here is the first sentence of one vicinal story:

Bedfast hedonist fights hoyden, foments bedlam; sport done, this undermost big-head sighted Jacobin post tabu documents on chipboards.

**visual word-unit palindrome**: a WORD-UNIT PALINDROME in which the text is arranged on the page to reflect the meaning visually as well as verbally. The following shows—and tells—the myth of Sisyphus:

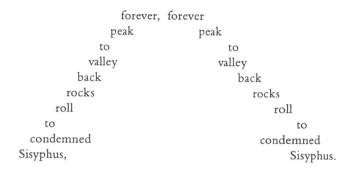

## SISYPHUS

<pre>
            forever,  forever
         peak            peak
          to              to
         valley          valley
         back            back
         rocks           rocks
        roll              roll
         to                to
       condemned        condemned
      Sisyphus,           Sisyphus.
</pre>

See CONCRETE POETRY, SHAPED POETRY.


**vocabularyclept poetry**: verse made by "cutting up" the words of a poem written by someone else and putting them back together differently. This can be done in two main ways : (1) one person cuts the poem apart and, in spite of knowing the original poem, puts the words back together to make a new poem; (2) one person cuts the poem apart and gives it to another person who creates a new poem without knowing the source poem. The first vocabularyclept poem was constructed by the second method, using a 478-word list. See EXQUISITE CORPSE.


**vocalic alternating monotony**: a word with the same vowel in every other position for three or more occurrences.

TACAMAHACA (5 A's)      VISIBILITIES (5 I's)
TELEMETERED (5 E's)     MONOGONOPOROUS (6 O's)
        HUMUHUMUNUKUNUKUAPUAA (8 U's)


**vocalic invariant**: see UNIVOCALIC.


**volatile words**: two words that change their pronunciation radically although they differ by only one letter. See SINGLE-LETTER DIFFERENCE PAIR.

PARISH      HIDEOUT      COMBINE      BELL YACHT
PARIAH      HIDEOUS      COMBING      BELLYACHE

**vowel-consonant pattern**: an arrangement of consonants and vowels in a word according to a mathematical pattern. The simplest pattern is one in which the consonants and vowels alternate in a 1 : 1 ratio throughout the word.

| | |
|---|---|
| HONORIFICABILITUDINITATIBUS | (1 consonant : 1 vowel) |
| HEEBIE-JEEBIES | (1 consonant : 2 vowels) |
| CRYSTALLOGRAPHERS | (2 consonants : 1 vowel) |
| SWEETHEART | (2 consonants : 2 vowels) |
| THRIFTLESSLY | (3 consonants : 1 vowel) |

**vowelindrome**: a set of PALINDROMES in which each of the five vowels appears between a pair of the same consonants to make five different words.

PAP PEP PIP POP PUP
TAT TET TIT TOT TUT
MAM MEM MIM MOM MUM

See DOUBLE VOWELINDROME.

**vowel mates**: a man and a woman whose names have all five vowels once each in the same order—a marriage made in alphabet heaven.

FRANÇIS POULENC (composer) + ALISON UTTLEY (children's book writer) (AIOUE)

ARLO GUTHRIE (singer) + MARY OF GUISE (mother of Mary, Queen of Scots) (AOUIE)

See LAST-NAME VOWEL MATES, OPPOSITES-ATTRACT VOWEL MATES.

**vowel-sequence word**: a word spelled with an unusually long, unbroken string of vowels and one or more consonants.

AEAEAN     COOEEING     QUEUEING     ZOUAOUA

**wacky medical term**: a genuine medical term given a new definition based on a tongue-in-cheek reinterpretation of its sound, spelling, or both.

> ANTABUSE = stepping on an anthill
> CLAUSTROPHOBIA = fear of Santa
> ENEMA = someone who is not your friend
> HICCUP = what a yokel drinks from
> PROTEIN = someone who favors adolescents
> URINALYSIS = different than my analysis

**Websterian word**: a word that can be found in any of the three unabridged dictionaries published by the Merriam-Webster Company. These three dictionaries are among a select group regarded as the most reputable sources of words in English.

**weight**: ALPHABETIC VALUE of a letter, used in discussions of LIGHTWEIGHT WORDS and HEAVYWEIGHT WORDS.

**well-mixed transposal**: a TRANSPOSAL in which no more than three consecutive letters in one word appear consecutively in the other. WHAT-THAW is a well-mixed transposal. A much longer example is this pair of 17-letter words:

> BASIPARACHROMATIN = MARSIPOBRANCHIATA

**wind name**: a term used to identify a specific wind in a specific locale.

> HABOOB: of the Sudan, the black roller of the upper Nile
> GHOST OF GOUDA: local gust on a calm night, South Africa
> CAT'S PAW: barely ripples mill ponds in America
> SZ: first faint breeze of the Chinese autumn

**witches' prayer**: a prayer that can be read backwards and forwards and that curses in one direction and blesses in the other.

**word chain: 1.** a sequence of four-letter words in which the last two letters of one word become the first two letters of the next word.

> CONE
>   NEAR
>     ARID
>       IDEA
>         EACH

**2.** a sequence of words in which the last letter of one word is the same as the first letter of the next, as in

AT THE ENDS, SEVERAL LOW WORDS SHARE EACH HOT TERMI-NAL LETTER.

**3.** a sequence of words in which each word has its first letter dropped and a new last letter added to make the next word.

> BAG
>  AGE
>   GEM
>    EMU
>     MUD

**word cluster**: a set of words that break down into all consecutive strings of the same length, each of which is a word in its own right. In this example, TONE starts in the first row. It breaks into two-letter words in the second row, three-letter words in the third, and a four-letter word in the fourth, which is itself.

> T    O    N    E
>   TO   ON   NE
>    TON   ONE
>     TONE

**word cycle**: a RING of words in which each adjacent pair of words, including last-first, forms a familiar compound word or two-word expression.

GROUND WATER MARK TIME PIECE WORK HORSE PLAY
GROUNDWATER, WATERMARK, . . . PLAYGROUND

**word deletion**: the deletion of a word from a longer word that leaves a third word.

>    PERFORMANCE—MAN, PERFORCE

**word deletion sentence**: a sentence in which one or more letters can be deleted from each word, resulting in a new sentence.

>    Hone shallowed feather acorns wise restrained.
>    On    all        the   corn   is    rain.

**word dice**: dice that have one or more letters on each face. A number of games (Boggle™, Scrabble™ Cubes, Perquackey™, Tuf-Abet™, and Agony™) use dice with letters on them. Word dice can be used in various ways in poetry writing and in wordplay. Also called "letter cube," "lettered dice."

**word dice problem**: a problem in which letters are placed on blank dice in order to roll letters to achieve a certain goal. One word dice problem requires placing any 24 letters on four dice to maximize the number of four-letter words they can spell on their upturned faces. The best allocation generates 420 words in the *Pocket Merriam Webster*. Each of the four dice has one of these sets of six letters on it:

>    AEIOTU, AEGHKO, BLPRST, CDMNRS.

**word fragment**: a part of a word, consisting of one or more of the word's letters, but not all. There are three main types of word fragment:

>    Letters in order, adjacent
>    Letters in order, not necessarily adjacent
>    Letters not necessarily in order, not necessarily adjacent

**word girder**: a pair of words in which every other letter can be exchanged to form two new words.

>    M O N A D                  P O L A R
>    | | | | |     becomes      | | | | |
>    P I  L E R                 M I N E D

**word graph**: a graph in which the letters of a word are arranged according to a specific procedure. In the basic type of word graph, each different letter is printed on a piece of paper, and then a line is drawn from one letter to the other in spelling order. For a repeated letter, a new line is drawn to the original letter. Here are word graphs for STATE, WOULD, and GOING:

```
   E                W – O – U – L – D          G – O
   |                                           |   |
S – T = A                                      N – I
```

See H-GRAPH, K-GRAPH, OS-GRAPH, Q-GRAPH, R-GRAPH, T-GRAPH.

**word interlocks**: two or more words that can be found in a longer word and that use all of its letters in order of appearance. Compound words are trivial cases. Here are two nontrivial word interlocks:

```
D R A W I N G S          M A G N E T I C
D   A W   N              M A G       I C
    R   I   G S                  N E T
```

**word ladder**: a series of words formed by changing a single letter of the starting word to make the next word and continuing this process at each step until reaching the final word. The goal of a word ladder is to connect two given words, usually related or contrasted in meaning, in as few steps as possible.

In 1879, Lewis Carroll invented the word ladder as a pencil-and-paper game, calling it "DOUBLETS," and he published them on a regular basis in *Vanity Fair* magazine. Since then, many puzzle magazines and books have published their own examples using their own terminology. See NETWORK.

Also called "Transformations," "Laddergram," "Stepword," "Transition," "Word Chain," "Word Link," "Word Ping-Pong," "Word Golf."

**word ladder square**: a square of words in which all rows and columns are WORD LADDERs.

```
FAN  PAN  PEN  PET
FIN  PIN  PUN  PUT
FIG  PIG  PUG  PUS
DIG  BIG  BUG  BUS
```

**word line**: an imaginary straight line in three-dimensional space on which individual specific sets of words can be plotted as irregularly spaced points. These include LETTERSHIFT WORDS and COLLINEAR WORDS. On a word line, the ALPHABETIC VALUES are treated as geometric coordinates.

**word molecule**: the representation of a word as a pattern of circles, each having a letter of the word in it. The circles are arranged so that they touch at points where their letters are next to each other in the word. The only letters used twice are doubled letters; otherwise, letters repeated later on in a word must be reused. If a word molecule can't be constructed, the word is an EODERMDROME.

**word network**: a NETWORK in which each word has one letter different from the words connected to it. All words in a word network are the same length. If two words can be joined by a WORD LADDER, they are in the same word network.

**word oblong**: a rectangular variation on the WORD SQUARE having a different amount of letters in each direction. One challenge is to take a pair of related words going down and see how far they can be extended by intermediate letters forming words going across. THE and END form the square below, which can be extended by word oblongs measuring 4 x 3, 5 x 3, and 6 x 3:

```
T H E     T H E E     T H E R E     T R A I S E
H E N     H E R N     H E R O N     H E R D E N
E N D     E Y E D     E N D E D     E X T E N D
```

**word pack**: a NETWORK of letters placed as densely as possible in a rectangular grid in order to spell the words in a specific set. Three kinds of word packs are the CROSSWORD PACK, the KING'S MOVE PACK, and the WORD-SEARCH PACK.

**wordplay**: the interplay of one or more elements of language that achieves a linguistic "special effect" beyond ordinary communication. *Webster's Collegiate Dictionary* defines *wordplay* as "verbal wit." This is perhaps one of the most simplified definitions in the dictionary. Because language itself is complex, wordplay is complex, too. The main types of wordplay involve LETTERPLAY, SOUND PLAY, and MEANING PLAY. They can occur individually or jointly to achieve effects that aren't usually associated with language usage ranging from everyday speech to literary writing. Wordplay can be accidental or intentional. Either way, it is a natural part of language, every language. In English, it is often associated with puzzles, games, jokes, and poems, which emphasize the *play* in *wordplay*. In *Language on Vacation,* Dmitri Borgmann suggested that it could also be an intellectual pursuit of its own. Also called "recreational linguistics," it is perhaps more complex than linguistics itself. Comparing wordplay to number play, Ross Eckler wrote, "Number play explores curious combinations of elements in the formal system of arithmetic. Wordplay explores curious combinations of elements in the informal system of natural language."

**word pyramid**: an arrangement of words with their letters in a triangular format to better illustrate certain types of wordplay, such as a TRANSDELETION CHAIN.

**word record**: as with world records, word records include the longest, the shortest, the first, the last, and any other attribute that can be measured and compared. Here are five word records using words from *Webster's Third Unabridged*:

> Longest word: pneumonoultramicroscopicsilicovolcanoconiosis (45 letters)
> Longest PALINDROME: kinnikinnik (11 letters)
> Longest ISOGRAM (no letters repeated): dermatoglyphics (15 letters)
> Longest UNIVOCALIC: strengths (9 letters)
> Longest TRANSPOSAL: cinematographer, megachiropteran (15 letters)

**word repetition**: the multiple use of the same word(s) within the same sentence.

> He used it over and over and over and over and over and over and over and over and over and over.

> After all these years, Duran Duran keeps keeps coming coming back back.

**word reversal**: a REVERSAL of a single word that forms another word, phrase, or sentence.

**word ring**: a WORD STRING joined at the ends. The last letter of the string leads back to the first letter, and every letter starts a word of equal length. The word ring ASP contains the words ASP-SPA-PAS-(ASP). Two other word rings are:

> ARE-REA-EAR-(ARE)
> APER-PERA-ERAP-RAPE-(APER)

**word-rubric rebade**: a REBADE in which the clue generates two or more words whose alternate letters form a two-word answer rebade.

**word-rubric rebus**: a REBUS in which the clue is a single word.

CARTS = concertinas (C once, RT in AS)

**word-search pack**: a WORD PACK in the format of a WORD-SEARCH PUZ-ZLE. Words can be printed in eight directions—forward or reverse on a hor-izontal, a vertical, or either of two diagonal lines. Letters of words can overlap, and not all adjacent letters have to form words. In this example, the names of the colors of the rainbow fit into a rectangle measuring 11 x 3 letters.

```
I N D I G O R A N G E
G R E E N Y E L L O W
V I O L E T D B L U E
```

**word-search puzzle**: a popular form of solitaire word puzzle in which the player looks for words in a grid of letters. The words usually go in any of eight directions, and they belong to a certain topic, such as that of food names. Some word-search puzzles provide the list of words that have to be found.

**word square**: an arrangement of letters in a square format to make words of equal length horizontally and vertically. The earliest known word square is the Latin SATOR SQUARE, which was found in various archeological digs, including excavations at Pompeii, Italy, destroyed in 79 A.D. by the eruption of Mount Vesuvius, and at sites in England and Mesopotamia. Some people think it was early graffiti; others think it was a secret Christian symbol. Its words can be read in all four directions—right, left, down, up. If the Latin words are written in a single row, their letters read form a PALINDROME: SATOR AREPO TENET OPERA ROTAS. Dmitri Borgmann translated it as "The sower, Arepo, guides the wheels with care." The letters can also be arranged to form a cross that has the first two words of "The Lord's Prayer" and the letters A and O in both directions. A and O stand for "Alpha" and "Omega," the first and last letters of the Greek alphabet. They signify the Christian belief that God is the beginning and the ending of all things:

```
S A T O R                              A
A R E P O                              P
T E N E T                              A
O P E R A                              T
R O T A S                              E
                                       R
                 A P A T E R N O S T E R O
                                       O
                                       S
                                       T
                                       E
                                       R
                                       O
```

Word squares didn't appear in English until the early 1850s, when the following square was published in "a little volume for the curious." Curiously, the mother of all English word squares is only three words long:

```
C A T
A T E
T E A
```

Before the invention of the CROSSWORD PUZZLE, word squares were popular diversions. They were usually presented as empty grids with clues to the words that made the square. They were called both "word squares" and "square words" until the 1879 Supplement to *Webster's Unabridged Dictionary* listed word square as an entry and made the term official. Nowadays, word squares are usually presented as a square of letters without grids or clues.

There are two basic kinds of word squares, the SINGLE SQUARE and the DOUBLE SQUARE. In the first kind, the same set of words goes across and down. In the second kind, a different set of words goes in each direction. The size of a word square is based on number of letters (or words) going in each direction. A FOUR-SQUARE has four letters on each side and spells four words. The larger a word square is, the more difficult it is to construct.

**word square poem**: a poem made by words arranged in a grid so that they read the same way across and down. This 5 x 5 word square poem begins with the first five words of Edgar Allan Poe's "The Raven":

|  |  |  |  |  |
|---|---|---|---|---|
| once | upon | a | midnight | dreary |
| upon | a | wintry | cyclone's | blackness |
| a | wintry | raven | soared | with |
| midnight | cyclone's | soared | cursing | endless |
| dreary | blackness | with | endless | nevermores |

**word stair**: a sequence of words in which each word is changed to the next by removing the first letter and inserting a new letter at the end (same as WORD CHAIN, third meaning). In a word stair, the words are printed in full. Nowadays, the words are condensed into a WORD STRING. In this example, the word stair on the left represents the same words as the word string on the right:

```
SPA              SPALETEA
 PAL
  ALE
   LEA
    EAT
     ATE
      TEA
```

**word stepladder**: a WORD LADDER in which one word becomes another by changing its letters to their alphabetic neighbors. Thus, HAT can change to GAT or HAS, but not HIT. The goal is to create the longest stepladder.

```
L I K E          B U R R I N G
M I K E          C U R R I N G
M I L E          C U R S I N G
M I M E          C U S S I N G
M I N E          B U S S I N G
L I N E          B U S T I N G
K I N E          B U T T I N G
K I N D          C U T T I N G
```

**word string**: a sequence of letters that represents words of a specific length. For three-letter words, every three adjacent letters in the word string spell a word. A word string is a more compact way of representing a WORD STAIR.

The longest strings of three- and four-letter words in the *Pocket Merriam-Webster* appear below. The first string of each length allows repeated letters; the second doesn't.

> 3-letter: WASPANTHERAYEATEAREVEX     SPALEGOBINK
> 4-letter: TSARIDESK                  ATOMENDS

**word substitution**: the change of a word or phrase containing a shorter one within it into a new word or phrase, by removing the shorter word and substituting another word for it.

> WANDER REMOVING AND—WISER REMOVING IS

**words un-in-one-breath-utterable**: long compound words. Ben Jonson coined this term to make fun of them.

# Words within Words

**Words within Words**: a pencil-and-paper game in which each player makes as many words as possible from the letters of a starting word. The winner is the person who makes the greatest number of words none of the other players have. This game is related to many wordplay forms—ANAGRAM, DELETION, KANGAROO WORD, and others involving letter manipulation.

> BRIDGE = BIDE, BIER, BIRD, BRED, BRIDE, BRING, DIRE, DIRGE, DREG, GRID, RIDE, RIDGE, and numerous two- and three-letter words.

Also called "Hidden Words," "In-Words," "Keyword," "Multiwords," "Target," "Word-Builder," "Word-Hunt," "Word-Making," "Words."

**word tiles**: restricted forms of WORD GRAPHS in which the positions of the different letters are placed in a regular geometric array called a PAVEMENT.

**word-to-name reversal**: a first name that is the REVERSAL of a word.

> SINNED = DENNIS          TREBLE = ELBERT
> NO, SIRRAH! = HARRISON   TREBLED = DELBERT

**word-to-names charade**: a word that can be divided to make two or more shorter names.

| | | |
|---|---|---|
| AbNormAl | JackAl | DesAliNatEd |
| BoGus | RicoChet | EmaNatIonAl |
| DotTed | RegAlEd | DeConTamInaTed |

**word-to-name transposal**: a first name that is a TRANSPOSAL of a word.

> CLASHER = CHARLES
> NAILED = DANIEL
> LEARNED = DARLEEN, DARLENE, LEANDER

**word-to-phrase reversal**: a phrase made by reversing the letters of a word or a name.

> NAVAJOS = SO JAVAN
> AMARYLLIS = SILLY RAMA
> ADELBERTA = A TREBLED "A"

**word-to-sentence reversal**: a sentence made by reversing the letters of a word or name.

> NAOMI = I MOAN.
> MAHARAJAH = HA! JAR A HAM!
> SEPARATION = NO, I TAR APES.
> DEGENERATIVE = EVITA RENEGED.

**word transformation**: a systematic change of one or more words to one or more other words. There are four simple forms of word transformations: substitution, addition, deletion, and transposal. Here are examples using the word FOUR:

> **Substitution**: the replacement of one letter with another (e.g., FOUR—SOUR).
> **Addition**: the insertion of a letter at any position. (e.g., FOUR—FLOUR).
> **Deletion**: the removal of a letter (e.g., FOUR—FOR)
> **Transposal**: the rearrangement of the letters (e.g., FOUR—O, FUR).

**word tree**: a diagram of a word (the trunk) connected to its successive TRANSADDITIONS (branches) and TRANSDELETIONS (roots).

**word-unit** (*adj.*): having words as the basic building blocks of the form. Also called "word-by-word," "word-order."

**word-unit palindrome**: a sentence whose words read the same in both directions.

> So patient a doctor to doctor a patient so.
> You can swallow a cage, can't you, but you can't cage a swallow, can you?

Also called "pseudodrome."

**word-unit palindromic-anagrammatic epitaph**: an epitaph that is a word-unit palindrome from start to finish and a word-unit anagram from line to line. It can also be read in columns going down to achieve the same results. The original appears at St. Winwalloe's Church at Gunwalloe in Cornwall.

> Shall we all die?
> We shall die all;
> All die shall we—
> Die all we shall.

**word-unit palindromic double square**: a WORD SQUARE consisting of PALINDROMIC WORDS with one set of words going across and the other going down. Some of the words have to be repeated to form this kind of square.

**word-unit palindromic poem**: a poem whose words but not letters read the same in both directions from the first word to the last. The poem "Ladies Long in the Tooth" begins with the first couplet  below and ends with the second couplet:

> Widows ate wives once?
> That believe I well.
> ....
> (Well, I believe that
> Once wives ate widows!)

**word-unit palindromic sentence**: see WORD-UNIT PALINDROME.

**word-unit palindromic single square**: a WORD SQUARE consisting of palindromic words with the same set of words going across and down.

> A N N A
> N O O N
> N O O N
> A N N A

**word-unit palindromic double square**: a PALINDROMIC SQUARE made of palindromic words with the same set of words going across and down.

```
A N N A
B O O B
B O O B
A N N A
```

**word-unit reversal ladder**: a WORD LADDER in which each word on one side is the reversal of the corresponding word on the other side. This ladder is broken into two halves to show the reversal pairs.

| | |
|------|------|
| TRAM | MART |
| TRAP | PART |
| TROP | PORT |
| TROT | TORT |

**word-unit reversal**: a text whose words form a different sentence in reverse.

> Scandalous society and life make gossips frantic.
> Frantic gossips make life and society scandalous.

**word-weight**: the sum of the ALPHABETIC VALUES of the letters in a word. The following words and their word-weights were selected from a list of word-weights of 1 to 250:

| | | |
|----------|----------------|--------------------|
| A = 01   | PUN = 51       | PALINDROME = 107   |
| CAB = 06 | LANGUAGE = 68  | LOGOLOGIST = 131   |
| BABE = 10 | SONNET = 87   | KNUCKLEDUSTER = 164 |

**word worm**: a single geometric representation for words of all lengths, based on the mathematical concept of the vector. A word worm is a set of 267 cubelets stacked in a 3 x 3 cubic lattice with the letters assigned to cubelets as shown below. Using the lattice as a template, the letters of a word can be traced in three-dimensional space to form the word worm.

| **Top Layer** | **Middle Layer** | **Bottom Layer** |
|---------------|------------------|------------------|
| A B C         | J K L            | R S T            |
| D E F         | M . N            | U V W            |
| G H I         | O P Q            | X Y Z            |

**would-be acronym**: a contrived ACRONYM that would probably never be a real acronym. For instance, MIT is the acronym of Massachusetts Institute of Technology, and MASSACHUSETTS INSTITUTE OF TECHNOLOGY becomes this would-be acronym:

> Many A Science Student At Cambridge Hoped, Unless Stopped Educationally by Terrible Test Scores, to Initiate Noteworthy Scientific and Technological Inquiries, To Uncover Truths, Explain Observations and Facts, and To Examine Critical Hypotheses, but Never Once to Linger Over the Glories of Yesterday.

**would-be phobia word**: a coined PHOBIA WORD. Each of these would-be phobia words is followed by the thing that could be feared:

CACOPHONOPHOBIA (bad music)
LUNAEDIESOPHOBIA (Mondays)
MEGADEKAPHOBIA (the Big Ten)
NADAPHOBIA (nothing)

**X-name**: a first name that begins with the letter X, the letter least used at the beginning of words and names. Xavier and Xaviera are well-known X-names, but there are many more. The following are from an X-file of 100 masculine and 50 feminine X-names gathered from various sources:

| Masculine | Feminine |
|---|---|
| Xagus | Xanthella |
| Xenarchos | Xara |
| Xenik | Xenodice |
| Xenombrotus | Xie Mae |
| Xopher | Xiutlaltzin |

**xzwamfeujho**: an undefined literary form whose name is unpronounceable.

**Y-invariant**: a UNIVOCALIC with Y as the only vowel.

GYPSYFY                    MYNYDDYSLWYN

**Yogi Berra quote**: a funny, thought-provoking, and slightly off-base quote attributed to Hall-of-Fame baseball catcher, coach, and manager Yogi Berra.

> "Nobody comes to this restaurant—it's always too crowded."
> "Baseball is ninety percent mental. The other half is physical."
> "A nickel ain't worth a dime anymore."
> "I didn't really say half the things I said."

**Yreka Bakery**: the most legendary business establishment in the world of PALINDROMES. Located at 322 West Miner Street, Yreka, Californina, and founded over a century ago, the bakery's name was an unintentional palindrome. After the bakery went out of business in 1990, there was a brief palindromic void. However, when the new occupants opened up an art space, they named it YRELLA GALLERY.

**zazzification**: the substitution of a Z-sound for another consonant sound to convert a non-slang word into a slang word or to make a slang word even slangier.

| | |
|---|---|
| BONKERS—ZONKERS | SLAP—ZAP |
| JILLION—ZILLION | SNAPPY—SNAZZY |
| SCUM—SCUZZ | YIPPIE—ZIPPIE |

**zeugma**: connecting any two parts of speech by any other part of speech. The word comes from *zeugos*, the Greek word for "yoked." A zeugma can be serious, as in the first example below, or humorous, as in the second example.

> Much he the place admired, the person more (Milton, *Paradise Lost* 9.444)
> "Well, I'll be damned and rich!" he said. "I won a million dollars."

**zeugma tale**: a story written with a myriad of ZEUGMAS. Here are the first and the last paragraphs of "Going Crazy and to the Store":

> William was going crazy and to the store. For two months, his wife Gloria had been badgering him about getting fired and a new job or lost. It wasn't his fault or in the cards. It was fate, embarrassing, and a surprise.
> [...]
> They kissed each other and their old lives goodbye. And they lived high on the hog, it up, like there was no tomorrow, on Easy Street, and happily ever after.

**zigzag word**: a words in which the direction in the alphabet from letter to letter changes with each new letter. In the word WORD, W-O goes toward the beginning of the alphabet, O-R goes toward the end, R-D goes toward the beginning.

DECLIVITOUS MILITARIZATION

**ziticorumbatous 15-square**: a comical WORD SQUARE made of fifteen 15-letter words, all created and defined specifically for the square. Three of the words and their definitions follow:

ISOPETOLURNETTE: a small device for measuring the equality of sideburn lengths in a wax factory.

ROISTOSTOMULOUS: speaking with feathers or rubber-bands in the mouth.

ZITICORUMBATOUS: compounded in more ways than one, and for no discernible reason.

**zoological homophonic pair**: a pair of words that are HOMOPHONES, one of which is the name of a living creature. In first column below, each animal name is paired off with an adjective, in the second with a verb, and in the third with a noun (although some of the words can be used as other parts of speech, too).

| | | |
|---|---|---|
| DEER—DEAR | DOES—DOZE | AUNT—ANT |
| FOWL—FOUL | EWES—USE | HARE—HAIR |
| GRIZZLY—GRISLY | FLEA—FLEE | MUSSEL—MUSCLE |

**Z-to-A word list**: a list of words that have all 26 letters of the alphabet appearing in reverse order. Here is the minimum list of *Pocket Merriam-Webster* words (allowing no single-letter words except I and A and no spelled-out words like XYZ and BB).

haZY oX WaVe oUT SiR QuiP ON MiLK Jig HoG FED CuB A

**zzyxjoanw hoax**: a wordplay hoax involving the last entry in Rupert Hughes's *The Musical Guide* (later, *Music-Lovers Encyclopedia*), published in various editions between 1905 and 1956. The entry reads:

ZZYXJOANW (*shaw*) Maori **1.** drum **2.** fife **3.** conclusion

No one questioned the word for more than 70 years until Philip Cohen pointed out some of the unusual properties of the entry, including the punctuation, the pronunciation (*shaw*), the three different meanings, and the fact that the name of Hughes's wife was JOAN. Until it was debunked, *zzyxjoanw* was considered to be the first legitimate dictionary word to have broken the two-Z barrier.

**ZZZZZZZZZZZZZZZZZZZZZZZZZZZZZZZZZZZZZZZZZZZZZ**: the longest published all-Z word. Clocking in at 43 Z's, it represents the sound of snoring. It appears within a citation in the *Oxford English Dictionary*, but not as a main entry. Its inclusion here makes it the final main entry that has ever appeared in any reference book, the very last word of all.

# After Word

Abraham Abulafia, a thirteenth-century cabalist, taught that the key to transcendence is language itself. Abulafia believed that, by concentrating on letters, the mind could loose itself from its shackles to commune with a presence greater than itself. Wordplay is one way we have of extending our reach beyond our grasp and touching something that transcends our coil of mortality.

Beyond our day-to-day use of language—"Please pass the butter"; "How much does that cost?"—gleams the realm of wordplay—"I'd rather have a bottle in front of me than a frontal lobotomy"; "What's the longest word in the English language? *Smiles*, because there's a mile between its first and last letter."

Wordplay appears to be programmed into our DNA and hardwired into our nervous system, one indication being that we have been messing around with words for a very long time.

In the ninth book of Homer's *Odyssey*, composed around 800 B.C., the wily Odysseus is trapped in the cave of Polyphemus, the one-eyed giant with 20/ vision. To fool the Cyclops, Odysseus gives his name as Outis, Greek for "No Man." When Odysseus attacks the giant in order to escape from the cave, Polyphemus calls out to his fellow monsters for help, crying "No man is killing me!" Naturally, his fellow big guys take him literally and make no attempt to aid him.

Remember Oedipus? He was a complex king who married a woman just like the girl that married dear old dad. He was a prince of a guy who married a woman old enough to be his mother—and that's what she turned out to be. Before he did that, Oedipus was challenged by a piece of wordplay put to him by the Sphinx: "What goes on four legs in the morning, two at noon, and on three at night?" Oedipus, one of the first game-show contestants in history, gave as his final answer: "Man. In infancy he crawls, in his prime he walks, and in old age he leans on a staff." His prize was that he became Rex, which turned out to be very bad for his eyesight.

The Catholic Church is founded on another Greek pun, this one in Matthew 16:18, where Jesus says, "Thou art Peter (*petros*) and upon this rock (*petra*) I will build my church."

And we are getting even better at this stuff. In 1892, William Walsh stated in his *Hand-Book of Literary Curiosities*: "After centuries of endeavor, so few really good anagrams have been rolled down to us. One may assert that all the really superb anagrams now extant might be contained in a pillbox." Look at the field of logology since 1965, the year Dmitri Borgmann's *Language on Vacation* was published, shortly before the birth of *Word Ways*, and compare this work with what came before. You'll see that we have an ineluctable rendezvous with logological destiny.

Wordplay unites us as an American culture. It is a great part of the folklore of a nation that was founded long after the invention of the printing press. Americans born generations apart and thousands of miles apart will still collectively recognize the likes of "Fuzzy wuzzy was a bear . . . ," "How much wood would a woodchuck chuck? . . . ," and "A sailor went to C-C-C to see what he could C-C-C. . . ."

As Peter Farb points out in *Word Play*, "The majority of American children are strikingly punctual in acquiring a repertoire of riddles at about age six or seven." One of those riddles has been and still is: "What's black and white and red [read] all over?" Through that question and its answer—"a newspaper"—many of us first experienced the epiphany that two meanings can occupy the same space at the same time.

This concision is one of the elements that wordaholics, logolepts, and verbivores so love about wordplay. Have you heard about the successful perfume manufacturer? His business made a lot of sense [scents, cents]. Within the brief compass of a single syllable repose three different spellings and relevant meanings. Have you heard about the man who gave his male offspring a cattle ranch and named it Focus? Because it was the place where the sun's rays meat [sons, raise meat]. Here six meanings inhabit the space ordinarily lived in by three.

In matters logological we also enjoy cramming the large into the small. We find it satisfying that within the word *rambunctious* lurks the synonymous *raucous*, with all its letters in perfect order. In a palindrome such as ELK CITY, KANSAS, IS A SNAKY TICKLE—just the kind of loopy, wiggy content merged into a syntactically perfect statement that I love—we find the same meaning running twice through the space ordinarily reserved for a single meaning.

There is yet one more satisfaction that comes with an elbow book like *The Dictionary of Wordplay*. It thrums with the human passion to name. Take another look at the book of *Genesis,* and you'll find that God doesn't just snap His fingers to make everything happen. He calls them into existence and then He names them: "And God said: Let there be light. . . . And God called the light Day, and the darkness He called Night." And what is one of the first thing that Adam does, after introducing himself to Eve by saying (in English; how convenient) MADAM, I'M ADAM, thus creating the world's first palindrome? He names all the creatures that run and crawl and fly and swim over the face of the earth.

This may be what is meant by our being made in God's image. Like Him, we are the speakers, and we are the namers. *The Dictionary of Wordplay* is an act of naming the creatures in a beautiful universe. You won't find some of the words between these covers in standard dictionaries, but they are known by those who play the game of words. This lexicon is a testament to the greatest miracle of language: its ability to name itself.

—*Richard Lederer*
 *San Diego, California*

## Appendix A: Alphasets

An alphaset is a group of symbols that includes at least one letter of the alphabet standing alone. The group was not assembled for wordplay but for other reasons. It must vary from the regular alphabet. Of the 26 alphasets below, some have been used in wordplay and some haven't. There would also be a very short, usually one-line description or explanation.

**Diatonic scale**: ABCDEFG
**Federal Reserve Notations**: ABCDEFGHI
**Temperature**: CH
**Telephone letters**: ABCDEFGHIJKLMNOPRSTUVWXY (no Q, Z)
**Elevator directions**: UD
**Deciduous teeth**: ABCDEFGHIJKLMNOPQRST (no U-Z) (used in children's dentistry)
**Compass directions**: NEWS
**Roman numerals**: IVXLCDM
**Amino acid symbols**: ABCDEFGHIKLMNPQRSTVWYZ (no J, O, U, X)
**Blood types**: A, B, AB, O
**Egg grades**: A, AA, AAA
**Playing cards**: A, K, Q, J, 10, 9, 8, 7, 6, 5, 4, 3, 2
**Days of the week**: SMTWTFS
**Shirt sizes**: S, M, L, XL, XXL, XXXL
**Condiments**: SP (salt, pepper)
**Shoe width sizes**: AAAAA, AAAA, AAA, AA, A, B, C, D, DD, DDD, DDDD, DDDDD
**Political Parties**: DRI
**Truth Values**: TF
**Sex**: MF
**Automatic Gearshift Settings**: PRNDL
**Marital Status**: SMD
**Grading System**: ABCDF (this is one of several grading system alphasets)
**Hexadecimal Notations**: 0, 1, 2, 3, 4, 5, 6, 7, 8, 9, A, B, C, D, E
**Record sides**: AB
**Chess Notation**: KQRBNP
**Tic-Tac-Toe**: OX

—*Dave Morice*

# Appendix B: "Interesting" Number Names

In the February 1977 issue of *Word Ways*, Dmitri Borgmann wrote, "All English words and names—all, without a single exception—are logologically interesting." He didn't define "interesting," and his examples didn't clarify matters. If the concept is applied to number names, the results are interesting. Because both logological and numerical properties can be considered, interestingness takes many strange twists and turns. The list below is limited to facts about 26 number names between 1 and 99. The first 10 numbers have two or three facts apiece, and the remaining 16 have one each. They come from a longer list that includes all number names under 100.

"Interesting" means that a number name has a property that makes it the only example, or the highest or lowest in numerical value, or the longest or shortest in letter-count, with respect to all nameable numbers, from ONE to ONE THOUSAND VIGINTILLION MINUS ONE, and not just the numbers under ONE HUNDRED. All wordplay in the list stays within the boundaries of the set of number names; non-numeric words aren't included. For example, "ONE subtransposes to TEN" qualifies, but "ONE transposes to EON does not." Numerical value of the numbers and their separate digits are used only when they relate directly to the letters. This would disqualify the fact that the names of the 13 different playing cards in each suit are spelled with 52 letters, since this is not a property of the number names but of the card names.

For each property, the number is the only example unless stated otherwise by inclusion of the term lowest, highest, shortest, or longest. Thus FOUR is listed as "Truthful number," which means that it is the only truthful number. One of the most interesting aspects of this list is the view it gives of the number names. Out of the myriad of possibilities, for example, only one number, THREE, ends in two vowels. That's the mathematics of language.

    **One**: Highest vowel-to-consonant ratio (2:1)
        Lowest total alphabetic value of letters (15 + 14 + 5 = 34)
        Lowest that counts its consonants
        In Morse code, only one that divides into dashes on left and dots on right
        (- - - - . .)
    **Two**: All last-half letters
        All vertical mirror letters
        Typed on only one row of typewriter keyboard
    **Three**: Most consonants at the beginning
        Most vowels at the end
        Letters shift to a well-formed Roman numeral (THREE = XLVII = 47)

**Four**: Truthful number (equalling its amount of letters)

Lowest bisquare (square number, square number of letters)

**Five**: Romantic truthful number (fIVe has IV = 4 in it, which equals the amount of letters)

Alphabetic value of final letter same as the number (E = 5)

**Six**: All upside-down letters

Alternating tall and narrow letters in lowercase

**Seven**: First spelled with letters that have appeared in previous numbers

Longest with letters alternating from first half and last half of the alphabet

**Eight**: Alphabetically first number name

Most vowels at the beginning

Most consonants at the end

Highest number whose Scrabble values multiply to itself (1 x 1 x 2 x 4 x 1 = 8)

**Nine**: Longest monoconsonantal number name (NiNe)

Highest number with letters typed alternately on two rows of the typewriter keyboard

**Ten**: Highest number requiring a different telephone keypad entry for each letter

Most frequently appearing number name in the reverse string of all number names (first appears at ONETWO = OWTENO)

**Twelve**: Scrabble truthful number (Scrabble values = 1+4+1+1+4+1 = 12)

**Thirteen**: Kangaroo having two joeys that add up to itself (THiRtEEn = 3, ThirtEeN = 10; 3 + 10 = 13.)

**Fifteen**: Morse truthful number (15 dots and dashes: ..-. .. ..-. - . . -.)

**Seventeen**: Longest univocalic (sEvEntEEn)

**Twenty-three**: Lowest reverse snowball word (TWENTY has 6 letters, THREE has 5)

**Twenty-eight**: Highest in which number of vowels times number of consonants equals itself (7 consonants x 4 vowels = 28)

**Thirty-seven**: Highest Braille truthful number (using 37 dots)

**Forty**: Letters in increasing alphabetic order

**Forty-four**: Highest with no Roman letters

**Forty-five**: Highest dishonest number: each digit counts the number of letters in other unit (FORTY has 5 letters, FIVE has 4 letters)

**Fifty**: All tall letters in lowercase (fifty)

**Fifty-eight**: Highest having amount of alphabetically consecutive letters equal to amount of letters in either unit (EFGHI, 5 letters)

**Sixty-two**: Highest zigzag number (direction in the alphabet from letter to letter changes with each new letter: S–I goes down, I–X goes up, X–T goes down, etc.)

**Seventy-two**: Second unit contained as a joey in lettershift of first unit (SEVENTY shifts 1 step to TFWFOUZ)

**Eighty-eight**: Highest typed with alternating hands (left, right, left, right, etc.)

**Ninety-seven**: Longest with alternating vowels and consonants.

*—Dave Morice*

# Appendix C: Inventors, Authors, and Sources for the Entries

## Abbreviations of Inventors and Authors

*(These appear in the "Index of the Entries with Inventors, Authors, and Sources," which begins on page 266.)*

AA = Anonymous Author,
    unknown author,
    undetermined author,
    common usage, etc.
AB = Alfred Butts
ALB = Alastair Brotchie
AC = Alan Davies
AD = Augustus de Morgan
AE = "Arty Ess"
AF = Alan Frank
AG = "Arty Fishel"
AH = Arthur Harris
AI = Arthur Holt
AK = A. Langdon Root
AL = Alan Levine
AM = "Allez"
AN = "Anonyme"
AP = A. Cyril Pearson
AQ = "Archimedes"
AR = "Air Raid"
AS = Aristophanes
AT = Rev. William A. Spooner
AV = "All Wrong"
AW = Arthur Wynne
BA = Barry Chamish
BC = Bill Cooley
BG = Bob Grant
BJ = "Blue Jay"
BK = Brian Lake
BL = Blake Greenlee
BM = Bruce Monrad
BO = "Bolis"
BP = Bruce Pyne

BR = Boris Randolph
BW = Bob Worgul
CB = Charles W. Bostick
CA = "Charlie B."
CC = Charles Bombaugh
CD = Carol DeLugach
CE = Christopher Edgar
CG = Clifford Goldstein
CH = Charles Holding
CL = Charles Linnett
CK = Cynthia Knight
CM = Chris McManus
CN = Charles N. Crowder
DAC = Dierdra Colzie
DB = Dmitri A. Borgmann
DC = "D.C. Ver"
DD = Danny Morice
DE = "Deacon"
DF = Darryl Francis
DG = Dave Glew
DGR = David Grambs
DH = Douglas Hofstadter
DK = Douglas Fink
DL = Darrel Gray
DM = Dave Morice
DN = Daniel Nussbaum
DO = Don Marquis
DR = David Rosen
DS = Dave Silverman
DT = Dan Tilque
DU = David Schulman
DV = Dona Telore
DW = David Williams

EA = Eric Albert
EB = Ethel H. Blackledge
EC = Eric Chaikin
ED = Edward Scher
EK = Elizabeth Kingsley
EL = "Ellsworth"
EN = Edgar Wilson Nye
EP = E. Pinnock
ES = Emily Schlesinger
EU = Eugene Ulrich
EV = Ernest Vincent Wright
EW = Edward R. Wolpow
EX = "Emmo W."
FA = "Fanacro"
FC = Fletcher Copp
FE = Faith Eckler
FI = "Fiddle"
FL = Frederick Landers
GA = Gilbert Adair
GC = George Carlin
GD = Guido d'Arezzo
GG = George Grieshaber
GH = George Herbert
GK = George S. Kaufman
GL = George Marvill
GM = Guy Murchie
GN = Gerard Malanga
GP = George Perec
GQ = g. p. skratz
GR = "Grandmother"
GS = George H. Scheetz
GT = George Starbuck
GU = "Grulla"
GX = Grelling
HB = Howard Bergerson
HC = H. C. Dodge
HD = Henry E. Dudeney
HE = "H.E.P." (probably Harriet
    Eleanor Phillimon)

HG = H.H. Gyde
HH = Harry W. Hazard
HM = Harry Mathews
HO = "Hoho"
HP = Harry Partridge
IB = Irwin M. Berent
IFM = Frank Mankiewicz
IK = Isabel Kadison
IM = "Imperial"
IS = ira steingroot
IX = "Ixaxar"
JA = Jan Ackerson
JB = John Brooks Tenney
JC = John E. Connett
JD = John David
JE = James Brunot
JEL = Jean Lescure
JF = John Foster
JG = Jeff Grant
JH = Joyce Holland
JI = Joan Griscom
JJ = J. L. Lundgren
JK = "Johank"
JL = J. A. Lindon
JM = Sir Jeremy Morris
JN = J.A. Morgan
JO = John Holgate
JP = John Boulten
JQ = John Coe
JR = James Rambo
JS = Dr. J. H. Marshall
JT = John Taylor
JU = J. A. H. Hunter
JV = John Walker
JW = Jonathan Swift
JX = J. E. Surrick
JZ = Jed Martinez
KB = John Roulstone
KC = "King Carnival"

KE = "Kenneth"  
KL = Kurt L. Loening  
KN = Kit Robinson  
KR = K. F. Ross  
LA = Leonard R. N. Ashley  
LB = Leslie Card  
LC = Lewis Carroll  
LD = Louis B. Delpino  
LE = L. M. Conant  
LFM = Leroy F. Meyers  
LG = Leonard Gordon  
LH = Louis Braille  
LJ = Les Jenkins  
LL = Lawrence Levine  
LM = Leigh Mercer  
LP = Louis Phillips  
LS = Lee Sallows  
LT = L. M. N. Terry  
MA = "Matilda"  
MB = Maxey Brooke  
MC = "Macropod"  
MD = Milton Bradley Co.  
ME = "Mrs. Ev"  
MF = Marjorie Friedman  
MAG = Mariah Green  
MG = Mike Griffin  
MH = Mary J. Hazard  
MI = Mardell Grothe  
MO = "Molemi"  
MP = Murray Pearce  
MR = Mike Reiss  
MS = Mark Saltveit  
MU = Michael Sussna  
MV = M. Vatriquant  
MW = Melvin O. Wellman  
MY = Mary J. Youngquist  
NA = Nugarum Amator  
NI = "Nightowl"  
NY = "Nyas"  

OD = Oren N. Dalton  
OJ = Otto Jespersen  
OM = Ove Michaelsen  
PA = Paul Dixon  
PC = Philip M. Cohen  
PD = Prince Djoli Kansil  
PE = Peter H. Gott, M.D.  
PF = "Professor Hoffman"  
PG = "Pearlie Glen"  
PH = Patrick Hunt  
PN = Peter Newby  
PP = Palitoy Parker  
PR = Paul R. Hanna  
PS = Peter Stickland  
RA = Russell Ash  
RB = Ralph Beaman  
RC = "R."  
RD = Richard E. Douglass  
RE = Ross Eckler  
RF = Robert Funt  
RG = Roger Lancelyn Green  
RH = Ray Bongartz  
RJ = Robert Cass Keller  
RK = Robert Kurosaka  
RL = Richard Lederer  
RN = "Roving"  
RO = Rudolf Ondrejka  
RP = Robert A. Palermo  
RR = R. Robinson Rowe  
RS = Richard Sheridan  
RT = Robert L. Ward  
RU = R. Tisdale  
RV = Rod L. Evans  
RW = Roger W. Wescott  
SA = "Sally"  
SB = Steven Cushing  
SC = Steve Chism  
SD = Sarah Josepha Hale  
SF = Samuel Goldwyn

SG = Sheila Heldenbrand
SH = Scott Hattie
SI = Simmias of Rhodes
SJ = Sol Hurok
SK = "Sibyl"
SL = "Sol, Jr."
SM = "Swamp Angel"
SN = Samuel F. B. Morse
SO = Sotades of Maronia
SP = Stanley L. Payne
SR = Steve Root
ST = Susan Thorpe
SW = Stevie Wonder
SX = "Sphinx"
TB = Thomas L. Bernard
TC = Ted Clarke
TD = "The Duke"
TE = Tom Clark
TF = The Artist Formerly
    Known as Prince
TG = "That Gal Nell"
TH = "T.H."
TJD = Jordan Davis
TK = Trudi Katchmar
TL = "T.L."
TP = Tom Pulliam
TQ = Thomas De Quincy
TR = "Treesong"
TU = "Tunste"
TV = Tom Veitch
TW = Thomas Wyatt
TZ = Te-Zir-Man
VA = "Vesta"
VE = Victor Eijkhout
VH = Virginia R. Hager
VI = "Viking"
VM = Vernon MacLaren
VN = Vladimir Nabokov
WE = Willard R. Espy

WG = William Gillespie
WM = William Shakespeare
WR = William R. Webster
WS = Will Shortz
WSH = Walter Shedlofsky
WT = William Tunstall-Pedoe
WW = W. S. Walsh
XS = "X. Spellary"
YN = "Y. Knott"

## Abbreviations of Sources

*(These appear in the index beginning on the next page.)*

*ALP = Alphabet Avenue*
*ANG = Anguished English*
*ARC = Archyology: The Long Lost Tales of Archy and Mehitabel*
*BSG = A Book of Surrealist Games*
*BUD = Budget of Paradoxes*
*BUZ = Buzzwords*
CNN = Cable News Network
*CZE = Crazy English*
*ECS = Ecstatic Occasions, Expedient Forms*
*FIN = The Final E*
*GAA = Glossary of Art, Architecture, and Design Since 1945*
*GAM = Games* magazine
*GET = Get Thee to a Punnery*
*GFC = Gleanings for the Curious from the Harvest Fields of Literature*
*GYW = Getting Your Words' Worth*
*KTP = A Key to Puzzledom*
*LOV = Language on Vacation*
*MAD = Making the Alphabet Dance*
*MW3 = Merriam Webster's 3rd Unabridged*
*MWC10 = Merriam Webster's Collegiate Dictionary, 10th Edition*
*NAN = The New Anagrammasia*
*NWN = Number Words and Number Symbols*
*NYO = The New Yorker*
*OAC = Oddities and Curiosities of Words and Literature*
*OGW = Oxford Guide to Word Games*
*OUC = Oulipo Compendium*
*PAA = Palindromes and Anagrams*
*PAL = The Palindromist*
*PAR = Parade* magazine
*PEP = Princeton Encyclopedia of Poetry and Poetics*
*POW = The Play of Words*
*PPW = Pictured Puzzles and Word Play*
*RED = Reader's Digest*
*SCI = Scientific American*
*TOP = The Top Ten of Everything*
*TLG = Through the Looking-Glass*
*WAP = Words at Play*
*WAW = Words about Words*
*WOC = The Word Circus*
*WOR = Word Ways* magazine

# An Index of the Entries with Inventors, Authors, and Sources

**A-invariant:** DB, in *LOV,* p. 174; **abbreviated rhyme:** WE in *ALP,* p. 173; **abstemious word:** concept, term, DS, examples, RE, in *WOR,* Feb72, p. 51; **accidental acrostic:** concept, AA, term, example, DB, in *BYL,* p. 5; **acro-equation:** concept, term, GG, examples from lists by PC, AH, DR, in *WOR*-Nov78, pp. 239–240; **acronymic palindrome:** concept, example, AA, term, MD, in ILM, p. 10; **acrostic:** term, definition, AA, example 1, LC, in *TLG*; example 2, HM, example 3, ES, in *MAD,* pp. 13–15; **acrostic dictionary:** term, definition, AA, in MAD, p. 78; example, DM; **acrostic equation:** DM, in *ALP,* p. 145; **acrostic poem:** AA; **acrostic puzzle:** AA, in *OGW,* p. 35; **add-a-line couplet:** concept, AA, examples, TA, in *OGW,* p. 137; term, DM; **adjacent-letter switch:** DB, in *LOV,* p 99; **adjacent pronoun speller:** concept, example, RL, in *WOC,* p. 241; term, DM; **adjacent word speller:** concept, example, RL, in *WOC,* p. 240; term, DM; **AEGINRST transposal problem:** concept, term, DB, in *LOV,* p. 90–91, examples, JG, in *MAD,* pp. 125–131; **AEIOU abbreviation:** concept, examples 1–2, FR; example 3, DB; derived term, DM; **AEIOU word:** DB, in *LOV,* p. 160; derived term, DM; **AEIOUY word:** concept, example, DB, in *LOV,* p. 162; derived term, DM; **Agamemnon word:** EW, in *WOR*-May80, pp. 104–105; **aibohphobia:** RL, in *WOC,* p. 60; **ailihphilia:** RL, in *WOC,* p. 54; **Alberti disc:** AA, in *BOP,* p. 205; **all-consonant word:** DB, in *LOV,* pp. 177–178 (synonym: no-vowel word, RE, in *MAD,* p. 12); **alliterative acrostic:** concept, AA, term, CC, in *OAC,* p. 45; example, DM; **alliterative eulogy:** concept, example, AA, term, CC, in *OAC,* p. 218; **all-vowel pun pair:** DM, in *ALP,* p. 42; **all-vowel word:** concept, examples 6–9, DB, in *LOV,* p. 156; examples 1–5, DM; **alphabet-crashing word:** EW, in *WOR*-Feb79, p. 59; **Alphabet Cube:** DM, in *MAD,* pp. 247–248; **alphabetical advertisement:** concept, example, AA, term, CC, in *OAC,* pp. 29–30; **alphabetically-ordered AEIOU word:** concept, example, DB, in *LOV,* p. 160; derived term, DM; **alphabetically-ordered AEIOUY word:** concept, examples, DB, in *LOV,* p. 162; derived term, DM; **alphabetically-ordered consonant word:** concept, example, DB, in *LOV,* p. 167. term, DM; **alphabetic equality names:** concept, examples, LG, in *ALP,* p. 185–187, term, DM; **alphabetic neighbor:** EU, in *MAD,* p. 168; **alphabetic pattern:** RE; in *MAD,* p. 173; **alphabetic poem:** concept, term, AA, example, AW, in *OGW,* p. 128; **alphabetic recital:** concept, example 1, HM; example 2, LP; term, RE, in *MAD,* p. 163 (synonym: alphabet story, RE, in *WOR*-May81, p. 85); **alphabetic sentence:** concept, AA, term, DB, in *LOV,* p. 133; example, AA, in *OGW,* p. 130; **alphabetic sequence (1):** concept, DB, examples, term, RE, in *MAD,* pp. 154–155 (synonym: alphabetic letter sequence, DB, in *LOV,* p. 168); **alphabetic sequence (2):** PC, in *MAD,* p. 169; **alphabetic substitute-letter transposal chain:** concept, WS, example, KC, term, RE, in *MAD,* pp. 149–150; **alphabetic tetragram:** JG, in *WOR*-May99, pp. 101–103; **alphabetic transaddition:** RE, in *MAD,* p. 148; **alphabetic trigram:** JG, in *WOR*-May99, pp. 101–102; **alphabetic value:** concept, DB, in *LOV,* p. 140, term, AA; **alphabetic word:** concept, examples 3–5, term, DB, in *LOV,* p. 166; examples 1–2, DM; **alphabetic word challenge:** concept, DS, example, MH, in *MAD,* pp. 181–182 (derived term, DM); **alphabetic wordplay:** term, RE, in *MAD,* p. 5; **alphabetized integers:** concept, examples 1–3, DB, in *LOV,* pp. 256–257; example 4, EW, in *WOR*-Feb80, p. 55 (derived term, DM); **alphabet of silent letters:** concept, AA, examples, RL, in *WOC,* pp. 23–24; derived term, DM; **alphabet of silent hosts:** concept, AA, examples, term, RL, in *WOC,* p. 24; **alphabet rearrangement:** term, RE, in *MAD,* p. 239; **alphabet ring:** RE, in *WOR*-Aug77, p. 189; **alphabet shift:**

RE, in *MAD* 170; **alphamagic square**: LS, in *MAD*, p. 238; **alphametic**: concept, example, AA, term, JU in *OGW*, p. 124; **alphanumeric value**: AA; **alphapositional value**: AA; **alphatoon**: DM, in *ALP*, p. 201; **alphome**: ST, in *WOR*-Aug98, p. 178; **alphomic word**: ST, in *WOR*-Aug98, p. 184; **alternade**: DB, in *LOV*, p. 170 (synonym: drop-letter reversal, DB, in *LOV*, p. 170); **alternating alphabet**: LG, in *MAD*, p. 186; **alternating monotony**: RB, in *WOR*-May71, p. 77; **alternating vowel-consonant number name**: concept, examples, EW, in *WOR*-Aug81, p. 166; derived term, DM; **amalgam**: PN, ST; **ambigram**: concept, term, SK, example, TZ, in *WAP*, p. 93; **anagram**: concept, LY, term, AA, in *LOV*–example 1, DC, example 2, AA, example 3, AR, example 5, JK, example 6, TD, example 7, EL, example 8, TH, example 9, SA, example 10, AA, in *NAN* various p; example 4 and 11, DM, example 12, ST, in *ALP*, p. 10, 15, 19 (synonyms: apt anagram, apposite anagram, DB, in *LOV*, p. 267); **anagram classification system**: concept, term, RE, in *MAD*, p. 119 and *WOR*-Feb70, p. 24; example, DM; **anagram equation**: concept, example 1, EX, examples 2 and 3, LS, term, DM, in *ALP*, p. 144 (synonym: apposite numerical transposition, OM, in *WAP*, p. 113); **anagrammar chain**: CM, in *MAD*, p. 109; **anagrammatic cross-reference**: concept, example 1, AG, example 2, AA, example 3, DM, in *WAP*, p. 112; example 4, JZ, in *FNI*; **anagrammatic definition**: concept, term, example 1, DR, example 2, FE, in *WOR*-Aug81, p. 175; **anagrammatic pangrams**: concept, example, EF, in *PAA*, p. viii (derived term, DM); **anagrammatic sonnet**: concept, term, example 1, LC; example 2, AA, example 3, RG; **anagrammatic translation**· PD, in *WOR*-May87, p. 116; **anagrammatic verse**: concept, term, AA, example, DM, in *ALP*, pp. 20–21; **anagrammed story**: WR, in *WOR*-Aug98, p. 233; **anagram puzzle verse**: concept, example, HP, term, TA, in *OGW*, p. 81; **anagram word square**: **(1)**: PN, in *PWG*, p. 180; **(2)** PN, in *PWG*, p. 180; **(3)** PN, in *PWG*, pp. 180–181; **ananym**: concept, AA, example, term, DB, in *LOV*, p. 46; **anatonym**: concept, term, IK, examples, OJ, from RL, in *WOR*-May79, p. 80; **anchored palindrome**· DB, in *LOV*, p. 25; **anchored transposals**: DB, in *LOV*, p. 98; **anchored word**: RE, in *MAD*, p. 35; **animultitude**: LM, in *WOR*-Feb70, p. 45; **animal anagram**: RL, in *WOC*, pp. 28–29; **animal beheadment**: RL, in *WOC*, pp. 116–117; **animal charade**: RL, in *WOC*, p. 92; **animal curtailment**: RL, in *WOC*, pp. 116–117; **animal kangaroo**: RL, in *WOC*, pp. 126–127; **animal letter substitution**: RL, in *WOC*, p. 145; **animal looper**: RL, in *WOC*, p. 45; **animal palindrome**: concept, AA, example 1, JC, example 2, KB, example 3, LM, example 4, MT, term, RL, in *WOC*, pp. 56–57; **animal-within-animal beheadment**: concept, examples, RL, in *WOC*, p. 118; derived term, DM; **animal-within-animal charade**: RL, in *WOC*, p. 92; **animal-within-animal kangaroo**: RL, in *WOC*, pp. 127–128; **antibeheadment**: RL, in *WOC*, p. 114; **anticharade**: concept, examples 1–2, DB, in *LOV*, p. 112; example 3, term, DM, in *ALP*, p. 131 (synonym: charade-antigram, DB, in *LOV*, p. 112); **antidisestablishmentarianism**: AA, in *CZE*, p. 39; **antigram**: AA (synonyms: antonymogram, antonymous anagram, opposite anagram, OM, in *WAP*, p. 92.); **antikangaroo**: RL, in *WOC*, p. 130; **anti-lettershift pair**: DM, in *ALP*, p. 118; **anti-lettershift sentence**: concept, term, DM, example, DM and FE, in *ALP*, p. 118; **antiphonetabet**: concept, AA, examples, term, IB & RV, in *GYW*, pp. 25-26; **antiphonetic spelling**: concept, example 1, GS, term, examples 2-3, IR & RV, in *GYW*, pp. 25-26; **anti-rebus**: DM, in *ALP*, pp. 67–68; **antonymic reversal**: DB, in *LOV*, pp. 44–45; **antonymic substitution**: concept, HM in *OUC* p. 50, (derived term, examples TJD); **antonymic transdeletion**: concept, example 2, term, DB, in *LOV*, p. 121; example 1, DM; **apostrophic poem**: DM, in *ALP*, p. 171; **apostrophic sentence**: DM, in *ALP*, pp. 263–264; **apostrophe word**:

concept, examples, DM, term, RL, in *WOC*, p. 22; **aptronym**: concept, term, AA, examples, RL, in *CZE,* p. 58; **aptly named author**: RA & BK, in *WAP,* p. 33; **artagram**: DM; **art movement name**: JV, in *GAA*; **asymmetrical letters**: DM, in *ALP,* p. 197; **A-to-Z word list**: RE, in *MAD,* p. 259; **augmented number name**: concept, examples, EU, in *MAD,* p. 235; **autological**: concept, term, GX, in *BYL*, pp. 111–112, examples, DM, in *ALP,* pp. 222–223; **automobile noise**: GE, in *WOR*-Aug81, p. 176; **automynorcagram**: concept, term, example 2, HB, in *MAD,* p. 16; example 1, DM; **autoshiftgram**: concept, example 1, TP, in *WOR*-Feb80, p. 24; example 2, term, RE, in *WOR*-May80 (synonym: identity shiftgram, TP, in *WOR*-Feb80, p. 24); **avenumenclature**: concept, examples 1–2, AA, examples 3–4, PN, term, DM, in *WOR*-May98 p. 145; **average letter weight**: concept, term, ST, in *WOR*-Nov94, p. 206; example, DM; **average numerical value of the alphabet**: concept, DB, in *LOV,* p. 169; term, RE, in *MAD,* p. 186; **backward alphabet**: BR, in *WOR*-May69, p. 67; **backward multiple charades**: concept, example, DB, in *LOV,* p. 111 (derived term, DM); **backward spiraling alphabet**: BR, in *WOR*-May69 p. 67; **backward substitution code**: AA, in *BOP,* p. 203–204; **bad mixer**: HK, in *BOP,* p. 20; **balanced word**: concept, example 2, term, DB, example 3, ST, in *MAD,* p. 186; example 1, DM (synonyms: alphabetically balanced combination, alphabetically balanced collocation, DB, in *BYL,* p. 26); **bananagram**: EC, in *WOR*-May98, p. 139; **base 27 number system**: LS, in *MAD,* pp. 243–245; **base 26 number system**: PC, in *MAD,* pp. 243–244; **base 26 word**: PC, in *MAD,* pp. 243–244; **baseword**: concept, term, AA, examples, DM; **beastly English**: RL, in *POW,* pp. 39–40, 42–43, 73; **beau présent (beautiful in-law)**: HM in *OUC,* p. 56; **beautiful English word**: concept, AA, examples, see entry, term, RL, in *CZE,* pp. 138–139; **beauty parlor/barber shop nomenclature**: RE, in *WOR*-May79, pp. 67–77; **beheadment**: concept, AA, examples, term, DB, in *LOV,* p. 113 (synonyms: apheresis, decapitation, decollation, DB, in *LOG,* p. 113); **beheadment homophone**: concept, AI, examples, RL, in *WOC,* p. 8; derived term, DM; **beheadment poem**: concept, example, GH, in *OGW,* p. 114 (derived term, DM); **beheadment sentence**: DB, in *LOV,* p. 114 (derived term, DM); **belle absente (beautiful outlaw)**: HM in *OUC,* p. 56; **Bermuda Triangle of definitions**: concept, examples, PN, in *ALP,* p. 75 (derived term, DM); **bialphabetic order**: concept, PC, in *MAD,* p. 169 (derived term, DM), (synonyms: dialphabetic order, PC, in *WOR*-Nov79, p. 236); **bialphabetic word**: concept, example, PC, in *MAD,* p. 169 (derived term, DM); **biconsonantal word**: EW, in *WOR*-Aug79, p. 165; **bicycle**: DS, in *WOR*-May69, p. 119; **bidigital word**: DM, in *ALP,* p. 147, **bigram**: AA, in *MAD,* p. 64; **bigram-frag square**: LG, in *WOR*-May95, pp. 78–79, **bilingual palindrome**: JP, in *WAP,* p. 143; **binary cipher**: AA, in *BOP,* p. 210; **birthday terminology**: concept, example 1, term, LC, examples 2–3, DM, in *ALP,* p. 278; **bisogram**: concept, example, RE, in *MAD,* p. 56; term, EC, *WOR*-Nov98, p. 290; **blank sonnet**: DU, in *OGW,* p. 135; **Boggle**: concept, term, PP, example, AF & SR, in *OGW,* pp. 69–70; **bookend word**: AA; **Book of Truth, the**: DM, in *ALP,* p. 224; **boustrophedon word**: PC, in *WOR*-Nov79, p. 236; **bout-rimés**: concept, DU, term, AA, example, TA, in *OGW,* pp. 135–137; **bow-wow theory**: concept, term, AA, examples, MB, in *WOR,* p. 176; **braille alphabet**: LH; **brand-name palindrome**: RF, in *WOR*-Nov81, pp. 220–221; **brand-name reversal**: RF, in *WOR*-Nov81, pp. 220–221; **British back slang**: concept, term, AA, examples, DB, in *LOV,* p. 46; **British broadcast blunder**: concept, AA, examples, term, OM, in *WAP,* p. 23; **buildup reversal**: DB, in *LOV,* pp. 48–49; **burlesque**: AA, in *MWX,* p. 112; **BW**: ST, in *WOR*-Nov94, p. 206; **cadence**: RE, in *MAD,* pp. 73–74; **Caesar's alphabets**: AA, in *BOP,* p. 205; **calli-**

**graphic portrait**: DM, in *ALP*, p. 206; **Canada Dry**: HM in *OUC*, p. 118; **capitonym**: concept, examples 1–3, DB, in *BYL*, p. 19; examples 4–6, term, RL, in *WOR*-Feb80, p. 50, p. 63; **capitonym poem**: concept, example, RL, in *WOC*, p. 23; derived term, DM; **car-name anagram**: DM, in *ALP*, pp. 17–19; **car-to-car anagram**: DM, in *ALP*, p. 17; **catch riddle**: AA, in *BOP*, p. 154; **caudation**: concept, term, RE, in *MAD*, p. 88; **celebrity palindrome**: concept, AA, example 1, DK, example 2–4, example 6, MG, example 7, in *ALP*, pp. 32–33; **centered lettershift pyramid**: DM, in *ALP*, p. 116; **cento**: concept, AS, term, AA, example, JN, in *OGW*, pp. 138–140 (synonyms: mosaic, patchwork verse, AA, in *OGW*, p. 138); **central number**: EW, in *WOR*-Aug81, p. 167; **C-graph**: LG, in *MAD*, p. 48; **chain-link sentence**: concept, term, WS, in *MAD*, p. 19, examples, AA; **chain verse (1)**: AA, in *OGW*, pp. 140–141 (synonym: concatenation verse); **chain verse (2)**: AA, in *OGW*, pp. 140–141; **challenge**: AA, defined by PC, RE, in *WOR*-Feb79, p. 3; **Chandlerism**: concept, RC, examples, AA, term, DM; **"characteristic initials" method**: DB, in *LOV*, p. 269; **charactonym**: concept, term, AA, examples, RL, in *CZE*, p. 59; **charade**: concept, term, AA, examples 1–5, DB, in *LOV*, p. 110; example 6, in *ALP*, p. 129; **charade-anagram**: DB, in *LOV*, p. 112; **charades**: AA, in *OGW*, pp. 21, 29 30; **charade sentences**: concept, AA, term DB, example 1, IID, in *LOV*, p. 112; example 2, DM, in *ALP*, p. 130; **charade square**: DB, in *LOV*, p. 111; **charadist**: DB, in *LOV*, p. 111; **charitable word**: DB, in *LOV*, p. 111; **cheater's**: DM; **cheater's amalgam**: ST, PN, in *WOR*-May95, p. 119; **cheater's anagram**: concept, example, DE, term, OM, in *WAP*, p. 112; **cheater's palindrome**: concept, term, DM, examples 1–3, DF, examples 4–6, JG, examples 7–9, PN; in *ALP*; **cheater's palindrome play**: concept, example, DM, in *ALP*, p. 35 (derived term, DM); **checkerboard word square**: SK, in *WAP*, p. 185; **chemical element word-weight**: DF, in *WOR*-May95, p. 93; **chemical element word-weight group**: DF, in *WOR*-May95, p. 93; **chemical symbol equivalent**: concept, example, AA, term, DB, in *LOV*, p. 275; **chess notation symbols**: AA, in *OCC*, p. 92; **chess word**: DM, in *WOR*-May98, pp. 147–148 (synonym: chess piece word, DM, in *WOR*-May98, p. 147); **children's alphabet**: AA, in *OGW*, p. 127; **chronogram**: concept, term, AA, example 1, RU, example 2, AA, in *OGW*, p. 93; **chronogrammatic epitaph**: AA, in *OGW*, p. 94; **chunnelism**: DM, in *WOR*-May95 p. 103; **cipher**: AA in *BOP*, p. 204; **cipher alphabet**: AA, in *BOP*, p. 203; **circular alphabet**: AA; **circular palindrome**: concept, term, DB, in *LOV*, p. 30; examples, DM; **circular reversal**: concept, term, example 2, DB, in *LOV*, pp. 50–51; example 1, DM; **clock alphabet**: AA, in *ALP*, 109; **code**: AA, in *BOP*, p. 204; **collinear words**: concept, term, RT, example, CB, in *MAD*, p. 177; **colorful rhyme**: concept, AA, term, examples, OM, in *WAP*, p. 10; **comic alphabet**: AA, in *OGW*, pp. 129–130; **comic book onomatopoeia**: RE, in *ALP*, p. 255; **compound epithet**: concept, AA, term, CC, in *OAC*, p. 211; **compound epithet epigram**: concept, example, IY, in *OAC*, p. 211; derived term, DM; **commonest letters**: AA; **common-gender pronoun**: list, PC, in *WOR*-Aug77; **complementary transposal**: concept, term, example 1, HB, example 2, DB; **compound palindrome**: DB, in *LOV*, p. 26; **computer-error poetry**: DM, in *ALP*, p. 213; **computer spelling algorithm**: PR, in *ALP*, pp. 212–213; **concealed cardinal**: DB, in *LOV*, p. 222; **concrete poetry**: AA; **connected diamonds**: concept, term, WI, in *WAP*, p. 195; example, DM; **consecutive dotted letters**: RL, in *WOC*, p. 178; **consecutive-identical-letter sentence**: AA, example 1, JI, example 2, DG, in *MAD*, pp. 72–73 (derived term, DM); **consecutive-identical-letter word**: concept, examples 1–2, term, FE, examples 3–6, JG, in *MAD*, p. 71–72; **consecutive letter-pairs**: concept, examples 1–3, term, DB, example 4, HB, in *LOV*, p. 166; **consecutive**

**paragraph acrostic**: concept, WS, example, ST, in *WOR*-Aug81, p. 162; derived term, DM; **consecutive pronoun speller**: concept, example, RL, term, DM, in *ALP*, p. 131; **consistent sesquipedalianism**: DB, in *LOV*, p. 164; **consonym**: concept, term, AA, examples, RL, in *CZE*, p. 60; **constant sum pair**: concept, examples 2–3, term, DB, in *LOV*, p. 140; example 1, DM; **constrained verse**: AA; **contronym**: concept, term, AA, examples, OM, in *WAP*, pp. 69–70 (synonyms: antilogy, contranym, Janus-faced word, AA, in *WAP*, p. 69; autantonym, FE, in *WOR*-Aug81, p. 175); **conundrum**: AA, in *OGW*, p. 1011 (synonym: punning riddle, HK, in *BOP*, pp. 152–153; **crash**: DS, in *MAD*, p. 210; **croaker**: RH, in *GET*, p. 76; **crossword**: AA, in *OGW*, p. 52; **crossword pack**: concept, term, RE, in *MAD*, pp. 219–222; example, DM; **crossword puzzle**: concept, term, AW, in *OGW*, pp. 52–58 (synonym: cross-word, word-cross, AW, in *OGW*, p. 52); **cryptarithm**: concept, AA, term, MV, in *OGW*, p. 124; **cryptographic sentence**: DB, in *LOV*, p. 134; **curtailment**: AA; **curtailment homophone**: concept, AI, examples, RL, in *WOC*, p. 8; derived term, DM; **cyclic transposal**: DB, in *LOV*, pp. 93–94 (synonyms: RE, in *MAD*, p. 136); **cyclic transposal sequence**: DB, in *LOV*, pp. 92–93; **cylinder** HM in *OUC*, p. 132; **daffynition**: concept, term, AA, examples, RL, in *GET*, p. 93–95; **definitional literature**: HM in *OUC*, p. 133; **deletion**: concept, AA, examples, term, DB, in *LOV*, p. 116 (synonyms: elision, syncopation, DB, in *LOV*, p. 116); **deletion antonyms**: DM, in *ALP*, p. 254; **diagonal square**: RQ, in *WAP*, p. 188; example, DM; **diamond**: AA, in *WAP*, p. 192; **difference pyramid**: TP, in *MAD*, p. 185; **difference word**: concept, DB, in *BYL* p. 221; **different end-letter rhyming poem**: concept, example, GT; in *NYO*-Jul22-72, and *WOR*-Aug 86 p. 135 (derived term, DM); **different end-letter rhymes**: concept, GT, in *NYO*-Jul 22, 1972, and in *WOR*-Aug86, p. 135, examples (derived term, DM); **digital anagram**: DM, in *WOR*-Feb89, p. 51 and *WOR*-Aug90, p. 175 (synonyms: numbergram, DM, in *WOR*-Feb89, p. 51; n-gram, DM in *WOR*-Aug89, p. 177); **digital charade**: TP, in *WOR*-Aug89, p. 178 (synonyms: numbergram charade, TP, in *WOR*-Aug89, p. 177; d-charade, DM, in *WOR*-Aug90, p. 175); **digital palindrome**: concept, example 1, term, DM, in *WOR*-Feb89, pp. 51–52; example 2, LG, in *WOR*; example 3, TP, in *WOR*-Aug89 (synonyms: numberdrome, DM, in *WOR*-Feb89 p 51; n-drome, DM, in *WOR*-Aug89, p. 177; digital palindrome, d-palindrome, DM, in *WOR*-Aug90, p. 175); **digital reversal**: TP, in *WOR*-Aug89, p. 178 (synonyms: numbergram reversal, TP, in *WOR*-Aug89, p. 178; d-reversal, DM, in *WOR*-Aug90, p. 175); **digital wordplay**: concept, DM, in *WOR*-Feb89, p. 51, term, DM, in *ALP*, p. 145; **digram**: AA; **disassembled poem**: RE, in *MAD*, p. 142; **doctored name**: concept, examples, VH, in *WOR*-Nov77 (derived term, DM); **domunym**: PA, in *CZE*, p. 60; **double acrostic**: AA, in *OGW*, p. 4; **double beheadment**: concept, example, HD, term, RE, in *MAD*, p. 108; concept, examples, AA, in *WOC*, pp. 113–114; derived term, DM; **double croaker**: RH, in *GET*, p. 78; **double-crostic**: concept, term, EK, in *OGW*, p. 62; **double dactyl**: AA; **double half-square**: TO, in *WAP*, p. 188; **double homoliteral**: concept, term, EA, in *MAD*, p. 18; example, DM; **double mirror letters**: DM, in *ALP*, p. 199; **double mirror palindome**: DM, in *ALP*, p. 199; **double mirror word**: DM, in *ALP*, p. 199; **double oxymoron**: RL, in *CZE*, p. 33; **double-play word**: MK, DM, in *WOR*-May99, p. 86; **double shiftword**: MB, in *WOR*-Aug79, p. 161; **double square**: IM, in *WAP*, p. 169; **double-sound pun**: concept, term, AA, examples, RL, in *GET*, p. 29; **doublet**: LC, in *OGW*, pp. 184–186; **double transposal square**: PC, in *WOR*-Nov79, p. 240; **double vowelindrome**: JG, in *WOR*-Nov94, p. 251; **doubly-intertwined alternating monotony**: RB, in *WOR*-May71, p. 77; **drop-letter reversal**: DB; in *LOV*, p. 50; **dual**

**identity word**: term, RD, in *WOR*-Aug81, p. 145; **echo verse**: concept, term, AA, example, GH, in *OGW*, pp. 142–144; **editorial kangaroo**: RL, in *WOC*, pp. 136–137; **eight-square**: concept, term, AA, example, DV, in *WAP*, p. 177; **E-invariant**: DB, in *LOV*, p. 174; **elementally-spelled element**: concept, examples, NI, in *WAP*, p. 67 (derived term, DM); **elemental word**: MY, in *WOR*-Feb71, p. 51; examples, MY, PC, MP; **embedded double letter removal**: ST, in *WOR*-May98, p. 128; **embedded number name**: DM, in *MAD*, p. 236; **embedded palindromic sequence removal**: ST, in *WOR*-May98, pp. 132–133; **embedded tautonymic sequence removal**: ST, in *WOR*-May98, p. 129; **emblematic poetry**: AA, in *OAC*, p. 92; **emoticon**: AA; **ender**: RE, in *MAD*, p. 109; **English/foreign language blend**: DF, in *WOR*-Aug79, p. 174; **enigma**: (1) example, TW, concept, term, AA, in *OGW*, p. 15; **enigmatic rebus**: concept, term, AA, example 1, GU, and VA, example 2, AV, example 3, AQ, example 4, MC; **eodermdrome**: GB, JK, and PW, in *MAD*, pp. 44–45; **"equation" equation**: HB; **equiliteral numbers**: concept, examples 2–4, term, DM, example 1 (758 letters), EW, in *WOR*-May95, pp. 102–103 (synonym: equiliteral number words, DM, in *WOR*-May95, p. 102); **equivalency**: MU, in *ALP*, p. 142; **equivoque**: concept, term, CR, in *OGW*, p. 144 (synonym: equivocal verse, Jesuitical verse, AA, in *OGW*, p. 144); **Ernulphus curse**: AA, in *OGW*, p. 44; **ETAOIN SHRDLU**: AA, in *LOV*, p. 173, AA; **ETAOIN SHRDLU poetry**: DM, in *WOR*-Aug98, p. 226; **euonym**: concept, term, AA, examples, RL, in *CZE*, p. 60; **even letters**: DB, in *LOV*, p. 166; **even-letter word**: DB, in *LOV*, p. 166; **everyday phrase professional terminology**: AA; **exclamation point name**: PC, in *WOR*-Nov79, p. 241; **exonym**: concept, term, AA, examples 1–3, RL, in *CZE*, p. 60, example 4, CE; **extended metaphor riddle**: concept, AA, term, HK, example, LC, in *BOP*, pp. 156–159; **extensive mutation pair**: HB, in *WOR*-Feb69, p. 13; **exquisite corpse**: ALB in *BSG*, p. 25; **ex-word**: CL, in *ALP*, p. 48; **eye-rhyme**: HM in *OUC*, p. 147; **false number name**: DM, in *WOR*-Aug98, pp. 225–226; **false past tense**: EA, in *WAP*, p. 80; **family of palindromes**: concept, term, DB, in *ILM*, p. 132; examples, DM; **famous last anagram**: JO, in *WOR*-May88, pp. 77–79; **famous last words**: AA, in *WAP*, pp. 74–77; **feminist surname**: DM, in *ALP*, p. 184; **Fibonacci letters**: DF, in *WOR*-May72, p. 110; **Fibonacci word**: concept, term, examples 3–4, DF, in *WOR*-May72, p. 110; examples 1–2, DM; **film title oxymoron**: concept, examples, AA, in *WAP*, pp. 39–40 (derived term, DM); **first-half letters**: DB, in *LOV*, p. 165; **first-half word**: concept, examples 3–5, term, DB, in *LOV*, p. 165; examples 1–2, DM; **first lady anagram**: concept, examples, MF, in *ALP*, p. 16; term, DM; **first-name lettershifts**: DM, in *ALP*, p. 114; **first-and-last-name lettershifts**: concept, term, DM, examples, RE, in *ALP*, pp. 114–115; **first-and-last name partial lettershifts**: concept, term, DM, examples, RE, in *ALP*, pp. 114–115; **five-square**: concept, term, AA, example, CA, in *WAP*, p. 169; **five-vowel word**: DB, in *LOV*, pp. 160–162; **flip-flop definition**: DM, in *ALP*, pp. 75–76; **floccinaucinihilipilification**: AA, in *CZE*, p. 39; **foldable permutation**: MG, in *MAD*, pp. 137–138 (synonym: roadmap anagram, MB, in *WOR*-Aug79, p. 161); **forbidden letter**: concept, term, RE, in *MAD*, p. 1; **form**: AA, in *WOR*-Feb80 p. 3; **formist**: AA, in *WOR*-Feb80, p. 3; **forward-and-backward multiple charades**: concept, example, DB, in *LOV*, p. 111 (derived term, DM); **found poem**: AA, in *OGW*, p. 147; **four-square**: AA, example, HE, in WAP, p. 167; **four-word pangram problem**: DB, in *ALP*, p. 103; **four-word word**: LM, in *WOR*-Feb70, p. 44; **frag**: RE, LG, in *MAD*, p. 115; **frame words**: DM ; **frequency-alphabet**: AA, in *LOV*, p. 174; **frequency value**: AA; **friendlier word**: DM, in *ALP*, p. 125; **friendliest word**: DM, in *ALP*, p. 125 (synonym: garble group, DM, in *ALP*, p. 126); **friendliest word pair**: concept, example, RE, in *MAD,* p. 93; term, DM (synonym: friendliest word, RE, in *MAD,* p. 93); _____-**friendly alphabet**: term, concept, example 1, RE, example 2, AF, in *MAD,* pp. 180–182; **friendly word**: DM, in *ALP,* pp. 125–126 (Antonym: isolano, DS, in *ALP,* pp. 125–126); **function shift**: AA, from RL, in *WOR*-May79, p. 79; **Game of Conditionals, the**: ALB, in *BSG,* p. 28; **Game of Definitions, the**: ALB, in *BSG,* p. 26; **gematria**: concept, term, AA, example, BA, in *MAD,* pp. 184–185; **gender-neutral term**: concept, term, AA, example 1, SB, examples 2–5, AA, in *ALP,* p. 275; **geographical link-o-gram**: AA; **geographic name speller**: concept, examples, DB; in *LOV,* p. 32 and *WOR*-Feb85, p. 50 (term, DM); **geographic name-to-word reversal**: concept, examples, DB, in *LOV,* p. 45 (derived term, DM); **geographic partial letter-shift**: DM, in *ALP,* pp. 115–116; **geographic reversal**: DB, in *LOV,* p. 45; **geographic spelling variants**: concept, example 1, DB, example 2, FC, in *ALP,* p. 198 (term, DM); **geographic transposal**: DB, in *LOV,* pp. 80–81; **giant synonym square**: EW, in *WOR*-Nov79, p. 252; **glyphic personal name**: TF; **Goldwynism**: concept, examples, SF, term, AA, in *WAP,* pp. 15–16; **goodbye pun**: concept, examples, DM, in *ALP,* p. 49 (derived term, DM); **graphic palindrome**: concept, AA, term, HB in *PAA,* p. 92; **grammagram**: AA, in *WOC,* p. 4; **grammatical substitution**: HM, in *OUC,* p. 150; **Greco-American graffiti**: concept, examples, AA, term, DM, in *ALP,* p. 44; **Grelling's paradox**: concept, term, GX, extension of concept, DB, term, AA, in *BYL,* pp. 111–112; **-gry place name**: examples, GS, MP, HP, RE, in *MAD,* pp. 69–70; **-gry question**: BG, reported by GS, in *MAD,* p. 69; **-gry surname**: examples, RE, in *MAD,* p. 71; **-gry word**: examples, GS. MP, HP, in *MAD,* pp. 69–70; **half-switch alphabet**: LG, in *MAD,* p. 186; **halfway word**: CM, in *MAD,* p. 178; **heavyweight word**: DF, in *MAD,* p. 184; **Herman**: concept, term, examples 1–2, DM, examples 3–4, VM, examples 5–6, OD, examples 7–8, JZ, in *ALP,* pp. 44–45; **Hermanette**: concept, examples 1–2, term, OD, in *WOR*-May91, pp. 107–108, examples 3–5, VM, in *WOR*-Aug91, p. 172; **Hermione**: concept, OD, DM, examples 1–2, OD, examples 3–4, DM, term, DM, in *WOR*-Nov91, p. 240; **heterogram**: ST, in *WOR*-Aug98, p. 178; **heteroliteral text**: concept, term, example 2, RE, in *MAD,* p. 17; example 1, DM; **heterological**: concept, term, GX, extension of concept, examples, DM, in *ALP,*. pp. 222–223; **heteronym**: concept, term, AA, examples, RL, in *WOC,* pp. 17-18; **heteronym poem**: concept, example, RL, in *WOC,* p. 20; derived term, DM; **hexagon**: GH; **hex-word**: RE, in *WOR*-May80, p. 124; **H-graph**: LG, in *MAD,* p. 47; **hidden middle name**: DM, in *WOR*-May98, p. 144; **Hidden Words**: AA, in *OGW,* p. 122 (synonym: Buried Words, AA, in *OGW,* p. 122); **hideaway number name**: DM, in *ALP,* p. 144; **Hieroglyphic Bible**: AA, in *OGW,* pp. 87–88; **high-contrast spelling set**: concept, example 1, HB; example 2, term, DM; in *WOR*-May99, p. 137; **high-scoring Scrabble**: JG, in *WOR*-Aug79, p. 134; **homoantonyms**: AA; **homoconcominyms**: AA; **homoconsonantal sequences**: HM in *OUC,* p. 153, derived term TJD; **homograph**: concept, term, AA, example 1, EB, example 2, RR; **homoliteral text**: concept, term, example 2, RE, in *MAD,* p. 17; example 1, DM; **homophone**: concept, term, AA, examples, RL, in *GET,* p. 28; **homophonic**: AA; **homophonic anagram pair**: concept, example, RL, in *WOC,* p. 11; derived term, DM; synonym: anagrammed homophones, RL, in *WOC,* p. 41; **homophonic opposites**: concept, AA, examples, RL, in *WOC,* p. 11; derived term, DM; **homophonic pair**: concept, term, AA, exam;ples, RL, in *WOC,* p. 8–9; **homophonic poem**: concept, example, RL, in *WOC,* p. 13; derived term, DM; **homophonic sentence**: concept, example 1, term, PC; *WOR*-Aug72, p. 131; example 2, AA; **homophonic translation**: HM in *OUC,* p. 154; **homovocalic sequences**: HM in *OUC,* p. 156, derived term TJD;

**homosynonyms**:AA; **honorificabilitudinitatibus**: WS, anagram, AA, in *LOV,* p. 145; **horizontal mirror letters**: concept, DB, in *LOV,* p. 28; term, DM, in *ALP* p 197; **horizontal mirror word**: concept, examples, DB, in *LOV,* p. 28; term, DM, in *ALP,* p. 199 (synonym: mirror palindrome (type B), DB; in *LOV,* p. 28); hospitable word: DS, in *MAD,* p. 88; **hybrid animal name**: DM; **hydration**: RE; in *MAD,* p. 88; **hyperhyphenation**: concept, AA, example 1, CG, example 2, AA, term, DM, in *ALP,* p. 262; **iber**: AA, discussed by PC, in *WOR*-Aug79, p. 138; **ideal word ladder**: JP, in *WOR*-Nov98 p. 248; **I-E word**: concept, AA, examples, term, RL, in *WOC,* pp. 221–222; **impromptu writing**: AA, in *OAC,* p. 89.; **insertion–deletion network**: RE, in *MAD,* p. 89; **I-invariant**: DB, in *LOV,* p. 174; **Illôt-Mollo**: ALB in *BSG* p. 33; **imaginary language**: JH, in *ALP,* p. 240; **imperative noun**: DS, in *WOR*-May73 p. 106; **incide word**: concept, examples, PN; term, DM; in *WOR*-Aug93 p. 178; **infinite array**: RE, in *MAD,* pp. 215–216; **infinite sentence**: DH, in *GEB;* **inflationary language**: concept, term, VB, examples, RL, in *GET,* p. 69; **inflationary language story**: concept, example, RL, in *GET,* p. 69; **interchangeable letters**: AA, in OM, in *WAP,* p. 97; derived term, DM; **internal deletion homophone**: concept, AI, examples, RL, in *WOC,* p. 8; derived term, DM; **insect sign language**: concept, example, DO; in *ARC* pp. 50–51 (term, DM); in *WOR*-Feb99, p. 67; **Insertion**: concept, AA, examples, term, DB, in *LOV,* p. 116; **insertion–deletion network**: RE, in *MAD,* p. 89; **intercalation**: AA, from MB, in *WOR*-May79, p. 101; **interchangeable vowel set**: JF, in *WOR*-Feb94, p. 57; **interior palindrome**: DB, in *LOV,* p. 25; **inter-language reversal**: DB, in *LOV,* p. 43; **interlock**: AA; **internal palindrome**: RE, in *MAD,* p. 82; **internal tautonym**: RE, in *MAD,* pp. 83–85; **internal-tautonym sentence**: concept, example, EW, in *MAD,* p. 85 (derived term, DM); **interrupted sentence**: concept, example, AA, term, CC, in *OAC,* p. 277; **invariant letter**: RE, in *MAD,* p. 170 (synonyms: alphabet-crashing word, EW, in *WOR*-Feb79, p. 59); **invariant sentence**: TP, in *WOR*-May79, p. 92; **inverted half-square**: concept, term, SK, in *WAP,* p. 186; example, DM; **inverted pyramid**: concept, term, CO, in *WAP,* p. 198; example, DM; **invisible definition**: DM; **invisible sonnet**: JH, in *FIN;* **isogram**: concept, examples 10–14, DB, in *LOV,* pp. 125–126; examples, DM (synonyms: nonpattern word, DB, in *LOV,* p. 125); **isogrammatic name**: RE, in *MAD,* p 50; **isogram set**: RE, in *MAD,* pp. 55–56; **isolano**: DS, in *MAD,* pp. 92–93; **isomorph**: concept, example, DGR, in *WAW,* p. 85; **Jabberwock**: DM, in *ALP,* p. 233; **Janeism**: LM, in *WOR*-Nov81, pp. 204–205; **Japanglish T.V. program title**: concept, example, OM, in *WAP,* p. 23 (derived term, DM); **JKQXZ word**: DF, in *WOR*-Aug70, p. 180; **joey**: term, RL, in *ALP,* p. 132; **JQXZ word**: concept, example 1, term, DB, in *WOR*-May68, p. 69; example 2, DF, in *WOR*-Aug70, p. 180; **kangaroo word**: DB, in *LOV,* p. 117, in *ALP,* p. 132 (synonyms: marsupial, multiple deletion, DB, in *LOV,* p. 117); **key**: MK, DM, in *WOR*-May99, p. 85; **keypunch word**: MK, DM, in *WOR*-May99, p. 87; **keyword substitution code**: AA, in *BOP ;* **K-graph**: concept, examples 3 and 4, term, LG, in *MAD,* p. 46; examples 1 and 2, DM; **kidspeak**: concept, AA, example 1, MN, term, OM, in *WAP,* p. 57, example 2, DD; **king's-move pack**: RE, in *MAD,* p. 222; example, DM; **Knave's English**: DM, in *ALP,* p. 157, 318; **Knight's Tour Letter Puzzle**: PF, in *OGW,* pp. 49–50; **knock, knock joke**: term, concept, AA, in *OGW,* pp. 211–212; example, DM; **language name**: AA, discussed by HP, from CIW, in *WOR*-Aug81, p. 169; **language-name palindrome**: HP, from CIW, in *WOR*-Aug81, p. 169; **language-name tautonym**: concept, examples, HP, from *CIW,* in *WOR*-Aug81 p. 169; derived term, DM; **larding**: HM in *OUC* p. 163; **last-half letters**: DB, in *LOV,* p. 165; **last-half number-name**: EW, in *WOR*-Aug81, p. 166; **last-half word**: DB, in

*LOV,* p. 165; **last-name vowel mates**: ST, in *WOR*-Aug96, p. 174; **leapfrog word**: DM, in *WOR*-May99, p. 137; **left-sided lettershift pyramid**: DM, in *ALP,* p. 116; **legal palindrome**: concept, A, example 1, JL, examples 2–5, term, DM, in *ALP;* **letter-change reversal**: DB, in *LOV,* p. 48; **letter conundrum**: AA, examples provided by RE & WS, in *ALP,* p. 65; **letter distribution**: Definition, term, DB, in *MAD,* p. 59; example, DM; **lettered dice**: TA, in *OBG,* p. 69; **letter kickoff word**: RL, in *WOC,* p. 210; **letter maze**: HK, in *BOP,* p. 38; **letter pattern**: Definition, term, DB, in *MAD,* p. 29; example, DM; **letterplay**: AA; **letter-plural word**: RL, in *WOC,* p. 211; **letter rebus**: AA, in *WAP,* p. 67; **letter riddle**: TA, in *OGW,* p. 12; **lettershift (n.)**: DB, in *LOV,* pp. 137–140; **lettershift (v.)**: DB, in *LOV,* p. 138; **lettershift (adj.)**: DB, in *LOV,* p. 137; **Lettershift Calculator**: DM, in *ALP,* p. 111; **lettershift form**: DM, in *ALP,* p. 116; **lettershift multiple**: term, RE, in *MAD,* p. 175; **lettershift pair**: term, AA, in *ALP,* p. 109; **lettershift reversal**: DM, in *ALP,* p. 118; **lettershift sentence**: concept, example, DB; in *LOV,* p. 139 (derived term, DM); **lettershift set**: AA; **lettershift word**: term, LG, in *WOR*-Feb90, p. 59; **lettershift word square (1)**: concept, example, DB, in *LOV,* p. 140 (derived term, DM); **(2)**: concept, example, DM, in *ALP,* p. 116 (derived term, DM); **letterstring**: concept, term, AA, examples, DM; **letter-unit transposal**: AA, in *MAD,* p. 142 (synonym: letter-by-letter transposition, RE, in *MAD,* p. 142); **letter word**: RL, in *WOC,* p. 210; **Lewis Carroll's alphabet cipher**: LC, in *BOP,* pp. 211–212; **Liar's Paradox**: AA, in *ALP,* p. 221 (synonym: Epimenedes' Paradox); **lightweight word**: DF, in *MAD,* p. 184; **limergimmick**: concept, term, AA, example, LM, info, MB, in *WOR*-Feb80 p. 34; **line repetition**: concept, term, AA; **Linear Logic**: DM, in *ALP,* p. 224; **line-unit**: JL, in *BAA* p. vii; **line-unit anagram**: concept, AA, example, DU (derived term, DM, in *WAP,* pp. 118–119); **line-unit palindrome**: concept, term, JL, in *PAA,* p. 118; example, DM; **linkade**: DGR, in *WAW,* p. 85, example 1, AA, example 2, DGR; **lipogram**: concept, term, AA, examples, DB, in *LOV,* p. 239; info, RE, in *MAD,* p. 2, CC, in *OAC,* pp. 25–26 (synonym: anti-frequency word, DB, in *LOV,* p. 239); **lipogrammatic dialogue**: CK, in *MAD,* pp. 6–7, derived term, DM; **lipogrammatic interview**: HB, in *MAD,* pp. 4–6; **lipogrammatic novel**: concept, EV, examples, EV, GP, GA, term, AA, in *MAD,* pp. 2–3; **lipogrammatic palindrome**: HB, in *PAA,* p. viii–ix; **lipogrammatic pangram**: concept, example, WW, in *OGW,* p. 110 (derived term, DM); **lipogrammatic poem**: AA; **lipogrammatist**: AA, in *MAD,* p. 2; **lipogrammetry**: term, RE, in *MAD,* p. 2; **liponymous text**: HM in *OUC,* p. 175, derived term, TJD; **literary anagram**: concept, term, AA, example 1, HG, example 2, EP, in *WAP,* pp. 116–117; **literary fellow's anagram**: concept, example 1, AA, example 2, BO, example 3, AA, term, OM, in *WAP,* pp. 117–118; **literary oxymoron**: RL, in *CZE,* p. 34, p. 36; **literary tongue-twister**: DM, in *ALP,* p. 261; **locally invariant letters**: RE, in *WOR*-Aug72, p. 140; **logocide**: DB, in *LOV,* p. 277; **logogram**: AA, in *OGW,* p. 115; **logograph**: concept, AA, term, CC, in *OAC,* p. 298; **logogriph**: AA, in *OGW,* p. 119 (synonym: logogram, AA, in *OGW,* p. 115); **logology**: AA, in *LOV,* p. 169; **logomotive**: PN, in *WOR*-May95, p. 104; **logophile**: DB, in *LOV,* p. 102; **longest word**: AA; **looping anagram**: concept, DB, in *LOV,* p. 92, term, RL, in *WOC,* p. 47; **looping anagram progression**: RL, in *WOC,* p. 47; **lost positive**: JF, in *WOR*-Aug79, p. 151 (synonym: unce word, AA, cited by PS, in *WOR*-Aug79, p. 151); **low-scoring Scrabble™**: AF, in *WOR*-Aug81, p. 184; **lucky number name**: DM; **lucky unlucky equation**: DM; **ludicrous acronym**: concept, examples, AA, term, OM, in *WAP,* pp. 34–35; **macaronic verse**: concept, term, AA, example, JW, in *OBG,* translation, DM; **magic sentence grid**: HK, in *BOP,* p. 89; **malapropism**: concept, example 1, term, RS, example 2, SJ, example 3, GK, example 4, EN; in *WAP*, p. 15; **malonym**: concept, term, AA, examples, RL, in *CZE*, p. 60; **many-spellings-for-the-same-sound sentence**: concept, example, RL, in *WOC*, p. 14; derived term, DM; **many-sounds-for-the-same-spelling poem**: concept, example, RL, in *WOC*, p. 14; derived term, DM.**"Mary Had a Little Lamb"**: original, KB or SD, lipogram, RE, in *MAD*, p. 4; **master word**: AA, in *MAD*, p. 146; **matched homonyms**: MB, in *WOR*-Aug79, p. 161; **mathematical English**: RL, in *GET*, p. 101; **meaning play**: AA; **melodic pun**: EA, in *WOR*-Feb86, p. 21; term, DM; **meronym**: concept, term, AA, examples, RL, in *CZE*, p. 60; **mesostich**: AA, in *OAC*, p. 45; **metric prose**: concept, example, WC, term, CC, in *OAC*, p. 223. synonym, poetic prose, CC, in OAC, p. 223; **middle of an alphabetic list**: AF, in *WOR*-Aug94, pp. 144–145; **midpoint of the alphabet**: DB, in *LOV*, p. 169; **minimal pairing triplet**: concept, example, PN, in *PWG*, p. 191; derived term, DM; **minimal word ladder**: concept, example 1, term, DB, in *LOV*, p. 155; example 2, KC, in *ALP*, p. 124; **minimum-length pangrammatic ladder**: LG, in *WOR*-May90, p. 125; **mirror letter**: concept, DB, in *LOV*, pp. 27–28; term, DM, in *ALP*, p. 197; **mirror word**: (synonyms: mirror palindrome, DB, in *LOV*, pp. 27–28; lipogrammatic optical trick, ML, in *ILM*, p. 202); **mischmasch**: LC, in *OGW*, pp. 191–192; **misnomer**: concept, term, AA, examples, OM, in *WAP*, p. 55; **mixed cliché**: LM; **mocking word**. WT, in *WOR*-Feb89, p. 24; **modified alphabet**: CB, in *WOR*-May80, p. 114; **monetary name**: DM, in *ALP*; **monoconsonantal**: DF, in *WOR*-Feb79, p. 55; **monosyllabic**: AA, in *OAC*, p. 98; **monosyllabic passage**: concept, AA, term, CC, example, AO, in *OAC*, p. 98; **Morse code**: SN; **Morse code square**: DM, in *ALP*, p. 90; **Morse dot-and-dash halfsquare**: DM, in *ALP*, p. 91; **Morse all-dot pyramid**: DM, in *ALP*, p. 91; **multi-generational kangaroo words**: RL, in *WOC*, p. 129; **multiple charades**: DB, in *LOV*, p. 111; **multiple embedded number names**: DM, in *WOR*-Nov94, p. 243; **multiple joeys**: RL, in *ALP*, p. 133; **multiple kangaroos**: RL, in *ALP*, p. 133; **multiple number name transposal**: concept, examples, DF, in *MAD*, p. 237; term, DM; **multiple plurals**: DS, in *WOR*-Aug69, p. 182; **multiple singulars**: concept, examples, DS, in *WOR*-Aug69, p. 182, 191; term, DM; **multiple transposals**: Examples, RE, in *MAD*, pp. 124–125 (synonym: multiple transposition, RE, in *MAD*, p. 125); **multiplicative numerical tautonym**: DF, in *WOR*-Feb70, p. 13; **multipuns**: concept, example 1, AA, example 2, DM, in *ALP*, p. 41; **musical syllable**: GD, in *MWE*, p. 2169; **musical syllable poetry**: DM; **mutation**: HB; **N + seven**: concept, JEL, term, definition, HM in *OUC*, p. 198; **name anagram**: DB, in *LOV*, pp. 105–106, 294; term, DM; **name-meaning duplication**: TB, in *WOR*-Aug96, p. 201; **name speller**: concept, example, DF, in *WOR*-Feb78, p. 39, 63; term, DM; **names-to-words lettershift**: DM, in *ALP*, p. 115; **narrow letters**: AA; **narrow word**: AA; **natural oxymoron**: RL, in *CZE*, p. 34, p. 36; **neo-adage**: concept, tiles, BW, term, JA, in *WOR*-Nov88; examples, DM; **network**: RE, in *MAD*, p. 89, 93; **never seen postmark**: concept, examples 1–4, term, CR, examples 5–6, HR, from LIN, in *WOR*-Aug81 p. 174; **new merology**: concept, AA, term, LS, in *WOR*-Feb90, p. 12; **new punctuation mark**: DM, in *ALP*, p. 273; **nine-square**: concept, term, AA, example, AH, in *WAP*, p. 181; **non-alphabetical order**: DM, in *WOR*-Nov89; **noletter Poem**: DM, in *ECS*, p. 151; **noncrashing word list**: DS, in *MAD*, p. 211; **noncrashing word pair**: DS, in *MAD*, p. 210; **non-overlapping stately word**: concept, DS, term, RB, in *WOR*-Feb76, p. 42; examples, DF, in *WOR*-May76, pp. 91–92; **nonsense spelling**: DM, in *ALP*, p. 239; **nontrivial**: AA; **nontrivial transposal**: KC, in *MAD*, pp. 133–134; **non-vicinal**: EU, in *MAD*, pp. 168–169; **non-vicinal story**: EU, in *MAD*, pp. 168–169; **normal word line**: LG, in *MAD,* p. 177; **noun–adjective–adverb–verb matrix**: RL; **noun of multitude**: LM, in *WOR*-Feb70, p. 44; **no-word alphabet**: concept, examples, DS, in *MAD,* pp. 179–180; term, DM; **number grid**: concept, term, DM, example 1, LQ, example 2, DM, in *ALP,* pp. 138–140; **number lattice**: DM, in *ALP,* p. 141; **number name**: DM; **number-name speller**: concept, example, DF, in *MAD,* pp. 336–337, term, DM; **number-name transaddition**: concept, examples, DF, in *MAD,* p. 236; derived term, DM; **number-name transposal**: concept, examples, DF, in *MAD,* p. 236, derived term, DM; **number tree**: DM, in *ALP,* p. 142; **numerical kangaroo**: AA; **numerical palindrome**: concept, term, AA, examples, ML, in *ILM,* pp. 238–239 (synonyms: number palindrome, numberdrome, ML, in *ILM,* p. 204, p. 238; **numerical near-tautonym**: DF, in *WOR*-Feb70, p. 13; **numerical tautonym**: DF, in *WOR*-Feb70, pp. 10–13; **numerical unit**: concept, example, AA, discussed by EW, in *WOR*-Aug81, p. 167; term, DM; **numerical wordplay**: DB, in *LOV,* p. 220; **numerical word square**: DB, in *LOV,* pp. 237–238; **obligatory letter**: RE, in *MAD,* p. 1; **odd book title**: RA and BK, in *WAP,* p. 32; **odd letters**: DB, in *LOV,* p. 165; **odd-letter sentence**: concept, example, DB; in *LOV,* p. 166 (derived term, DM); **odd-letter word**: DB, in *LOV,* p. 165; **odd-numbered letter**: AA; **O-invariant**: DB, in *LOV,* p. 174; **onalosi**: DS, in *MAD,* p. 93; **one-consonant word**: concept, example, DB, in *LOV,* p. 157, derived term, DM; **one-cycle word**: concept, term, examples 2–4, RE, in *LOV,* p. 164; example 1, DM; **one-letter liporebus**: TR, in *WOR*-Aug79, p. 137; **one-letter palindrome**: DB, in *LOV,* p. 14; **one-letter poem**: DM, in *ALP*; **one-move Scrabble score**: DF, RJ, JG, in *WOR*-May79, p. 105; **old style pyramid**: BH, in *WAP,* p. 198; **one-switch reversal**: DB, in *LOV,* p. 48; **one-syllable word**: concept, term, example 1, AA, examples 2–7, JM, in *WOR*-Aug79, p. 153; **one-to-one triplet**: PN, in *OGW,* p. 191; derived term, DM; **one-word anagram**: concept, AA, example 1, KE, example 2, KC, example 3, TL, example 4, NY, example 5, AN, example 6, VI, example 7, AA, example 8, RC; term, OM, in *WAP,* pp. 90–91; **one-word celebrity anagram**: concept, examples 1–3, MR, examples 4–5, AL, in *ALP,* p. 17; term, DM; **one-word pangram**: RE, in *MAD,* pp. 53–55; **one-word poem**: concept, term, example 1, AS, example 2, DL, example 3, FC, example 4, GQ, example 5, TE, example 6, GN, example 7, TV, example 8, KN, example 9, IS, example 10, CD, example 11, AC, example 12, SG, example 13, TK, in *ALP,* p. 275; **one-word sentence**: DM, in *ALP,* p. 267; **opinion oxymoron**: RL, in *CZE,* p. 36; **opposites-attract vowel mates**: ST, in *WOR*-Aug96, p. 174; **orthinology**: AA, in *WAP,* p. 18; **OS-graph**: LG, in *MAD,* p. 47; **OUGH**: concept, term, AA, example, CC, in *OAC,* p. 186.**Ouija word**: DM; **overlapping stately word**: concept, DS, term, RB, in *WOR*-Feb76, p. 42; examples, DF, in *WOR*-May76, pp. 91–92; **overlapping word**: PN, in *WOR*-May98, p. 144; **oxymoron, oxymora**: concept, term, AA, example, GC, in *CZE*; **oxymoronic**: AA, in *CZE,* p. 33; **pairagram**: concept, AA, example 1, VI, example 2, SL, example 4, MO, example 5, RC, example 6, SM, example 3, term, OM, in *WAP,* p. 71; **paired-key word**: MK and DM, in *WOR*-May99, p. 86; **pair isogram**: DB, in *LOV,* p. 128 (synonym: diplogram, JS, in *MAD,* p. 59); **palindromania**: (1) AA; (2) concept, EL and MD, term, EL, in *ILM,* p. 263; **palindddrome challenge**: AA; **palindrome**: concept, SO, examples 1–3, AA, example 4, DM, example 5, DAC, 2, 3, term, PN, examples 1, 4, JG, example 6, FE, example 5, DM, examples 6–22, DB, example 23, JT, example 24, LM, examples 25–27, example 28–29, JL, example 30, DB, example 31, LM (synonyms: anacyclic, bifrontal, cancrine verse, carcinoi, 'drome, pal, P/D, PD verse, versus anacyclici, versus diabolici, versus echoici, all listed by DB, in *LOV* pp. 57–58; inversion, reciprocal, Sotadic, Sotadcan phrase, Sotadean verse, all listed by OM, in *WAP* p. 123; adreverbum, WSH, in *WOR*); **palindrome pair**: SH, in *WOR*-Aug79, pp. 131–133; **palindromic dialogue**: JL, in *MAD*, pp. 34-36; **palindromic double square**: RE, in *ALP*, p. 89; **palindromic initials**: DB, in *LOV*, pp. 28–29; **palindromic interview**: concept, AA, term, example, DM, in *ALP*, p. 33; **palindromic ladder**: JF, in WOR-Aug79, p. 151; **palindromic tautonymic monoliteral square**: concept, term, example 1, DB, in *LOV*, p. 202; example 2, DM, in ALP. p. 89 (synonym: total palindromic single square, DM, in ALP. p. 89); **palindromic name**: DB, in *LOV*, pp. 23–24, examples, DAC, DB; **palindromic novel**: LL, mentioned in *MAD*, p. 36; **palindromic palindrome**: DM; **palindromic pangram**: term(s), HB, in *PAA*, p. ix; **palindromic pattern**: DB, in *LOV*, pp. 241–242; **palindromic play**: term, DM, in *ALP*, p. 27; **palindromic poem**: OM, in *WAP*, p. 78; **palindromic poetry**: AA, in *LOV*, pp. 66–71; **palindromic pun**: DM; **palindromic pyramid**: DB, in *LOV*, p. 31; **palindromic reversal**: (1) DB, in *LOV*, p. 49; **palindromic sentence**: AA, in *PAA*, p. 82; **palindromic single square**: concept, example, DB, in *LOV*, p. 203, term, RE, in *ALP*, p. 88; **palindromic slide rule**: DM, in *ALP*, p. 29; **palindromic square**: concept, term, AA, example, NJ, in *ALP*, p. 88; **palindromic tautonymic monoliteral square**: concept, term, example 1, DB, in *LOV*, p 202; example 2, DM; **palindromic word**: AA, in *ALP*, p. 6; **palindromist**: AA, in *PAA*, p. 92; **Panama parody**: concept, AA, examples 1–3, JEC, examples 4–6, term, DM; **pangram**: Examples, DR, in *MAD*, pp. 51–53; **pangrammatic crossword**: RE, in *MAD*, p. 57, **pangrammatic highway**: concept, term, UP, revised concept, FE, example, RE, in *ALP*, p. 102; **pangrammatic ladder**: LG, in *WOR*-May90, p. 125; **pangrammatic palindrome**: concept, term, HB, example, EF, in *PAA*, p. ix; **pangrammatic poetry**: concept, term, AA, example, HB, in *LOV*, pp. 132–133 (synonym: all-alphabet poetry , DB, pangrammatic rubai, pangrammatic verse, AA, in *LOV*, p. 133); **pangrammatic rebus**: JJ, in *ALP*, p. 105; **pangrammatic rebus poem**: concept, term, AA, example, DM, in *ALP*, p. 105; **pangrammatic window**: (synonyms: natural pangrammatic sentence, DB, in *LOV*, p. 132; panalphabetic window, HB, in *MAD*, p. 160); **panoramic number name**: DM, in *MAD*, p. 236; **paratransposition**: concept, examples 1–7, term, DB, in *WOR*-May78, pp. 79–85; example 8, DM, in *WOR*-Nov98, p. 247 (synonym: minimum substitute-letter transposal, DM, in *WOR*-Nov98, p. 247); **parody**: concept, term, AA, example 1, RE, example 2, DM, in *ALP*, p. 55, p. 58; **parody pangram**: PN, in *ALP*, p. 101; **paronomasia**: AA, in *MWX*, p. 613; **partial lettershifts**: DM, in *ALP*, pp. 113–114; **partially overlapping word group**: RE, in *MAD*, pp. 203–204; **partition**: PC, in *WOR*-Nov79, p. 235; **pasquinade**: AA, in *MWX*, p. 848; **patriotic number**: DM, in *ALP*, p. 144; **pavement**: LG, in *MAD*, p. 46; **pentagram**: AA, in *MAD*, p. 235; **perfect palindrome**: concept, term, DB, example, AA, in *LOV*; **perfect anagrams**: (1) AA, in *WOC*, pp. 277–278; (2) RL, in *WOC*, pp. 39–40; **permutable palindrome**: DB, in *LOV*, pp. 11–12, 285–286; **permutation**: DB, in *MAD*, p. 77; **permutation-containing word**: DB, in *MAD*, p. 77; term, DM; **permute**: DB, in *LOV*, p. 80; **-phobia word**: AA, in *WAP*, p. 53; **phonetically reversible word**: YC, in *PAA*, p. 92; **phonetically reversible word pair**: YC, in *PAA*, p. 92; **phonetic palindrome**: YC, in *PAA*, p. 91; **phonetically palindromic sentence**: YC, in *PAA*, p. 92; **phonetic rebus**: concept, term, example 1, RN, example 2, HO, example 3, IX and PG, example 4, BJ; **phonetic reversal**: concept, term, examples 3–5, DB, in *LOV*, p. 47; examples 1–2, DM (synonym: unit reversal, DB, in *LOV*, p. 47); **Phonetic Word Wheel**: MD, in *ALP*, p. 237; **phrase pyramid**: SS, in *WAP*, p. 199; **piano letters**: Term, DB, in *LOV*, p. 167; **piano sentence**: DM; **piano word**: DB, in *LOV*, p. 167; **Pig Latin poem**: DM, in *ALP*,

p. 177; **plaintext:** in *BOP*; **plaintext alphabet:** AA, in *BOP*; **place-name oxymoron:** RL, in *CZE,* p. 36; **playing card anagram:** concept, HB and DM, example, term, DM, in *WOR*-May99, p. 139; **playing card name sum:** AA, in *WOC*; **playing card suit sum:** DM; **PL8 SPEEK:** concept, examples, AA, term, JB, in *WOR*-May97, p. 84; **PL8 SPEEK writing:** concept, example, DN, term, JB, in *WOR*-May97, p. 84; **pneumonoultramicroscopicsilicovolcanoconiosis:** AA, in *LOV,* p. 147, *CZE,* p. 39; **poetry maze:** DM, in *ALP,* p. 249; **political issue anagram:** DM, in *ALP,* p. 17; **Polybius's checkerboard:** PO, in *BOP,* p. 206; **polyphonic substitution cipher:** AA, example, RE, in *MAD,* p. 20 (synonym: polyphonic cipher, AA, in *MAD,* p. 19); **possessive celebrity:** SC, in *ALP,* p. 185; **presidential anagram:** concept, AA, example 1, SX, example 2, DW, examples 3–4, MH, example 5, RL, in *ALP,* pp. 15–16; **presidential palindrome:** concept, AA, examples 1–3, 6, DM, example 4, DB, example 5, Edward Scher, example 6, AA, in *ALP,* p. 31; **presidential pun name:** DM, in *ALP,* pp. 40–41; **presidential reversal:** concept, example, DB, derived term, DM, in *ALP,* p. 31; **progressive half-square:** concept, term, KD, in *WAP,* p. 188; example, DM; **progressive word square:** PN, in *PWG,* p. 181; **pronoun speller:** concept, example, PN, in *WOC,* p. 239; term, DM; **prose equivoque:** AA, in *OGW,* p. 146; **prose poem:** AA, in *OGW,* p. 147; **pseudo-antonyms:** concept, term, examples 1 and 3, DS, example 2, LB, example 4, OM, in *WAP,* p. 70; **pseudo-comparative:** RL, in *WOC,* p. 240; **pseudo-heteronymic pair:** concept, AA, term, examples, RL, in *WOC,* p. 17; **pseudo-synonyms:** see *WOR*-Feb 95, form by PN, examples by ST; **pun:** concept, term, AA, examples, RL, in *GET,* pp. 23–30, DM; **pundrome:** DM, in *ALP,* p. 48; **pun name:** DM, in *ALP,* p. 41; **punnery:** RL, in *GET,* p. 26; **punning author's name:** concept, examples, AA, in *OGW,* pp. 210–211, derived term, DM; **punster:** AA, in *GET,* p. 6; **pure word:** PC, in *WOR*-Nov79, p. 235; **Puritan baptismal name:** concept, examples, AA, in *OAC,* pp. 150–151; derived term, DM; **Q-graph:** LG, in *MAD,* p. 47; **Q-not-followed-by-U word:** RE, in *MAD,* pp. 27–28; **quadrisogram:** concept, RE, in *ALP,* p. 56; example, term, EC, in *WOR*-Nov98, pp. 290–291; **quadruple homophone:** RL, in *WOC,* p. 11; **-quake word:** DF, in *WOR*-May79, p. 103; **quasi-antonyms:** see Borgmann in *WOR.* The above appears in *WAP,* p. 71; **quaternade:** DB, in *LOV,* p. 171; **QU-followed-by-a-consonant word:** RE, in *MAD,* pp. 26–27; **quick-change word:** MK and DM, in *WOR*-May99, p. 88; **quinade:** DB, in *LOV,* p. 171; **quintisogram:** concept, RE, in *ALP,* p. 56; example, term, EC, in *WOR*-Nov98, pp. 290–292; **qwaint:** concept, example 1, AA, examples 2–5, DF, example 6, AS, term, examples 1 and 7, PN, in *PWG,* pp. 202–203; **radio call letter word:** RP, in *WOR*-Aug79, p 179; **rare doubled letters:** JG, in *WOR*-Aug81, p. 154; **rare letters:** AA; **Reaganagram:** (synonym: Reagan anagram, OM, in *WAP,* p. 106); **real word square:** LG, in *WOR*-May95, p. 78; **rebus:** *WOR*-Aug79, p. 137; **rebus poem:** concept, AA, example, HC, term, DM, in *ALP,* p. 67; **reciprocal automynorcagram:** concept, term, JL, in *MAD,* p. 17; **reconstructed poem:** JL, in *PAA,* p. 24; **redivide:** MS, in *PAL*-Spring97, p. 5; **redivider:** MS, in *PAL*-Spring97, p. 4; **redundancy:** AA, in *WAP,* pp. 24–26; **redundant place name:** concept, AA, examples, term, OM, in *WAP,* pp. 30–31; **redundant quote:** concept, AA, examples, term, OM, in *WAP,* p. 26; **reflexicon:** LS, in *MAD,* p. 228; **regular pyramid:** CT, in *WAP,* p. 198; **restaurawntese:** LA, in *WOR*-Feb70, p. 33; term, DM, in *ALP,* p. 153; **repeated key-pattern word:** MK and DM, in *WOR*-May99, p. 89; **retronym:** FM, in *CZE,* p. 60; **reversal:** DB in *LOV,* pp. 76–79, example, RE (synonyms: anagram, ananym, antigram, HD; drow, PN; half-palindrome, JP; inversion, palinode, JC; recurrent palindrome, retronym, reversagram, JS; reversal pair, reversal sentence, reversible, reversible anagram, reversion, semordnilap, sotadic palindrome, HE; word reversal, all listed by JP in *WOR*-Feb00, pp. 28–30; **reversal charade**: OM, in *WAP*, p. 68; **reversal double square**: RE, in *ALP*, p. 88; **reversal lettershift**: concept, example, DB; in *LOV*, p. 139 (derived term, DM); **reversal pair**: term, DB, in *LOV*, p. 35, p. 287; **reversal pseudonym**: concept, AA, example, SW, in *OGW*, p. 101; term, DM; **reversal sentence**: concept, term, AA, example 1, DB, in *LOV*, example 2, HB, in *LOV*, pp. 76–77; **reversal single square**: RE, in *ALP*, p. 88; **reversal square**: RE, in *ALP*, p. 89; **reverse alphabetically-ordered AEIOU word**: concept, example, DB, in *LOV*, pp. 160–161 (derived term, DM); **reverse alphabetically consonant word**: concept, examples, DB, in *LOV*, p. 167; term, DM; **reverse alphabetically-ordered number name**: derived term, DM; **reverse alphabet**: AA, in *MAD*, p. 173; **reverse alphabetic sequence**: RE, in *MAD*, p. 157; **reverse alphabetic word**: concept, term, examples 3–4, DB, in *LOV*, p. 167; examples 1–2, RE, in *MAD*, p. 164 (synonym: reverse alphabetical word, DB, in *LOV*, p. 166); **reverse-alphabetized number names**: concept, examples, EW, in *MAD*, p. 234 (derived term, DM); **reverse alphomic word**: ST, in *WOR*-Aug98, p. 184; **reverse bialphabetic word**: concept, example, PC, in *WOR*-Nov79, p. 236 (derived term, DM), (synonym: reverse dialphabetical order, PC, in *WOR*-Nov79, p. 236); **reverse invariant sentence**: RE, in *MAD*, p. 173; **reverse-keyboard word**: concept, term, example 3, JG, in *WOR*-Aug79, p. 154; examples 1–2, DM; **reverse parallelism**: concept, term, AA, examples, MD, in *WAP*, p. 77; **reversible inverted half-square**: OM, in *WAP*, p. 187; **reverse trinade**: DB, in *LOV*, p. 171; **reversible tautonym**: MB, in *WOR*-Aug79, p. 161; **reversible word ladder**: RR, in *WOR*-Feb79, p. 45; **R-graph**: LG, in *MAD*, p. 48; **rhetorical irony question**: PN, in *WOR*-May95, p. 104 (derived term, DM); **rhopalic sentence**: AA; **rhopalic verse**: concept, term, AA, example, WE, in *OGW*, p. 150; **rhymatic writing**: DM, in *ALP*, p. 164; **rhyming puzzle**: TA, in *OGW*, p. 116; **riddle**: AA, in *OGW*, pp. 1–5; **riddle-contest**: AA, in *OGW*, p. 3; **riddle of the Sphinx**: TQ, in *OGW*, p. 4; **roller-coaster word**: DM; **roller-coaster word chain**: LG, in *MAD*, p. 109; **Roman numeral palindrome**: DB, in *LOV*, p. 220; **Roman numeral part-word**: DB, in *LOV*, p. 221; **Roman numeral word**: DB, in *LOV*, pp. 220–221; **Romanomagic square**: LS, in *WOR*-Feb92, p. 51; **Romantic equation**: concept, term, DM, in *ALP*, p. 144 (derived term, DM); **Romantic number**: DM, in *ALP*, p. 144; **Romantic word**: DM, in *WOR*-Aug91, p. 182; **Rorschach word pair**: EW, in *WOR*, pp. 236–237; **rotary telephone word**: MK and DM, in *WOR*-May99, p. 85; **same-initial shiftgram**: LG, in *WOR*-Feb80, p. 23; **same-length isogram set**: RE, in *MAD*, p. 57; **SATOR square**: AA, in *ALP*, p. 86; **Schwarzkopf Challenge, The**: concept, example 2, RK, example 1, AA, example 3, JB, example 4, term, DM; **Scrabble™**: concept, AB, term, JE, in *OGW*, pp. 63–66 (synonyms: Lexico, It, Criss-Cross, AB, in *OGW*, p. 63-66); **Scrabble™-friendly word square**: DA, in *WOR*-Nov98, p. 286; **Scrabble™ sentence**: PS, in *ALP*, p. 14; **scrambled alphabet**: concept, example, DR, term, RE, in *MAD*, p. 179; **second-order reduplication**: DB, in *LOV*, p. 176; **self-contradictory word**: AA; **self-descriptive crossword**: VE, LS, in *MAD*, pp. 228–230; **self-descriptive number name**: Original concept, HB, in *BYL*, p. 114; term, RE, in *MAD*, p. 239; concept 1, DM, example, LG, term, EW, in *MAD*, p. 239, concept 2, example, LS, in *MAD*, p. 240, concept 3, example, RE, in *MAD*, p. 243 (synonym: perfect number name, HB, in *BYL*, p. 114); **self-enumerating book**: LS, in *MAD*, p. 227; **self-enumerating sentence**: concept, examples 1–2, term, AA; example 3, RK, in *MAD*, p. 225; **self-invariant word**: concept, RE, in *MAD*, p. 173 (examples, derived term, DM); **self-referential**: AA; **semantic rhyming word set**: BP, in *WOR*-May84, p. 71; **sentence**

**reversal**: concept, term, AA, example 1, HB, example 2, DB, in *LOV,* pp. 76–77; **sequential word squares**: concept, term, OM, in *WAP,* p. 189; example, DM; **set-up pun**: RL, in *GET,* p. 129; **seven seas**: HB; **seven-square**: concept, term, AA, example, SE, in *WAP,* p. 175; **sex change charade**: DM, in *WOR*-Aug96; **semordnilap**: AA; **Shakespearean coined word**: concept, examples, WM, in *WAP,* pp. 48–49, derived term, DM; **Shakespearean palindrome**: DM, in *ALP,* p. 180, 320; **Shakespearean pangrammatic sonnet**: HB, in *ALP,* p. 105; **Shakespearean pun**: concept, example, WM, in *OGW,* p. 205, derived term, DM; **Shakespearean reversible sonnet**: DM, in *ALP,* p. 179; **shaped poetry**: concept, SI, term, AA, in *OGW,* pp. 152–157; **shape-shift**: DM, in *ALP*; **Shaw's tactic**: concept, example 1, GS, examples 2–3, term, RL, in *WOC,* p. 225–226; **shift**: DB, in *LOV,* p. 137; **shiftgram**: concept, example 2, term, HB, example 3, DB, in *MAD,* p. 179; example 1, DM; **shift pair**: term, RE, in *MAD,* p. 17; **shift-quadruple**: term, RE, in *MAD,* p. 175; **shift-triple**: term, RE, in *MAD,* p. 175; **shift value**: term, DM, in *ALP,* p. 109; **shift-word**: DS, in *MAD,* p. 137; **"Siamese" pyramid**: concept, term, SS, in *WAP,* p. 199; example, DM; **silly subject heading**: JL, in *ALP,* p. 280; **singing with words**: DD; **single-key word**: MK and DM, in *WOR*-May99, p. 86; **single-letter difference pair**: RE, in *WOR*-May69; **single-shift scode**: AA, in *BOP,* pp. 204–205; **single square**: concept, term, AA, example, DM; **single-step pair**: DM, in *ALP,* p. 125; **single transposal square**: PC, in *WOR*-Nov79, p. 240; **single square**: concept, term, AA, example, HE, in *ALP,* p. 86; **single-word oxymoron**: RL, in *CZE,* p. 34, p. 36; **singular plurals**: PN, in *ALP,* p. 75; **666**: Example, BR, in *WOR*-Aug77, p. 179; **six-square**: concept, term, AA, example, AK, in *WAP,* p. 171; **six-vowel translation word pair**: concept, examples, DB, in *LOV,* p. 162; term, DM; **six-vowel word**: concept, examples, DB, in *LOV*; derived term, DM; **skewed word line**: LG, in *MAD,* p. 177; **slanted word line**: LG, in *MAD,* p. 177; **slenderizing**: concept, term, HM in *OUC,* p. 225, example TJD; **sneeze word**: concept, AA, examples, term, MB, in *ALP,* p. 272; **snowball/melting snowball sentence**: concept, example, DB, in *LOV,* p. 137; term, DM; **snowball sentence**: concept, AA; example, term, DB, in *ALP,* p. 135 (synonyms: rhopalic sentence, rhopalism, DB, in *ALP,* p. 135; prose rhopalic, rhopalic prose TA, in *OGW,* p. 150); **solid cluster five-vowel word**: concept, example, DB, in *LOV,* p. 161 (derived term, DM); **soundplay:** AA; **specialty definition**: LD, in *WOR*-Feb70, p. 30; **spell-checker Jabberwocky**: DS, in *ALP,* p. 216; **spelled-out letter**: PC, in *WOR*-Nov79, p. 237; **spelling bee**: concept, term, AA, example, LP, in *OGW,* pp. 125–126; **spiraling alphabet**: BR, in *WOR*-May69, p. 67; **split definitive**: HR, in *WOR*-Nov94, p. 223; **spoonergram**: concept, term, example 1, EX, example 2, AM, example 3, AE, example 4, XS, example 5, JL, in *WAP,* p. 20 (synonyms: spannergroom, spammergroon, groonerspam, AA, in *WAP,* p. 20); **spoonergram opposites**: concept, term, AA, example 1, YN, example 2, ME, in *WAP,* p. 20, derived term, DM; **spoonerick**: TC, in *WOW*-July 97, p 13; **spooner-rhyme**: concept, AA, examples, term, TC, in *WOW*-July97, p. 13; **spoonerism**: concept, examples, AT, term, AA, in *WAP,* pp. 18–19; **spoonerism equation**: DM, in *ALP,* p. 145; **spoonerism poem**: DM, in *WOW*-Feb96; **square & diamond inside**: NP, in *WAP,* p. 187; **squaring the circle**: DB, in *LOV,* p. 232; **standard rebus**: concept, term, AA, example 1, ME, example 2, FI, example 3, GR, example 4, AA; **Star of David**: RE, in *MAD,* p. 215; **star's name**: concept, AA, examples, RL, in *POW,* p. 177–180, 213–214; **starter**: RE, in *MAD,* p. 109; **state double-three square**: DM, in *ALP,* p. 90; **state double-four square**: DM, in *ALP,* p. 90; **stately word**: concept, DS, term, RB, in *WOR*-Feb76, p. 42; **state name word-weight group**: DF, in *WOR*-May95, p. 93; **state palindrome**:

concept, AA, term, examples 1–5, 7, DM, in *WOR*-Nov96, p. 264; example 6, LM, in *PAL*, p. 87; **state postal abbreviation ambiguity problem**: RE, in *WOR*-May95, p. 96; **state single-four square**: RE, in *ALP*, p. 90; **state square**: DM, in *ALP* .p 90; **stereowords**: DM, in *ALP*, p. 205; **stinky pinky**: AA, in *WOR*-May95, p. 88; **stinky pinky buzzword**: AA, collected by JD, in *BUZ*, reported by RE, in *WOR*-May95, p. 88, derived term, DM; **strike-out**: SP, in *WOR*-Nov77, p. 251; **strike-out poetry**: SP, in *WOR*-Nov77, p. 251; **strike-out sentence**: SP, in *WOR*-Nov77, p. 251; **string**: AA; **suber**: concept, term, AA, examples, FA, TR, NI; **subletter**: DM, in *ALP*, p. 272; **substitute-letter transposal**: concept, term, example 3, DB, in *LOV,* p. 123; example 2, RE, in *MAD*, p. 149; example 1, DM; **substitute-letter word chain**: DB, in *LOV,* p. 123; **substitution code**: AA, in *BOP*, p. 204; **subtransposition**: HB, in *MAD*, p. 183; **subtransposition group**: FE, in *MAD*, p. 183; **successive beheadment**: concept, example, AA, term, DB, in *LOV,* p. 113; **successive bigram beheadment**: RL, in *WOR*-May98, p. 142; **successive beheadment sentence**: concept, example, DB, in *LOV,* p. 114, derived term, DM (synonyms: reductive anagram, subtractive anagram, OM, in *WAP*, p. 102); **successive buildup reversal**: concept, example, @DB, in *LOV,* p. 49; derived term, DM; **successive curtailment**: DB, in *LOV,* p. 115 (synonyms: apocope, paragoge, DB, in *LOV,* p. 115); **successive curtailment sentence**: concept, example 1, DB, in *LOV,* pp. 115–116, example 2, term, DM; **successive deletion**: concept, AA, term, example, DB, in *LOV* .p 116; **successive terminal deletion**: DB, in *LOV,* p. 118 (derived term, DM); **successive transaddition**: RE, in *WOR*-Aug79, p. 141; **successive transdeletion**: DB, in *LOV,* p. 11; **sumgrams**: PN, in *PWG*, p. 206; **sum word**: **(1)** CB in *MAD,* pp. 185–186; **(2)** PN, in *PWG*, p. 206; **sumword value**: concept, AA, term, PN, in *PWG*, pp. 205–205; **supercalifragilisticexpialidocious**: AA, in *TOP*; **super-charade**: DM, in *ALP*, p. 130; **supersentence**: concept, term, RL, example, BM, in *WOR*-Feb80, pp. 52–54; **super title**: TM, in *WOR*, concept, AA, term, RE, in *WOR*-May80, p. 117; example 1, DB, in *WOR*-Feb68, pp. 34–35; example 2, JG, in *WOR*-May80, p. 117; example 3, RE, in *WOR*-May80, p. 117, and KL, RO in *WOR*-Aug80, p. 151; **superultramegalosesquipedalia**: concept, AA, term, RE, in *WOR*-May80, p. 117; example 1, DB, in *WOR*-Feb68, pp. 34–35; example 2, JG, in *WOR*-May80, p. 117; example 3, RE, in *WOR*-May80, p. 117, and KL, RO in *WOR*-Aug80, p. 151; **syllabic rebus**: AA, in *ALP*, p. 66; **symmetric crash group**: RE, in *MAD*, p. 212; **synonym chain**: DB; **synonymic reversal:** DB, in *LOV,* p. 44 (synonyms: synonym reversal, MP, in *WOR*-Aug79, p. 161); **synonym square**: TP, in *WOR*-Aug79,, p. 157; **synonymic transdeletion**: concept, examples 23, term, DB, in *LOV,* p. 121; example 1, DM; **synonym square**: TP, in *WOR*-Aug79, p. 157; **tag**: AA, in *WOR*-Feb80, p. 4; **Syzygy**: AA; **tall writing**: concept, example, AA, term, CC, in *OAC*; **tautogram**: HM in *OUC*, p.229; **tautonym**: DB, in *LOV,* p. 175 (synonyms: reduplication, two-part tautonym, DB, in *LOV,* p. 175); **tautonymic ten-square**: concept, "Tunste," example, AI, term, AA, in *WAP*, p. 182; **telepalindrome**: MK and DM, in *WOR*-May99, p. 89; **telephomnemonic**: Examples, BR, in *WOR*-Aug81, p. 149; **telephone answer**: MB, in *WOR*-Feb79, p. 206; **telephone double-digit word**: DM, in *WOR*-Feb99, p. 67; **telephone isogram**: DM, in *WOR*-Feb99, p. 67; **telephone reversal**: DM, in *WOR*-Feb99, p. 67; **telephone word**: DB, in *LOV* pp. 162–163; **telestich**: AA, in *OGW*, p. 4; **tensquare**: AA; **terminal**: DB, in *LOV,* p. 119, example, DM; **terminal deletion**: DB, in *LOV*, pp. 117–118 (synonym: terminal elision, DB, in *LOV,* p. 118); **terminal man**: RE in *NAG*, pp. 45–51; last example, DT, in *WOR*-Nov93, p. 214; **terminal switch**: DB, in

*LOV,* p. 99; **tetragram:** AA, in *MAD,* p. 64; **"the" country:** DB, in *BYL,* pp. 15–16; **T-graph:** LG, in *MAD,* p. 47; **thedom:** puzzledom. SK, in WAP, p. 185; **Thinglish:** DM, in *ALP,* p. 204; **thousand-words problem:** concept, RE, example, JG, in *MAD,* pp. 147–148; term, DM; **three-letter body part:** concept, term, MI, in *RED*-Sep73, p. 90; examples, DS, in *WOR*-Feb75, p. 49; **three-letter switch:** DB, in *LOV,* p. 99; **three-square:** concept, term, AA, example, DM; **threnodials:** HM in *OUC* p. 229; **tic–tac–toe board letters:** DM, in *WOC;* **tic–tac–toe board palindrome:** DM; **tic–tac–toe board word:** DM; **tic–tac–toe board letters:** DM, in *WOC,* p. 178; **tic–tac–toe word:** DM; **Timely neologism:** term, examples, DF, in *WOR*-Aug77 pp. 180–185; **timely poem:** DM; **Tom Swiftie:** AA, in *OGW,* p. 214 (synonym: Tom Swifty, AA, in *GET,* p. 76; adverbial puns, AA, in *OGW,* p. 214); **tongue-twister:** AA, in *OBW,* pp. 160–162, 171; **tongue-twister limerick:** AA, in *OBW,* p. 170; **tongue-twister palindrome:** LM, in *WAP,* p. 79; **tongue-twister sobriety test:** concept, example, in *OBW* p. 169, derived term, DM; **top, the:** OM, in *WAP,* p. 188; **touchtone telephone word:** MK, DM, in *WOR*-May99, p. 85, 91; **town–state word:** aconcept, example, FE, in *WOR*-Aug81, p. 174; derived term, DM; **transaddition:** concept, term, DB, in *LOV,* p. 119; example, DM; **transbeheadment:** concept, term, DB, in *LOV,* p. 120; example, DM; **transcurtailment:** concept, term, DB, in *LOV,* p. 120, example, DM; **transdeletion:** concept, term, AA, in *LOV,* p. 119, example, DM; **transdeletion chain:** concept, term, DB, in *LOV,* p. 119; example, DM; **transdeletion pyramid:** concept, term, DB, in *LOV,* p. 119; example, DM; **translingual lettershift:** BL, HB; in *WOR*-Feb80, p. 27; **transmute** (*v.*): DB, in *LOV,* p. 83; **transposal:** MA, from MB, in *WOR*-Aug79, p. 160; **transposal form:** PC, in *WOR*-Nov79, p. 240; **transposal index:** RE, in *MAD,* pp. 134–135; **transposal name:** RE, in *MAD,* p. 136; **transposal poetry:** AA (synonym: transpositional poetry, RE, in *MAD,* p. 141); **transposal pseudonym:** DB, in *LOV,* pp. 97–98; term, DM; **transposal rectangle:** PC, in *WOR*-Nov79, p. 240; **transposal sentence:** DB, in *LOV,* pp. 95–96; **transposal square:** PC, in *WOR*-Nov79, p. 240; **transposal system:** DB, in *LOV,* p. 96-97; derived term, DM; **transpose (v.):** AA; **triad:** ST, in *WOR*-May95, p. 111; **trianagram:** concept, AA, example, EA, term, OM, in *WAP,* p. 92 (synonym: triplet, OM, in *WAP,* p. 92); **trictionary:** DM, in *MAD,* pp. 77–78; **tricycle:** DS, in *WOR*-May69, p. 119; **trigram:** AA, in *MAD,* p. 64; **trinade:** DB, in *LOV,* p. 170; **trigram-positioned word:** MK and DM, in *WOR*-May99, p. 89; **trilingual synonymic anagram:** MB, in *WOR*-May91, p. 107; **trio isogram:** DB, in *LOV,* p. 129; **triple charade sentence:** PN, in *WOR*-Nov91, p. 235; **tripartite color rhyme:** concept, AA, example, DM, term, OM, in *WAP,* p. 11; **triple acrostic:** AA, in *OGW,* p. 4; **triple homophone:** concept, example, RL, in *WOC,* p. 10; derived term, DM; **triple internal tautonym:** AA; **triplet:** PN, in *ALP,* p. 127; **triple oxymoron:** RL, in *CZE,* p. 33; **triple tautonym:** concept, examples 2-3, DB, in *LOV,* p. 175; example 1, RE, in *MAD,* p. 82; derived term, DM (synonym: three-part tautonym, DB, in *LOV,* p. 175; **triple transposal:** concept, AA, examples, EA, term, OM, in WAP, p 94. Synonym: triplet, OM, in WAP, p. 94; **triplets-in-parallel:** PN, in *ALP,* p. 127; **trisogram:** concept, RE, in *ALP,* p. 56; example, term, EC, in *WOR*-Nov98, pp. 290–291; **trivial:** AA; **true riddle:** concept, examples, AA, term, OP, in *BOP,* p. 150; **truthful number: (1)** AA, in *MAD,* p. 230; **(2)** AA; **Turkey Irish:** AA, noted by FL, in *WOR*-Nov79; **twenty consonant poetry:** WG, in *WOR*-May96, p. 74; **twenty-one consonant poetry:** WG, in *WOR*-May96, p. 74; **twinned reversal:** DB, in *LOV,* p. 49; **two-headed headline:** concept, AA, examples, term, RL, in *ANG,* p. 83, pp. 87–90; **two-letter alternation poem:** DM, in *ALP,* p. 138; **two-letter word:** concept, term, AA, examples 1 and 3–12,

HK, in *BOP*, p. 21; example 2, DM; **two-square**: concept, term, AA, example, DM; **two-syllable word**: concept, term, AA, examples 3–4, JM, in *WOR*-Aug79, p. 153, examples 1–2, DM. **type-collection**: term, AA, in *MAD*, p. 65; **type-collection of bigrams**: concept, term, RE, examples, RE, other, in *MAD*, pp. 65–66; **typewriter keyboard alphabet**: AA, in *ALP*, p. 186; **typewriter-keyboard order word**: concept, term, example 3, JG, in *WOR*-Aug79, p. 154; examples 1–2, DM; **typewriter sentence**: DB, in *LOV*, p. 173; term, DM; **typewriter word**: AA; **ugliest word**: concept, term, AA, examples, DM, in *ALP*, pp. 73–74; **U-invariant**: DB, in *LOV*, p. 174; **ultimate transposal set**: DB, in *LOV*, p. 86; **unattractive opposites**: DM, in *ALP*, p. 254; **undergrounder**: DB, in *WOR*-Feb86, pp. 23–26; **undominated alphabetic sequence**: RE, in *MAD*, pp. 154–155; **unfolded Platonic solid**: RE, in *MAD*, pp. 213–214; **-unfriendly alphabet**: PC, in *MAD*, p. 181; **unicycle**: concept, term, example 1, FE, in *WOR*-Feb70, p. 39; example 2–4, MB, in *WOR*-Aug79, p. 162; **unidigital word**: DM, in *ALP*, p. 147; **unit**: HB, in *PAA*, p. vi–vii; **univocalic**: concept, AA, examples, DB, in *LOV*, pp. 173–175; term, AA (synonyms: vocalic invariant, A-invariant, E-invariant, I-invariant, O-invariant, U-invariant, Y-invariant, DB, in *LOV*, pp. 173–175; monovocalic, DF, in *WOR*-Aug00, p. 224); **univocalic haiku**: HB, in *ALP*, p. 171; **univocalic palindrome**: GL; **univocalic poetry**: concept, term, AA, example, MH, in *MAD*, p. 7; **unlucky letter**: DM; **unlucky number name**: DM; **unparagraph**: DM, in *ALP*, p.158; **unquote**: DM, in *ALP*, p. 59; **unspeakable sentence**: concept, example, HB, in *WOR*-Feb70, p. 48 (Derived term, DM); **UN- word**: DF, in *WOR*-Aug79, p. 176; **upside-down letters**: concept, term, DB, in *LOV*, p. 29; **upside-down palindrome**: concept, term, examples 1–4, DB, in *LOV*, p. 29; example 5, AA, in *SCI*; example 6, DM, in *ALP*, p. 200 (synonym: four-way palindrome, DB, in *LOV*, p. 29); **unspeakable sentence**: concept, example, HB, in *WOR*-Feb70, p. 48. Derived term, DM; **UN- word**: DF, in *WOR*-Aug79, p. 176; **verb-adverb paradox**: RL, in *WOR*-Feb80, p. 47; **verb hypertense**: DM, in *ALP*, p. 273; **vertical mirror letters**: concept, DB, in *LOV*, pp. 27–28; term, DM (synonym: mirror palindrome (type A), DB, in *LOV*, p. 27); **vertical mirror word**: concept, examples 1–2, DB, in *LOV*, p. 28; term, DM, in *ALP*, p. 197; example 1, RE, examples 2, 3, 4, DM; **"V-14" problem**: DB, in *WOR*-May95, pp. 67–71; **vicinal**: EU, in *MAD*, p 168; **vicinal story**: EU, in *MAD*, p. 168; **visual word-unit palindrome**: PH, in *WOR*-Aug81, p. 163; **vocabularyclept poetry**: HB, in *PAA*, pp. 20–22; **vocalic alternating monotony**: RB, in *WOR*-May71, p. 77; **vocalic invariant**: DB, in *LOV* .p 173; **volatile words**: AA; **vowel-consonant pattern**: DB, in *LOV*, pp. 169–170; **vowelindrome**: concept, examples 1 and 2, term, SC in *WOR*-Aug93, p. 164; example 3, JF, in *WOR*-Feb94, p. 57; **vowel-mates**: ST, in *WOR*-Aug96, p. 174; **vowel-sequence word**: concept, example, DB, in *LOV*, p. 156 (derived term, DM); **wacky medical term**: concept, term, PE, examples, AA, in *ALP*, p. 277; **Websterian word**: AA, in *WOR*-Feb80, p. 4; **weight**: DF, in *WOR*-Nov72, p. 226; **well-mixed transposal**: concept, term, RE, example 2, CH, in *MAD*, p. 132; example 1, DM; **wind name**: GM, in *WOR*-May80,, p. 107; **Witches' Prayer**: AA, in *OAC*, p. 61; **word chain: (1)**: concept, term, HD, in *OGW*, p. 190; example, CM, in *MAD*, p. 109; **(2)**: concept, term, HD, in *OGW*, pp. 190–191; example, DM; **(3)**: HD, in *OGW*, p. 191; **word cluster**: DM, in *WOR*-Nov98, p. 308; **word cycle**: DS, in *WOR*-May69, pp. 118–119 (synonym: word chain, AA, in *OGC*, p. 191); **word dice**: concept, term, DS, in *MAD*, pp. 23–24 (synonym: letter cube, RE, in *MAD*, p. 24; lettered dice, TA, in *OBG*, p. 69); **word dice problem**: RE, in *MAD*, p. 24; **word fragment**: RE, in *MAD*, p. 64; **word girder**: DB, in *LOV*, p. 159; **word graph**: LG and RE, in *MAD*, p. 42; **word interlocks**: RE, in

*BOP*, p. 22; **word ladder**: LC (synonyms: transformations, PF, laddergram, JX and LE, stepword, transition, word chain, word link, word ping-pong, AA, word golf, VN, in *OGW*, pp. 187–188); **word ladder square**: JP, in *WOR*-Nov98, pp. 248–249; **word line**: LG, in *MAD*, pp. 176–177; **word molecule**: DM, in *MAD*, pp. 45–46; **word network**: RE, in *MAD*, pp. 93–94; **word oblong**: PN, in *PWG*, pp. 182–183; **word pack**: RE, in *MAD*, p. 219; **wordplay**: concept, term, AA, quote, RE, in *MAD*, p. 45; **word pyramid**: DB, in *LOV*, p. 119; **word-rubric rebus**: concept, term, PC, example, AA;**word record**: AA, assembled by CC, in *ALP*, p. 70; **word repetition**: concept, term, AA; example 1, HH, on NPR's "On the Connection" 10/16/97; example 2, AD & JS, on *NEW* Nov 3-97, p. 90; **word reversal**: term, DB, in *LOV*, p. 76; **word ring**: concept, HD, examples, term, TP, in *MAD*, p. 108; **word-search pack**: RE, in *MAD*, p. 219; example, DM; **word-search puzzle**: AA; **word square**: AA, in *WAP*, pp. 168–169; **word square poem**: HB, in *ALP*, p. 58; **word stair**: HD, in *MAD*, pp. 107–108; **word stepladder**: concept, term, example 1, DM, example 2, JM, in *ALP*, p. 124; **word string**: concept, HD, TP, examples, term, TP, in *MAD*, p. 108; **word transformation**: concept, AA, term, HK, in *BOP*, p. 40; examples, DM; **words un–in–one–breath–utterable**: term, BJ, in *OAC*, p. 211; **word–unit palindromic double square**: concept, example, DB, in *LOV*, p. 204, term, DM, in *ALP*, p. 89; **word–unit palindromic single square**: concept, example, DB, in *LOV*, p. 201, term, DM, in *ALP*, p 89; **Words within Words**: concept, term, AA, example, TA, in *OGW*, pp. 120–121 (synonyms: hidden words, in-words, keyword, multiwords, target, word-builder, word-hunt, word-making, words, AA, in *OGW*, pp. 120–121); **word tiles**: LG, in *MAD*, p. 46; **word-to-name reversal**: DB, in *LOV*, p. 83, pp. 289–290, term, example 1, DM; **word-to-names charade**: concept, examples 1–6, HR, examples 7–9, JG, in *ALP*, p. 184; term, DM; **word-to-name transposal**: DB, in *LOV*, p. 83, pp. 289–290; term, DM; **word-to-phrase reversal**: DB, in *LOV*, p. 76; **word-to-sentence reversal**: DB, in *LOV*, p .76; **word transformation**: concept, AA, term, HK, in *BOP*, p. 40; examples, DM; **word tree**: RE, in *WOR*-Aug79,, p. 141; **word-unit** (*adj.*): RE, in *MAD*, p. 142; AA; **word-unit**: AA (synonym: word-by-word, RE, in *MAD*, p. 142; word-order, AA); **word-unit palindrome**: JL, in *PAA*, p. 108; (synonym: PN, in PWG, p. 199); **word-unit palindromic-anagrammatic epitaph**: AA, in OGW, p. 103; term, DM; **word-unit palindromic double square**: DM, in *ALP*, p. 89; **word-unit palindromic poem**: concept, example, JL, in *PAA*, p. 109; contrived term, DM; **word-unit palindromic sentence**: JL, in *PAA*, p. 108; **word-unit palindromic single square**: DM, in *ALP*, p. 89; **word-unit reversal**: AA; **word-unit reversal ladder**: concept, term, AA, example, GY, discussed by PC, in *WOR*-Aug79, p. 138; **word-weight**: DF, in *WOR*-May95, pp. 91–93; **word worm**: KJ, GW, in *MAD*, pp. 248–252; **would-be acronym**: concept, AA, example, JQ, term, OM, in *WAP*, p. 36; **would-be phobia word**: concept, AA, examples 1–3, OM, in *WAP*, p. 53; example 4, AA, example 5, DM; **X-name**: DB, in NAG, pp. 51–52; **xzwamfeujho**: DM, in *ALP*, p. 164; **Y-invariant**: DB, in *LOV*, p. 174; **Yogi Berra quote**: concept, examples, YB, in *WAP*, pp. 16–17; derived term, DM; **Yreka Bakery**: AA; **zazzification**: RW, in *WOR*-Nov87, p. 216; **zeugma**: concept, term, AA, example 1, in *PEP*, example 2, DM, in *ALP*, p. 164; **zeugma tale**: DM, in *ALP*, pp. 163–164; **zigzag word**: DM; **ziticorumbatous 15-square**: EW, in *WOR*-May81, p. 91; **zoological homophonic pair**: concept, AA, examples, RL, in *WOC*, p. 9; derived term, DM; **Z-to-A word list**: RE, in *MAD*, p. 259; **zzyxjoanw hoax**: concept, example, RH, hoax discovery, PC, in *MAD*, p. 152; : JG, in *ALP*, p. 80; **ZZZZZZZZZZZZZZZZZZZZZZZZZZZZZZZZZZZZZZZZZZZ-ZZ**: JG, in *ALP*, p. 80.

## Appendix D: Bibliography

## BOOKS

Augarde, Tony. *The Oxford Guide to Word Games*. New York: Oxford University Press, 1984. This book explains almost every classic type of word game, with examples accompanying the text. It's one of the few scholarly, historical guides to the field. Moreover, in the best spirit of wordplay, it's entertaining.

Bergerson, Howard W. *Palindromes and Anagrams*. New York: Dover Publications, Inc., 1973. In this wide-ranging study, Bergerson gives a brief history of both forms and presents a generous selection of classical and modern examples, from one-liners to longer poems.

Bombaugh, Charles, ed. *Gleanings for the Curious from the Harvest Fields of Literature*. Detroit: Gale Research Company, 1985. Originally published in 1875, this 864-page book presents a huge variety of wordplay, including everything from puns to "Irish bulls," and discusses them in a homey, enjoyable fashion. It demonstrates an earlier attitude toward wordplay.

Borgmann, Dmitri A. *Beyond Language*. New York: Charles Scribner's Sons, 1967. Many authorities on recreational linguistics agree that Borgmann is the founder of modern wordplay. In this, his third book, he presents word puzzles in a unique three-part format—problems, hints, and solutions, within a maze of fascinating information that takes the reader to the fringes of language and beyond.

————. *Curious Crosswords*. New York: Charles Scribner's Sons, 1970. It would be hard to assemble a set of crossword puzzles more difficult than this collection. It's a treasure-house for the advanced cruciverbalist, and a slaughterhouse for the novice. If crossword puzzles can be considered an art form, this book is the Museum of Modern Art.

————. *Language on Vacation*. New York: Charles Scribner's Sons, 1965. A ground-breaking work, this is the first book treating wordplay as a field of knowledge to be studied in its own right. It discusses the basic elements of logology, the author's term for wordplay, in a witty, conversational fashion, chapter by chapter, word by remarkable word. It has been referred to as the bible of recreational linguistics.

Brotchie, Alastair (compiler) and Mel Gooding (editor). *A Book of Surrealist Games*. Boston and London: Shambhala Redstone Editions, 1991. An inventory of writing and drawing methods, ranging from random provocation to formal collage, collected from the work and history of the surrealists.

Byrne, Josefa Heifetz, ed. *Mrs. Byrne's Dictionary of Unusual, Obscure and Preposterous Words*. Secaucus, N.J.: Citadel, 1976. Byrne lists and defines thousands of words that she considers the most outlandish examples from other dictionaries. The book is a great resource for coming up with autoschediastic remarks to leave other people mommixed.

Dickson, Paul, *Words*. New York: Delacorte Press, 1982. Aimed specifically at people interested in wordplay, this book is an enthusiastic display of etymology and pseudo-etymology. Heavily illustrated, it presents a collection of unusual words, some real and others made up by the author.

Dudeney, Henry Ernest. *300 Best Word Puzzles*. New York: Charles Scribner's Sons, 1968. Based on Dudeney's *The World's Best Word Puzzles,* published in 1925, this collection shows the state of wordplay in the period between Bombaugh and Walsh (nineteenth century) to Borgmann (1965).

Eckler, Ross. *Making the Alphabet Dance*. New York: St. Martin's, 1995. This landmark book defines letterplay and synthesizes the many advances that have been made over the past thirty years. In progressing from simple to complex forms, Eckler discusses the work of many wordplay writers and includes dozens of illustrations, tables, and lists. No other book achieves such a complicated goal.

————, ed. *Names and Games*. University Press of America, Inc., 1986. The only book devoted entirely to onomastics, the field of the wordplay of names—personal names, town names, chemical names, business names, state names, and other names. Ninety-nine articles from *Word Ways* are reprinted in their entirety with occasional follow-up commentary.

————, ed. *The New Anagrammasia: A Collection of 8876 Anagrams and Antigrams Published between 1797 and 1991*. Morristown, N.J.: *Word Ways* Monograph Series 2, 1991. The largest collection of anagrams ever published. Each entry is presented alphabetically in four parts: Phrase, Anagram, Author, and

Date. Almost all the anagrams are restricted to phrases (instead of proper names), and often the same phrase is anagrammed into more than one new phrase.

―――――, ed. *Word Recreations: Games and Diversions from Word Ways.* New York: Dover, 1979. After the first ten years of *Word Ways,* the editor assembled the best articles representing some of the major concerns of modern wordplay. They discuss topics ranging from word networks to computerized pangram searches.

Espy, Willard. *An Almanac of Words at Play.* New York: Crown Publishers, Inc., 1975. Wordplay in prose, poetry, and puzzles appears here in the form of a daily almanac, with one or more entries for each day of the year. The presentation is highly original: it can be read in one day or 365 days!

―――――. *Another Almanac of Words at Play.* New York: Crown Publishers, Inc., 1980. The successor to the first book, it has all new material.

―――――. *The Game of Words.* New York: Grosset and Dunlap, 1972. Among the chapters, lettered from A to Z, the author displays a great variety of wordplay. From puzzle poems to punning headlines, he explores the structure of language to achieve his multifaceted effects.

Fisher, Leonard Everett. *Alphabet Art: Thirteen ABCs from around the World.* New York: Four Winds, 1978. A beautifully illustrated introduction to thirteen very different alphabets, ranging from the widely used (Greek) to the lesser-known (Eskimo). Each section includes a brief history of the origin of the specific alphabet or syllabary.

Gardner, Martin. *Aha! Gotcha!: Paradoxes to Puzzle and Delight.* New York: W H. Freeman and Co., 1982. This thorough presentation of mathematical paradoxes has linguistic elements, too. The reader goes step by step into the quicksand of problems involving logic, probability, time, and tricky topics. The cartoon-strip illustrations help to illuminate the puzzlement.

―――――. *The Annotated Night Before Christmas.* New York: Summit Books, 1991. Dozens of parodies of this Christmas classic show how a popular poem can inspire imaginative clones. Each parody comes with introduction and footnotes.

Grambs, David. *Words about Words*. New York: McGraw-Hill, 1984. This "dictionary of 2000 words—old, new, and surprising—for the styles, devices, defects, and oddities of the craft of prose writing" contains sections on word-game words, Irish bulls, propaganda devices, mixed metaphors, etc.

Hofstadter, Douglas R. *Gödel, Eschel, Bach*. New York: Vintage, 1989. In this multifaceted book, wordplay and logic are part of a larger whole that involves artificial intelligence, art, music, philosophy, language, and other things. Achilles and the Tortoise engage in a running narrative that serves as both point and counterpoint to the more abstract discussions.

Kim, Scott. *Inversions: A Catalog of Calligraphic Cartwheels*. Peterborough, N.H.: Byte Books, 1981. By distorting the shapes of letters, the artist has rendered words that can be rotated or reflected to form the same or other words. Kim shows how plastic the alphabet can be.

Kohl, Herbert. *A Book of Puzzlements*. New York: Schocken Books, 198 I. This compendium of word games ranging from easy to difficult is aimed at children as well as adults. Along with being an enjoyable read, it's a how-to book that gives directions for making palindromes, word squares, and other forms of wordplay.

Kuhn, Joaquin, and Maura Kuhn. *Rats Live on No Evil Star*. New York: Everest House, 1981. Palindromic crossword puzzles are featured in this unusual book. Not for rookie wordplayers, the games here challenge even the experts.

Lederer, Richard. *Anguished English*. New York: Dell, 1987. Student bloopers, courtroom blunders, and welfare gaffs fill the pages of this book, which became a wordplay bestseller. Over a thousand examples of disjointed English show that our language confounds even the natives.

———. *Crazy English*. New York: Pocket Books, 1990. Humorous essays that reflect the idiosyncracies of the English language, including odd plurals, animal names, and palindromes—in a style that uses the forms to talk about themselves.

———. *Get Thee to a Punnery*. New York: Dell, 1988. Twenty-five quizzes challenge, teach, and entertain the reader with nearly every type of pun—daffynitions, Tom Swifties, spoonerisms, knock-knock jokes, and more. The text explains the forms in a lively, punny fashion.

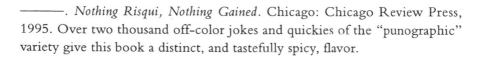
————. *Nothing Risqui, Nothing Gained*. Chicago: Chicago Review Press, 1995. Over two thousand off-color jokes and quickies of the "punographic" variety give this book a distinct, and tastefully spicy, flavor.

————. *The Word Circus*. Springfield, Mass.: Merriam-Webster, Inc., 1998. A lively survey of wordplay. Includes acrostics, anagrams, palindromes, spoooner-isms, kangaroo words, homophones, and many (more esoteric) forms, with illustrations by Dave Morice.

Lloyd, Sam. *Sam Lloyd's Cyclopedia of 5000 Puzzles, Tricks & Conundrums with Answers*. New York: Pinnacle, 1976. This work by an American puzzle genius is full of picture riddles, word games, mathematical problems, and other "species of mental gymnastics." The text is generously illustrated with intricate line drawings. Although not all puzzles are wordplay, charades, rebuses, puns, and riddles abound.

Mathews, Harry, and Alastair Brotchie, eds. *Oulipo Compendium*. London: Atlas Press, 1998. A comprehensive survey of the work of the Oulipo (*Ouvroir de Littérature Potentielle*) group, whose members included Georges Perec, author of the lipogrammatic novel *La Disparition* (translated into English as *A Void,* with nary an E in either version); Raymond Queneau, who assembled a mix-and-match book of sonnets entitled *100, 000, 000, 000, 000 Poems;* and Harry Mathews, whose *Selected Declarations of Dependence* consists entirely of neo-adages.

Michaelson, O. *Words at Play: Quips Quirks, and Oddities*. New York: Sterling, 1997. This book covers anagrams, palindromes, word squares, and numerous other forms, and it includes many wonderful examples by the author and others. Michaelson adds a historical perspective by citing (when known) the creator of each work and its original place of publication.

Morice, Dave. *Alphabet Avenue: Wordplay in the Fast Lane*. Chicago: Chicago Review Press, 1997. An exhaustive and exhilarating collection of wordplay from *Word Ways* magazine, especially from Morice's "Kickshaws" column.

————. *The Adventures of Dr. Alphabet*. New York: Teachers & Writers Collaborative, 1995. 104 innovative and highly unusual poetry exercises for school and community settings.

Newby, Peter, *The Mammoth Book of Word Games*. London: Pelham Books, 1990. This collection of more than ISO spoken and written games is the largest of its kind. From the classic "Ghost" to Newby's own "Pentery Web," the author discusses the games, gives the rules, and shows sample plays.

_____. *Pears Advanced Word-Puzzler's Dictionary*. London: Pelham Books, 1987. This 750-page volume gathers together words of particular interest to crossword puzzlers and word gamesters. The first section includes the most comprehensive anagram list in print, and the second section contains a dictionary of unusual words.

Steig, William. *CDB?* New York: Farrar, Straus, and Giroux, 1984. The single-page cartoons in this one-of-a-kind book have number-and-letter rebuses for the captions.

Train, John. *Most Remarkable Names*. New York: Clarkson Potter, 1977. A collection of unusual, often unbelievable, names, it combines the author's two previous books—*Remarkable Names of Real People* and *Even More Remarkable Names*—and includes new material, too.

Walsh, William Shepard. *The Handy-Book of Literary Curiosities*. Detroit: Gale Research Company. 1985. Another nineteenth-century classic (originally published by Lippincott in 1892), this I,I04-page book includes puzzles, games, and word facts from many magazines and books of the period. It's an excellent companion to Bombaugh's book (listed above).

Williams, Emmet. *An Anthology of Concrete Poetry*. New York, Villefranche, Frankfurt: Something Else Press, 1967. Concrete poetry is a twentieth-century development. The poets achieve their effects by manipulating the meaning, the shape, and/or the sound of words in nontraditional ways. This anthology provides a worldview of concrete poetry in its formative years, 1945 to 1967.

## MAGAZINES

*Games.* New York, 1976–present. Subscription rate $17.97 for 6 issues. Address: P.O. Box 605, Mt. Morris, IL 61054-0605. Available in many drugstores and supermarkets, this magazine offers all sorts of cleverly devised puzzles, contests, and games in a full-color glossy format. Several word games appear in every issue. Articles, game reviews, and other features make it stand out from all other game magazines.

*Logophile: The Cambridge Journal of Words and Language.* Cambridge, England: The Logophile Press, 1977–1979. This British quarterly, which lasted only about three years, dealt with a wide variety of wordplay, traditional as well as innovative. It covered topics such as computer "word" generators, Guinness advertising, and dyslexia, and it offered reader competitions and challenges.

*Verbatim: The Language Quarterly.* Essex, CT: 1974–present. Subscription rate $14 for four issues. This magazine focuses on spoken language—words, dialects, and etymologies—and shows the curious development that occurs in different environments, from the local to the international level. There is surprisingly little duplication of material between *Word Ways* and *Verbatim*.

*Word Ways: The Journal of Recreational Linguistics.* Morristown, NJ, 1968 to present. Subscription rate $20 ($22 foreign) for four issues. Address: Spring Valley Rd., Morristown, NJ 07960. The only magazine devoted to all aspects of written wordplay, from anagram to zeugma, it publishes essays, poems, puzzles, stories, and occasional artwork. Some of the more technical matter might not have been written if it weren't for the magazine providing a soapbox for the dedicated logologist. It charts the course of modern recreational linguistics.

## REFERENCE BOOKS

Babcock, Philip Gove (editor-in-chief). *Webster's Third New International Dictionary of the English Language.* Unabridged. Springfield, MA: G. & C. Merriam Co., 1966.

Baskin, Wade. *The Dictionary of Satanism.* New York: Philosophical Library, 1972.

British and Foreign Bible Society. *The Gospel in Many Tongues*. London: British and Foreign Bible Society, 1965.

Crabtree, Monica, ed. *Language Files*. Fifth edition. Columbus: Ohio State University Press, 1991.

Flexner, Stuart B. *The Random House Unabridged Dictionary of the English Language*. New York: Random House, 1987.

Gove, Philip B., ed. *Webster's Seventh New Collegiate Dictionary*. Springfield, Mass. : G. & C. Merriam Co., 1963.

Hanna, Paul R. *Phoneme-Grapheme Correspondences as Cues to Spelling Improvement*. Washington: U.S. Department of Health, Education, and Welfare, Office of Education, 1966.

Kirkpatrick, E. M., ed. *Chambers Twentieth-Century Dictionary*. Edinburgh: Chambers, 1983.

McWhirter, Norris. *The Guinness Book of Records*. New York: Sterling Publishing Co., 1989.

Mish, Frederick C., ed. *Merriam-Webster's Collegiate Dictionary*. Tenth edition. Springfield, Mass.: Merriam-Webster, Inc., 1994.

Neilson, William Allen (editor-in-chief). *Webster's New International Dictionary of the English Language*. Second edition. Unabridged. Springfield, MA: G. & C. Merriam Co., 1949.

Simpson, J. A., ed. *The Oxford English Dictionary*. New York: Oxford University Press, 1989.

*Times Atlas of the World*. London: Times Books, 1994.

Walker, John Albert. *Glossary of Art, Architecture and Design since 1945*. Third edition, Boston: G. K. Hall, 1992.

*Webster's Encyclopedic Unabridged Dictionary of the English Language*. New York: Gramercy Books, 1994.

*Webster's New Collegiate*. Sixth edition. Springfield, Mass.: G. & C. Merriam Co., 1961.

Wells, Evelyn. *What to Name the Baby*. Garden City, N.Y: Garden City Books, 1953.

Wentworth, Harold, and Stuart Flexner, eds. *The Pocket Dictionary of American Slang*. New York: Pocket Books, 1968.

Wright, Joseph. *The English Dialect Dictionary*. London: Oxford University Press, 1970.

Woolf, Henry Bosley, ed. *The Merriam-Webster Dictionary*. New York: Pocket Books, 1974 [*The Pocket Webster's*].

# OTHER T&W BOOKS YOU MIGHT ENJOY

**The Adventures of Dr. Alphabet** by Dave Morice. 104 amusing and imaginative poetry writing methods that have excited Morice's students for decades. Generously illustrated. "Teachers and parents will treasure this collection."—*School Enrichment Model Network News*. Rave review on National Public Radio.

**How to Make Poetry Comics** by Dave Morice. The popular guide by the author of *Poetry Comics* (Simon & Schuster) and *More Poetry Comics* (Chicago Review Press).

**The Handbook of Poetic Forms**, edited by Ron Padgett. 74 entries by 19 teaching poets. "A treasure."—*Kliatt*. "A small wonder."—*Poetry Project Newsletter*. Revised second edition.

**Poetry Everywhere: Teaching Poetry Writing in School and in the Community** by Jack Collom and Sheryl Noethe. This big and "tremendously valuable resource work for teachers" (*Kliatt*) at all levels contains 60 writing exercises, extensive commentary, and 450 examples. "A most informative, pedagogically sound, and yet friendly book on how to write poetry."—*Library Journal*.

**The List Poem: A Guide to Teaching & Writing Catalog Verse** by Larry Fagin. Defines list poetry, traces its history, gives advice on teaching it, offers specific writing ideas, and presents more than 200 examples. An *Instructor* "Poetry Pick." "An outstanding reference for teachers."—*Kliatt*.

**The Teachers & Writers Guide to Walt Whitman**, ed. Ron Padgett. Fifteen poets offer practical ideas for fresh ways to read Whitman and to write poetry and prose inspired by him. "A lively, fun, illuminating book."—Ed Folsom, University of Iowa, editor of *The Walt Whitman Quarterly Review*.

**The Teachers & Writers Guide to William Carlos Williams**, ed. Gary Lenhart. Seventeen practical and innovative essays on using Williams's short poems, fiction, nonfiction, and long poem *Paterson*. Contributors include Allen Ginsberg, Kenneth Koch, and Julia Alvarez. "Wonderful—such a thorough and fine job."—Robert Coles.

**Luna, Luna: Creative Writing Ideas from Spanish, Latin American, & Latino Literature**, ed. Julio Marzán. In 21 lively and practical essays, poets, fiction writers, and teachers tell how they use the work of Lorca, Neruda, Cisneros, and others to inspire students to write imaginatively. "Succeeds brilliantly."—*Kliatt*.

**Sing the Sun Up: Creative Writing Ideas from African American Literature**, ed. Lorenzo Thomas. Twenty teaching writers present new and exciting ways to motivate students to write imaginatively, inspired by African American poetry, fiction, essays, and drama. "Especially helpful to language arts teachers on both the elementary and secondary level."—*Kliatt*.

**For a free copy of the complete T&W publications catalogue, contact:**

Teachers & Writers Collaborative
5 Union Square West, New York, NY 10003-3306
tel. (toll-free) 888-BOOKS-TW
Visit our World Wide Web site at www.twc.org